GW00469383

Where to find adoption records

A guide for counsellors, adopted people and birth parents

Compiled by Georgina Stafford

103397185

BAAF
ADOPTION
& FOSTERING

Published by
British Agencies for Adoption & Fostering (BAAF)
200 Union Street
London SE1 0LX
www.baaf.org.uk

Third edition © BAAF 2001

British Library Cataloguing in Publication Data
A Catalogue record for this book is available from the
British Library

ISBN 1-9036 99-01-0

Cover design by Andrew Haig & Associates
Typeset by Avon DataSet Ltd, Bidford on Avon B50 4JH
Printed and bound by PIMS UK; cover printed by The
Russell Press, Nottingham

Contents

Note from BAAF

BAAF is particularly indebted to Georgina Stafford for revising this unique directory; her painstaking attention to detail, boundless patience and sheer determination to "get it right" are much valued. Those who will use this book in the years to come to locate their records and begin on their journeys and searches will also share that sense of gratitude.

Georgina worked with BAAF for 14 years *after* she retired in 1978! During that time, she compiled different and ever-growing editions of *Where to Find Adoption Records*. In 1999, I tentatively asked her if she would consider working with us in revising it yet again as records had no doubt moved following local government reorganisation. I am very grateful that Georgina was persuaded; it is evident that her commitment to making information available to those who were adopted many years ago is absolute.

The importance of this phenomenal contribution can best be illustrated by the following story. Three years ago I was contacted by Stephen Richardson, who had located his records some years previously thanks to this book. Over the following months and years, he embarked on a fascinating search to meet members of his birth family – a search that took him to many countries and changed his horizons for ever. The story is a compelling one, one made possible by this directory and one which he has now published; it is titled *Lost and Found: The search for my family* (The Book Guild Ltd, 2001). There are hundreds of others, like Stephen Richardson, who have succeeded in their searches thanks to this book.

A warm thank you to Georgina for making it happen once again.

Shaila Shah
Head of Communications

Author's acknowledgements

I am again indebted to the Directors of social services and social work departments, and to the staff of adoption agencies, who have answered questionnaires and questions. I owe a great deal to county and borough archivists and historians who have gone to considerable trouble to find missing records, to share with me the information which they do hold, and to suggest alternative sources.

Among many helpful people I would like to thank these individuals particularly: Mrs Judy Clark of International Social Service and Mrs Gill Howarth of Overseas Adoption Helpline with their encyclopaedic knowledge of facilities in other countries; Miss Phillida Sawbridge for the generous use of her computer and her particular expertise; Mrs Madeline Carriline for the hours she spent proofreading with me; Mrs Patricia White of Barnardo's, Dublin for her invaluable corrections and additional new information; Mr Rhys Griffiths of the London Metropolitan Archives and Mr R H A Cheffins of the British Library for their patience and time so generously given in the compilation of Chapters 4 and 9. I am also grateful to the Registrar General for facilitating the reproduction of official forms.

Preface

This book is designed to help counsellors in their work with adopted people, birth relatives and adoptive families. It may also help individuals, particularly those whose search is intricate or frustrating.

Although extensive research has been done in an effort to locate missing records, some have apparently disappeared without trace. However, from time to time records, indexes and registers emerge from attics, the backs of cupboards, auction rooms, and other unlikely places. When they are old, dusty, somewhat indecipherable, and totally uncatalogued, there is a great temptation to throw them away. It is then worth remembering that someone's emotional well-being and maturity may depend upon one tiny piece of information there (such as a date of birth). The horrendous task of sorting, collating and indexing records can sometimes be effectively undertaken by willing (or persuaded) volunteers such as retired social workers or administrators.

At present there are quite a number of people who were adopted in the 1930s and 40s and even 50s whose every channel to information seems to be frustratingly blocked. For them time is running out, so that the preservation and availability of records has become urgent.

Since the last edition of this book there have been many changes of geographical boundaries which have necessitated the movement of many records and which in some cases have probably further confused an already complicated search. We have tried to make clear both old and new boundaries and to put Homes in what would now be their current areas.

We have again tried to indicate possible, as well as known, sources of information. Although there is a small amount of cross-referencing, it is a general principle that if the required facts are not in one chapter it is worth taking a quick look in the others for further clues, because in adoption work so many agencies, organisations and individuals have intertwined in the stories of individual people.

BAAF has a little information about children's homes, foster mothers in London, the history of some voluntary organisations and their changes of address, and the Home Office list of registered adoption agencies from 1946. We welcome enquiries if the information in this book proves inadequate. We would also be glad to hear from anyone who uncovers further details. I am personally grateful to the many patient people who have generously contributed to the present edition.

Georgina Stafford
September 2001

List of abbreviations

Admin	Administration
Assocn	Association
BWT	Not yet traced (It is likely that this stands for British Women's Temperance)
CAFCASS	Children and Families Court Advisory Support Service
C ad L	Curator *ad Litem*
CB	County Borough
CC	County Council
C of E	Church of England
CSR	Council for Social Responsibility
DSW	Department of Social Work
FW	Family Welfare
FWA	Family Welfare Association
G ad L	Guardian *ad Litem*
GALRO	Guardian *ad Litem* Record Office
GLC	Greater London Council
HQ	Headquarters
Inc	Incorporated
LB	London Borough
LCC	London County Council
LDBSR	London Diocesan Board for Social Responsibility
LMA	London Metropolitan Archives
M&B	Mother and Baby
MBC	Metropolitan Borough Council
MD	Metropolitan District
MH	Maternity Home
Misc	Miscellaneous
MW	Moral Welfare
MX	Middlesex
NAS	National Adoption Society
NCAA	National Children Adoption Association
NCH	National Children's Home
NH	Nursing Home
NI	Northern Ireland
ONS	Office of National Statistics
RC	Roman Catholic
RSSPC	Royal Scottish Society for the Protection of Children
SR	Social Responsibility
SRN	State Registered Nurse
SS	Social Services
SSAFA	Soldiers', Sailors' and Airmen's Families Association
SSD	Social Services Department
SW	Social Work
SWD	Social Work Department
WRVS	Women's Royal Voluntary Service
WS	Women's Suffrage
YLU	Young Leaguers' Union
YWCA	Young Women's Christian Association

1 • Voluntary agencies (current and previous) by area

For many reasons, including the Second World War, agencies have changed their locations from time to time. There have also been considerable boundary changes in 1974 and, more comprehensively, between 1996 and 1998. This combination of changes has made it almost impossible to pin-point every current area in which an agency has worked at any time. Agencies have therefore been retained in pre-1996 areas with a note of how, and at what date, each area's boundaries changed. Maps are available in *The Social Services Year Book 2000*. Because agencies moved about their names may appear more than once. The letters C and P indicate whether they are current or previous agencies and in which chapters (2 or 3) they are listed. A few agencies which were not registered adoption agencies have been included where it is known that adoptions were arranged through them.

Northern Ireland, Isle of Man, Channel Islands and Eire have not had recent boundary changes.

ENGLAND

AVON

From 1 April 1996 Avon was abolished and replaced by four unitary councils: Bristol, South Gloucestershire, North Somerset, Bath and N.E. Somerset.

P   Avon and North Wiltshire (The Church's Association for Family Welfare)

P   Bristol Diocesan Moral Welfare Association

P   Bristol and Somerset Adoption Society

P   Bristol Women's Aid Association

C   Catholic Children's Society (Diocese of Clifton)

P   Church's Association for Family Welfare

C   Church of England Children's Society (Bristol)

C   Clifton Catholic Children's Society

C   Clifton Catholic Rescue Society

C   National Children's Home (Bristol)

C   National Children's Home Action for Children

P   Western National Adoption Society

P   West of England Adoption Society

BEDFORDSHIRE

From 1 April 1997 Luton became a unitary council. Remainder of Bedfordshire unchanged.

C   Church of England Children's Society (Luton)

C   Church of England Children's Society Find Me a Family (Dunstable)

C   Northampton Diocesan Catholic Child Protection and Welfare Society

C   St Francis Children's Society

BERKSHIRE

From 1 April 1998 Berkshire became six unitary councils: Reading, W Berkshire, Slough, Wokingham, Bracknell Forest, Windsor & Maidenhead.

P   National Children Adoption Association

C   Oxford Diocesan Council for Moral Welfare

C   Oxford Diocesan Council for Social Work Inc

C   PACT

BUCKINGHAMSHIRE

From 1 April 1997 Milton Keynes became a unitary council. Remainder of Buckinghamshire unchanged.

P   National Children Adoption Association

CAMBRIDGESHIRE

From 1 April 1998 Peterborough became a unitary council. Remainder of Cambridgeshire unchanged.

C   Adopt Anglia

C   Cambridge Association for the Care of Girls

C   Cambridge Association for Social Welfare

C   Cambridge Branch of Church League for Women's Suffrage

C   Church Adoption Society

C   Church League for Women's Suffrage

C   East Anglia Adoption and Family Care Association

P   Ely Diocesan Moral Welfare Association

C   Newark Moral Welfare Association

CHESHIRE

From 1 April 1998 Warrington and Halton each became a unitary council. Remainder of Cheshire unchanged.

C   Chester Diocesan Adoption Society

C   Chester Diocesan Adoption Services

C   Chester Diocesan Board for Social Responsibility

C   Chester Diocesan Board of Moral Welfare

C   Chester Diocesan Moral Welfare Adoption Society

C   Church of England Children's Society (Bowden)

P   Lancashire and Cheshire Child Adoption Council

C   National Children's Home (Warrington)

CLEVELAND

From 1 April 1996 Cleveland abolished. Replaced by four unitary councils: Middlesbrough, Hartlepool, Stockton-on-Tees, Redcar & Cleveland (formerly Langbaurgh)

P   Catholic Child Welfare Society (Diocese of Middlesbrough)

P   Cleveland Family Welfare

C   Church of England Children's Society (Middlesbrough)

P   Middlesbrough Diocesan Rescue Society

P   Stockton and District Branch, Durham Diocesan Moral Welfare Association

C   Stockton-on-Tees Deanery Adoption Society

CORNWALL (Unchanged)

P   Cornwall Social and Moral Welfare Association

CUMBRIA (Unchanged)

P   Carlisle Diocesan Family Welfare Association

P   Carlisle Diocesan Society of Moral Welfare

C   Catholic Caring Services (Diocese of Lancaster)

DERBYSHIRE

From 1 April 1997 Derby City became a unitary council. Remainder of Derbyshire unchanged.

P   Derby Diocesan Council for Moral Welfare

P   Derby Diocesan Council for Social Work Adoption Committee

DEVON

From 1 April 1998 Plymouth and Torbay each became a unitary council. Remainder of Devon unchanged.

C   Council for Christian Care

C   Diocesan Council for Family and Social Welfare

C   Exeter Diocesan Association for the Care of Girls

C   Exeter Diocesan Board for Christian Care

C   Exeter Diocesan Board for Family and Social Welfare

C   Exeter Diocesan Council for Moral Welfare Work

C   Families for Children Adoption Agency

C   North Devon Association for the Help and Protection of Girls

C   North Devon Association for Moral Welfare

C   North Devon Preventive and Rescue Work Association

C   Nursing Services Association

C   Plymouth Diocesan Catholic Children's Society Ltd

C   Plymouth Diocesan Children's Rescue Society

P   Plymouth and District Association for Girl's Welfare

C   South Devon Association for the Help and Protection of Girls

C   South Devon Association for Moral Welfare

C   South Devon Preventive and Rescue Work Association

DORSET

From 1 April 1997 Bournemouth and Poole each became a unitary council. Remainder of Dorset unchanged.

P   Mission of Hope for Children's Aid and Adoption

C   Plymouth Diocesan Catholic Children's Society Ltd

P   St. Gabriel's Adoption Society (Weymouth)

COUNTY DURHAM

From 1 April 1997 Darlington became a unitary council. Remainder of County Durham unchanged.

C   Catholic Care – North East

C   Durham and Easington Moral Welfare Association

P   Durham and Northumberland Adoption Society

C   Durham Diocesan Adoption Society

C   Durham Diocesan Family Welfare Adoption Society

C   Durham Diocesan Family Welfare Council

C   Durham Diocesan Moral Welfare Council

C   Family Welfare Council (Durham)

P   Northern Counties Adoption Society

C   Sunderland Deanery Adoption Society

C   Sunderland Social Services Welfare Co

EAST SUSSEX

From 1 April 1997 Brighton & Hove became a unitary council. Remainder of East Sussex unchanged.

P   Chichester Diocesan Association for Family Social Work

P   Chichester Diocesan Moral Welfare Association

ESSEX

From 1 April 1998 Southend and Thurrock each became a unitary council. Remainder of Essex unchanged.

C   Barnardo's

C   Barnardo's New Families project

P   Chelmsford Diocesan Committee for Family Care (Social Care)

P   Chelmsford Diocesan Moral Welfare Association

P   Children's Aid Society

P   Family Care

P   Welcare, Chelmsford

GLOUCESTERSHIRE (Unchanged)

P   Gloucester Diocesan Association for Moral Welfare

P   Gloucester Diocesan Association for Preventive and Rescue Work

P   Gloucester Diocesan Council for Social Work

GREATER LONDON (Unchanged)

C   Adoption Association

C   Adoption Society of the Church of England

C   Agnostics Adoption Society

P   Baker Street Society

P   Baptist Society

P   Baptist Union Adoption Society

C   Barnardo's

P&C   Bloomsbury Society

C   Bloomsbury Square Society

P   British Adoption Project

C   Catholic Children's Society (Arundel and Brighton, Portsmouth and Southwark)

C   Catholic Children's Society (Westminster)

C   Childlink

P   Children's Aid Society

C   Children's Society

P   Christian Family Concern

C   Church Adoption Society

C   Church League for Women's Suffrage

C   Church of England Children's Society

C   Church of England Waifs and Strays Society

C   Church Society

C   Coram Family Adoption Service

C   Crusade of Rescue

C   Dr Barnardo's

P   Family Care

P   Family Ties

P   F.B. Myer's Children's Home

C   Foundling Hospital

P   Harrow and Wealdstone Ruri-Decanal Association for Moral Welfare

P   Haven for Homeless Little Ones

P   Homeless Children's Aid and Adoption Society

P   Hong Kong Project

P   Hutchinson House Children's Home

C   Independent Adoption Service

C   Independent Adoption Society

P   International Social Service

C   Jewish Board of Guardians

C   Jewish Welfare Board

P   The Knightsbridge

P   Memorial Centre of Help for Babies

P   Mission of Hope

P   Mission of Hope for Children's Aid and Adoption

P   Muswell Hill Society

P   National Adoption Society

P   National Children Adoption Society

C   National Children's Home

C   National Children's Home and Orphanage

C   National Children's Home Action for Children

C   Northampton Diocesan Catholic Child Protection

C   Norwood Jewish Adoption Society

C   Parents for Children

P   Phyllis Holman Richards Adoption Society

P   The Retreat

P   Royal Society

C   St Francis Children's Society

C   Soldiers', Sailors' and Airmen's Families Association

C	Southwark Catholic Children's Society
C	Southwark Catholic Rescue Society
P	Spurgeon's Homes Adoption Society
C	Thomas Coram Foundation for Children
C	Waifs and Strays
P	Western National Adoption Society
P	West of England Adoption Society

GREATER MANCHESTER (Unchanged)

P	Ashton-under-Lyne Adoption Society
C	Catholic Children's Rescue Society (Diocese of Salford)
C	Church of England Children's Society (Manchester)
C	Manchester Adoption Society
P	Manchester and District Child Adoption Society
C	Manchester Diocesan Adoption Society
P	Oldham Adoption Society
P	Oldham Council of Social Service Adoption Committee
P	Oldham Council of Social Welfare
C	Salford Catholic Children's Society
C	Salford Catholic Protection and Rescue Society

HAMPSHIRE

From 1 April 1997 Portsmouth and Southampton each became a unitary council. Remainder of Hampshire unchanged.

P	Diocese of Portsmouth Catholic Children's Welfare Society
P	Diocese of Portsmouth Catholic Social Service Council
P	Portsmouth Catholic Social Service Council
P	Portsmouth Diocesan Catholic Child Welfare Society
P	Portsmouth Diocesan Children's Society
P	Portsmouth Diocesan Council for Moral Welfare
P	Portsmouth Diocesan Council for Social Responsibility
P	Portsmouth Diocesan Council for Social Work

HEREFORD AND WORCESTER

From 1 April 1998 Herefordshire became a unitary council on pre-1974 boundaries. Worcestershire unchanged.

P	Worcester Diocesan Association for Family and Social Services
P	Worcester Diocesan Association for Moral Welfare Work

HERTFORDSHIRE (Unchanged)

C	National Children's Home (Harpenden)
P	St Albans Diocesan Association for Girl's Aid
P	St Albans Diocesan Council for Moral Welfare Work
P	St Albans Diocesan Council for Social Responsibility
P	St Albans Diocesan Council for Social Welfare
P	St Albans Diocesan Council for Social Work

KENT

From 1 April 1998 Rochester upon Medway and Gillingham combined into a unitary council. Remainder of Kent unchanged.

C	Church of England Children's Society (Tunbridge Wells)
P	Spurgeon's Homes Adoption Society

LANCASHIRE

From 1 April 1998 Blackburn and Blackpool each became a unitary council. Remainder of Lancashire unchanged.

C	Blackburn Diocesan Adoption Agency Inc
C	Blackburn Diocesan Board for Social Responsibility
C	Catholic Caring Services to Children (Diocese of Lancaster)
C	Catholic Rescue Society
C	Church of England Children's Society
P	Lancashire and Cheshire Child Adoption Council
C	Lancaster Diocesan Catholic Children's Society Ltd
C	Lancaster Diocesan Catholic Child Welfare Society
C	Lancaster Diocesan Protection and Rescue Society
C	Lancaster, Morecambe and District Moral Welfare Association
C	National Children's Home
P	Oldham Adoption Society
C	The Rescue Society

LEICESTERSHIRE

From 1 April 1997 Leicester City and Rutland each became a unitary council. Remainder of Leicestershire unchanged.

C	Children's Society
P	Leicester Diocesan Board of Social Work
P	Leicester Diocesan Board for Social Responsibility
P	Leicester Diocesan Council for Social Work

P   Leicester Diocesan Moral Welfare Association

P   Leicester and Leicestershire Adoption Society

LINCOLNSHIRE (Unchanged)

P   Lincoln Diocesan Association for Moral Welfare

P   Lincoln Diocesan Board for Social Work

LONDON see Greater London

MANCHESTER see Greater Manchester

MERSEYSIDE (Unchanged)

C   Catholic Children's and Social Services (Liverpool)

P   Catholic Children's Society (Shrewsbury Diocese) Inc

C   Catholic Social Services (Archdiocese of Liverpool)

C   Children's Society

P   Diocesan Children's Rescue Society

P   Lancashire and Cheshire Child Adoption Council

C   Liverpool Catholic Children's Protection Society

C   Liverpool Catholic Social Services

C   Nugent Care Society

P   Shrewsbury Diocesan Catholic Children's Society and Family Advice Service Inc

P   Shrewsbury Diocesan Children's Rescue Society

NORFOLK (Unchanged)

C   Catholic Nursery Sheringham

C   Church of England Children's Society – The Child Wants a Home (Norwich)

NORTHAMPTONSHIRE (Unchanged)

C   Northampton Diocesan Catholic Child Protection and Welfare Society

C   St Francis Children's Society

P   St Saviour's Diocesan Maternity Home

NOTTINGHAMSHIRE

From 1 April 1998 Nottingham City became a unitary council. Remainder of Nottinghamshire unchanged.

C   Association for Moral Welfare Work (Retford, Bawtry, Tuxford)

C   Association for the Help and Protection of Girls (Retford, Bawtry, Tuxford)

C   Catholic Children's Society (Roman Catholic Diocese of Nottingham)

C   Mansfield Moral Welfare Association

C   Newark Moral Welfare Association

C   Nottingham Catholic Children's Society

P   Nottingham Day Nursery and Children's Homes

C   Nottingham Roman Catholic Diocesan Rescue Society

C   Retford, Bawtry and Tuxford Association for Moral Welfare Work

C   Retford Moral Welfare Association

C   Southwell Diocesan Association for Moral Welfare Work (Newark, Norwell, Southwell)

C   Southwell Diocesan Association for Moral Welfare Work (Retford, Bawtry, Tuxford)

C   Southwell Diocesan Board of Moral Welfare

C   Southwell Diocesan Council for Family Care

C   Southwell Diocesan Council for Moral Welfare

C   Worksop Moral Welfare Society

OXFORDSHIRE (Unchanged)

C   Oxford Diocesan Council for Moral Welfare

C   Oxford Diocesan Council for Social Work Inc

C   Parents and Children Together (PACT)

SHROPSHIRE

From 1 April 1998 The Wrekin became a unitary council. Remainder of Shropshire unchanged.

P   Catholic Children's Society (Shrewsbury Diocese) Inc

P   Shrewsbury Diocesan Catholic Children's Society and Family Advice Service Inc

P   Shrewsbury Diocesan Children's Rescue Society

SOMERSET (Unchanged)

P   Bristol and Somerset Adoption Society

STAFFORDSHIRE

From 1 April 1997 Stoke on Trent became a unitary council. Remainder of Staffordshire unchanged.

P   Burton-on-Trent Association for the Protection of Girls

P   Girls' Home

P   Lichfield Diocesan Association for Family Care

P   Lichfield Diocesan Association for Moral Welfare

SUFFOLK (Unchanged)

C   Church of England Children's Society (Ipswich)

SURREY (Unchanged)

C   National Children's Home (Woking)

P   Project Vietnam Orphans

P   Memorial Centre of Help for Babies

TYNE AND WEAR (Unchanged)

C   Barnardo's

C   Catholic Care – North East

P   Children – North East

C   Hexham and Newcastle Diocesan Rescue Society

C   Jarrow Deanery Adoption Society

C   Jarrow Deanery Moral Welfare Association

C   National Children's Home (Sunderland)

P   North East Children's Society

P   Northern Counties Adoption Society

P   Poor Children's Holiday Association and Rescue Agency Newcastle Upon Tyne Inc

P   Poor Children's Homes Association and Rescue Agency Newcastle Upon Tyne Inc

C   Sunderland Deanery Adoption Society

C   Sunderland Social Services Welfare Committee

WARWICKSHIRE (Unchanged)

P   Christian Outreach Adoption Society Ltd

P   Fairhaven

P   Hamilton Home

P   Leamington and Warwick Girls' Shelter Association

P   St Faith's Adoption Society

P   St Faith's Shelter

WEST MIDLANDS (Unchanged)

C   Barnardo's

C   Church of England Children's Society (Birmingham)

C   Church of Jesus Christ of Latter Day Saints

C   Father Hudson's Home Adoption Society

C   Father Hudson's Home for Homeless, Abandoned and Suffering Children

C   Father Hudson's Society

P   Lahai-Roi Adoption Society

P   Lichfield Diocesan Association for Family Care

P   Lichfield Diocesan Association for Moral Welfare

C   National Children's Home (Birmingham)

C   National Children's Home Action for Children

P   St Faith's Adoption Society

P   St Faith's Shelter

C   Trustees of Father Hudson's Homes

WEST SUSSEX (Unchanged)

P   Memorial Centre of Help for Babies

C   National Children's Home Action for Children

P   Worthing and District Council of Social Service

WILTSHIRE

From 1 April 1997 Swindon became a unitary council. Remainder of Wiltshire unchanged.

P   Avon and North Wiltshire (The Churches Association for Family Welfare)

YORKSHIRE

From 1 April 1996 W. Yorks & S. Yorks unchanged. In N. Yorks York, with extended boundaries, became a unitary council. Remainder of N. Yorks unchanged.

C   Barnardo's

P   Bradford Diocesan Family Welfare Committee

P   Bradford Diocesan Moral Welfare Council

C   Catholic Care (Diocese of Leeds)

C   Catholic Child Welfare Society (Dioceses of Leeds and Hallam)

P   Catholic Child Welfare Society (Diocese of Middlesbrough)

C   Catholic Social Welfare Society (Diocese of Leeds)

C   Church of England Children's Society (York)

C   Doncaster Adoption and Family Welfare Society Ltd

C   Doncaster and District Adoption Society

P   Downguard Ltd

P   Four Deaneries Family Welfare Association

P   Haven for Moral Welfare

C   Leeds Diocesan Rescue, Protection and Child Welfare Society

C   National Children's Home (Leeds)

C   National Children's Home Action for Children

P   Sheffield Council of Social Service

P   Sheffield and District Child Adoption Association

P   York Adoption Society

P   York Community Council

WALES

All the boundary changes in Wales took place on 1 April 1996.

CLWYD

Replaced by 4 unitary authorities: Flintshire County, Denbighshire County, Wrexham County Borough, Conwy County Borough Council (also made up of part of Gwynedd)

C   Barnardo's Derwen New Families Project

C   Menevia Family Social Service

DYFED

Replaced by 3 unitary authorities: Carmarthanshire County; Ceredigion County; Pembrokeshire County

P   St David's Adoption Society

P   St David's Moral Welfare Committee

GWYNEDD

Replaced by 3 unitary authorities: Conwy County Borough Council (also made up of part of Clwyd); Cyngor Gwynedd Council; Isle of Anglesey County

P   Bangor Diocesan Adoption Society

P   Bangor Diocesan Council for Moral Welfare

P   Bangor Diocesan Council for Social Work

POWYS

Became Powys County

P   Swansea and Brecon Diocesan Council for Social Work

SOUTH GLAMORGAN

Replaced by 2 unitary authorities: Cardiff City Council, Vale of Glamorgan Borough Council

C   Barnardo's (Cardiff) South Wales and South-West Division

C   Barnardo's Derwen Project, Cardiff.

C   Cardiff Archdiocesan Rescue and Moral Welfare Society

C   Cardiff Catholic Rescue Society

C   Catholic Children and Family Care Society (Wales)

C   Catholic Children's Society (Cardiff)

C   Catholic Children's Society (Wales)

C   Catholic Rescue Society (Cardiff)

C   Menevia Diocesan Rescue Society

C   Menevia Family Social Service

C   National Children's Home (Cardiff)

WEST GLAMORGAN

Replaced by 2 unitary authorities: Swansea County, Neath and Port Talbot County Borough.

P   Swansea and Brecon Council for Social Work

P   Swansea and Brecon Diocesan Moral Welfare Association

SCOTLAND

All the boundary changes in Scotland took place on 1 April 1996.

GRAMPIAN

Became 3 unitary authorities: City of Aberdeen Council, Aberdeenshire Council, Moray Council

P   Aberdeen Association of Social Services

P   Voluntary Service Aberdeen

LOTHIAN

Became 4 unitary authorities: East Lothian Council, City of Edinburgh Council, Midlothian Council, West Lothian Council

C   Barnardo's Family Placement Service, Edinburgh

C   Barnardo's New Families Project (Edinburgh)

C   Catholic Enquiry Office

P   Church of Scotland Committee on Social and Moral Welfare

P   Church of Scotland Committee on Social Responsibility
P   Church of Scotland Committee on Social Service
C   (Edinburgh) Catholic Social Service Centre
P   Episcopal Church in Scotland, Social Services Board
C   Family Care
C   Guild of Service
C   Guild of Service for Women
C   National Children Adoption Association and the Mothers' and Infants' Care Committee
C   National Vigilance Association of Scotland (Eastern Division)
C   St Andrew's Children's Society Ltd
C   Scottish Adoption Association Ltd
C   Scottish Association for the Adoption of Children
C   Scottish Branch of the National Association and the Mothers' and Infants' Care Committee
C   Scottish Children Adoption Association
P   Scottish Episcopal Church Adoption Society

STRATHCLYDE

Became 12 unitary authorities: Argyll and Bute Council, East Dumbartonshire Council, West Dumbartonshire Council, South Lanarkshire Council, North Lanarkshire Council, East Ayrshire Council, North Ayrshire Council, City of Glasgow Council, Inverclyde Council, South Ayrshire Council, Renfrewshire Council.

C   Barnardo's New Families Project, Glasgow
C   National Children's Home
P   National Vigilance Association, Glasgow
C   National Vigilance Association of Scotland (Eastern Division)
C   St Margaret of Scotland Adoption Society
C   St Margaret's Children and Family Care Society
C   Scottish Adoption and Advice Service, Glasgow

TAYSIDE

Replaced by 3 unitary authorities: Angus Council, Dundee City Council, Perthshire and Kinross Council.

P   Dundee Association for Social Services
P   Melville House
P   National Vigilance Association of Scotland
P   Perth and Dundee Association of Social Service

NORTHERN IRELAND

ANTRIM
C   Barnardo's
C   Catholic Family Care Society
C   Catholic Family Welfare Adoption Society
C   Church of Ireland Adoption Society
C   Church of Ireland Moral Welfare Association
C   Family Care Society

DOWN
C   Down and Connor Catholic Family Welfare Society

LONDONDERRY
C   Family Care Society
C   Sisters of Nazareth Adoption Society

ISLE OF MAN

C   Diocesan Council for Social, Moral and Religious Service
C   Manx Churches Adoption and Welfare Society
C   The Nugent Care Agency
C   The United Council of Christian Welfare

CHANNEL ISLANDS see Chapter 2

EIRE

In Eire the Health Boards cover more than one county and usually delegate their adoption work to voluntary agencies. They have therefore been included in this section although they are not voluntary agencies.

CLARE
C   Mid-western Health Board
C   St Catherine's Adoption Society

CORK
C   Cork and Ross Family Centre (Incorporating St Anne's Adoption Society)
P   Sacred Heart Adoption Society
P   Sean Ross Abbey
C   Southern Health Board

DONEGAL

C   St Mura's Adoption Society

DUBLIN

C   Barnardo's

C   Catholic Protection and Rescue Society of Ireland

P   Catholic Women's Aid Society

C   Cunamh

C   Eastern Health Board

P   Holles Street Hospital Adoption Society

C   Northern Area Health Board

C   PACT

C   Protestant Adoption Society

P   Rotunda Girls' Aid Society

P   St Brigid's Adoption Society

C   St Louise Adoption Society

P   St Patrick's Guild

P   St Rita's (not a registered agency but children adopted from it)

P   St Theresa's Adoption Society

GALWAY

C   Clann Western Regional Adoption Service

P   St Nicholas' Adoption Society

KERRY

P   St Mary's Adoption Society

C   Southern Health Board

C   The Kerry Adoption & Fostering Team

KILKENNY

P   Challenge Adoption Society

LIMERICK

P   Limerick Catholic Adoption Society

C   Mid-Western Health Board

LOUTH

C   North Eastern Health Board

MEATH

P   St Clare's Adoption Society

OFFALY

C   Midland Health Board

SLIGO

C   North Western Health Board

P   St Attracta's Adoption Society

WATERFORD

C   Challenge Adoption Society

P   St John's Adoption Society

P   St Kevin's Adoption Society

C   SEEK

C   South Eastern Health Board

WESTMEATH

P   Sacred Heart Adoption Society

P   St Clare's Adoption Society

2 • Voluntary agencies: current

Name of Agency	Registered	Records: Location/ Availability	Former Address(es)	Notes	Enquiries to

ENGLAND

Name of Agency	Registered	Records: Location/ Availability	Former Address(es)	Notes	Enquiries to
Adopt Anglia Project of Coram Family	1884 present name from 1996	At agency's office: 9 Petersfield, Cambridge CB1 1BB. None lost or destroyed.	2 Bridge Street & 60 St Andrews St, Cambridge	Now (from 1996) part of Coram Family Adoption Service	Project Leader
The Adoption Association		Scanty or non existent. Might be with Childlink.	124 Maple Road, Surbiton	This was the home of Mrs Westerman who worked at the Church Adoption Society. During WW2 she did some work from home and some mothers may have lived there.	
The Adoption Society of the Church of England	1931			Now Childlink	
Agnostics Adoption Society	1965–1969		23 Baalbec Road, London N5 (1964–5); 55 Dawes Street, London SE17 (1965–66); 69 Chaucer Road, London SE24 (1966–69); 160 Peckham Rye, London SE22	Now the Independent Adoption Service	
Association for Moral Welfare Work (Retford, Bawtry, Tuxford)	1933–62		55 Chancery Lane, Retford; 43 Chancery Lane, Retford (1949–); Yorkshire Penny Bank Chambers, Retford (1953–64)	Affiliated to Southwell Diocesan Council for Family Care	
Association for the Help and Protection of Girls (Retford, Bawtry, Tuxford)	1922–33			Affiliated to Southwell Diocesan Council for Family Care	
Barnardo's	1866	Cottage No 1, The Village, Barkingside, Ilford, Essex IG6 1BU. None lost or destroyed.	Barnardo's Homes, 18–26 Stepney Causeway, London E1 (1866–1969)		Counselling Service
Barnardo's Jigsaw Project 12 Church Street Walthamstow London E17 3AG		Cottage No 1, The Village, Barkingside, Ilford, Essex IG6 1BU. None lost or destroyed.			Counselling Service
Barnardo's New Families Project (Colchester) 54 Head Street Colchester CO1 1PB		Cottage No 1, The Village, Barkingside, Ilford, Essex IG6 1BU. None lost or destroyed.			Counselling Service
Barnardo's New Families Project (Newcastle) NE Divisional Office Orchard House Fenwick Terrace Jesmond Newcastle-upon-Tyne NE22 2JQ		Cottage No 1, The Village, Barkingside, Ilford, Essex IG6 1BU. None lost or destroyed.			Counselling Service

Name of Agency	Registered	Records: Location/ Availability	Former Address(es)	Notes	Enquiries to
Barnardo's New Families Project (Shipley) 4 Briggate Shipley W. Yorkshire BD17 7BP		Cottage No 1, The Village, Barkingside, Ilford, Essex IG6 1BU. None lost or destroyed.			Counselling Service
Barnardo's New Families Project (West Midlands) Owen House Little Cornbow W Midlands B63 3AJ		Cottage No 1, The Village, Barkingside, Ilford, Essex IG6 1BU. None lost or destroyed.			Counselling Service
Blackburn Diocesan Adoption Society				Now Blackburn Diocesan Adoption Agency	
Blackburn Diocesan Adoption Agency	First placement 12 April 1948 (by the original society)	St Mary's House, Cathedral Close, Blackburn BB1 5AA and Lancashire Record Office. Brief records of placements from March 1948.	7 Queen's Street, Lancaster	The agency grew out of a hostel for unmarried mothers	The Director
Blackburn Diocesan Board for Social Responsibility				Now Blackburn Diocesan Adoption Agency	
The Bloomsbury Society				Colloquial name for Church Adoption Society, Baptist Union Adoption Society or Spurgeon's Homes	
Bloomsbury Square Society				Colloquial name for Church Adoption Society	
Cambridge Association for the Care of Girls	1949–54			Now Adopt Anglia Project of Coram Family	
Cambridge Association for Social Welfare	1954–83			Now Adopt Anglia Project of Coram Family	
Cambridge Branch of Church League for Women's Suffrage	1913			Now Childlink	
Catholic Care (Diocese of Leeds) Covers W. Yorks, parts of N. Yorks, Cumbria, Greater Manchester, Humberside & Lancashire	1943 Adoptions arranged since 1926	At agency's central office, 31 Moor Road, Headingley, Leeds LS6 4BE Fax: 0113 278 9089 Records available from 1926.	9 Mount Preston, Leeds 2 (1947–61) Carmel House, Houghley Lane, Leeds; St Margaret's, Leeds 6	Records held for the Leeds & Hallam Diocese & Catholic Child Welfare Society	Team Leader (Homefinding Team)

Name of Agency	Registered	Records: Location/ Availability	Former Address(es)	Notes	Enquiries to
Catholic Care – North East				Now St Cuthbert's Care	The Administrator
Catholic Caring Services (Diocese of Lancaster). Covers Lancashire (North of River Ribble) and Cumbria	First adoption 1934	At agency's office, 218 Tulketh Road, Preston, Lancashire PR2 1ES. Fax: 01772 768726 None lost or destroyed.	Former addresses in Preston: Lune Street (1934–48); 28 Bairstow Street (1948–58); 236 Garstang Road (1958–71)	Also have offices in Carlisle, Workington and Barrow	Principal Officer, Children's Services
Catholic Children's Rescue Society (Diocese of Salford) Inc. Covers Greater Manchester and South East Lancashire between Ribble Valley & River Mersey	1942	At agency's office, 390 Parrs Wood Road, Didsbury, Manchester M20 5NA. Fax: 0161 445 7769	St Gerrard's, Denmark Road, Manchester (1943–52); St Joseph's Home, Patricroft, Eccles (1952–58); Our Lady of Lourdes, Parrs Wood Road, South Manchester 20	Catholic Moral Welfare transferred from 2 Anson Road, Manchester to Catholic Children's Rescue Society, 2 Galbraith Road, Didsbury, Manchester	Director of Social Work
Catholic Children's and Social Services	1972–76			Now the Nugent Care Society	
Catholic Children's Society (Arundel & Brighton, Portsmouth & Southwark) www.cathchild.org	Founded 1887	At agency's office, 49 Russell Hill Rd, Purley, Surrey CR8 2XB. None lost or destroyed.	59 Westminster Bridge Rd, London SE1 (1920s–1967)	Society covers London boroughs south of the Thames, Kent, Sussex, Surrey, Hants, Berkshire, Oxfordshire south of Thames, Dorset, east of original county boundary, Isle of Wight & The Channel Islands	The Director
Catholic Children's Society (Diocese of Clifton). Covers Gloucestershire, Somerset, Wiltshire, Swindon, Bristol, Bath, NE Somerset, S. Gloucester, N. Somerset	1943 (Records of informal adoptions from 1906)	At agency's office, 58 Alma Road, Clifton, Bristol BS8 2DJ Fax: 0117 923 8651	Pro Cathedral, Bristol 8; St Bernard's Presbytery, 43 Station Road, Shirehampton, Bristol; 4 Brookthorpe Avenue, Lawrence Westou, Bristol; 1 Tailor's Court, Broad Street, Bristol		The Administrator
Catholic Children's Society (Diocese of Nottingham). Covers counties of Nottingham (excluding Bassettaw), Derby (excluding Chesterfield), Leicestershire, (Rutland & Lincolnshire)	1948	At agency's office, 7 Colwick Road, West Bridgford, Nottingham NG2 5FR. Records probably intact.	Cathedral House, Derby Road; Garden Cottage, Colston Bassett; Colston Bassett Hall, Colston Bassett, Notts. (1950–1960/1)		The Administrator or Principal Social Worker

Current voluntary agencies

Name of Agency	Registered	Records: Location/ Availability	Former Address(es)	Notes	Enquiries to
Catholic Children's Society (Westminster). Covers London Boroughs North of the Thames and West of Waltham Forest, NW Surrey & Hertfordshire	1943 (Informal adoptions from 1900, first legal adoption 1927)	At agency's office, 73 St Charles Square, London W10 6EJ. Fax: 020 8960 1464 Some records before 1963 damaged or destroyed.	27 Tavistock Place, London WC1 (1900–53)	Post-adoption counselling available and advice and help in tracing	Post Adoption Team Leader
Catholic Child Welfare Society (Diocese of Leeds & Hallam)				Now Catholic Care (Diocese of Leeds)	
Catholic Nursery Sheringham				Always part of St Francis Children's Society	
Catholic Rescue Society				Now Catholic Caring Services (Diocese of Lancaster)	
Catholic Social Services (Archdiocese of Liverpool)				Now Nugent Care Society	
Catholic Social Welfare Society (Diocese of Leeds)				Now Catholic Care (Diocese of Leeds)	
Chester Diocesan Adoption Services	Before 1955	14 Liverpool Road, Chester CH2 1AE. Fax: 01244 390067. Records probably intact.	52 Tynedale Avenue, Crewe; Jasmine House, Woodside Lane, Wistaston; 3 Abbey Green, Chester; The Vicarage, Vale Road, Ellesmere Port, Wirral (1955–59); Diocesan House, Raymond Street, Chester; (Deanery Cottage, Chester, may have been quoted before 1955)		Post Adoption Social Worker
Chester Diocesan Adoption Society				Now Chester Diocesan Adoption Services	
Chester Diocesan Board of Moral Welfare		Some early records when children were placed through Children's Society may be with Children's Society.		Now Chester Diocesan Adoption Services	
Chester Diocesan Board for Social Responsibility				Now Chester Diocesan Adoption Services	
Chester Diocesan Moral Welfare Adoption Society				Now Chester Diocesan Adoption Services	

Name of Agency	Registered	Records: Location/ Availability	Former Address(es)	Notes	Enquiries to
Childlink www.childlink. org.uk	Founded about 1913. First adoption society after 1926 Act passed, about 1927	10 Lion Yard, Tremadoc Road, London SW4 7NQ. Intact from 1945. Sketchy information 1939–45. Most pre-war records destroyed in Second World War, but incomplete index cards available.	Church House, Westminster SW1; The Church House, 1 Bloomsbury Court, London WC1 (in the 1930's); 4a Bloomsbury Square, London WC1; 282 Vauxhall Bridge Road, London SW1. Also some addresses in Cambridge.		General Secretary
Children's Society	Probably 1933 (Recordings of informal adoption cases begun in 1910)	Edward Rudolf House, 69–85 Margery Street, London WC1X OJL. Fax 020 7837 0211. None lost or destroyed.	Old Town Hall, Kennington Road, London SE11 1QD; St Michaels, Joel Street, Pinner	Hold the records of Bristol Diocesan Moral Welfare Association	Post Adoption and Care Counselling and Research Project, 91 Queens Road, Peckham, London SE15 2EZ Tel: 020 7732 9089
Church Adoption Society				Now Childlink	
Church League for Women's Suffrage	1913			Now Childlink. Originated in 1913 as the Adoption Committee of the Cambridge Branch of the Church League for Women's Suffrage	
Church of England Children's Society				Now Children's Society	
Church of England Waifs and Strays Society				Now Children's Society	
Church of Jesus Christ of Latter Day Saints (LDS Social Services)	1980	399 Garretts Green Lane, Garretts Green, Birmingham B33 0UH Fax: 0121 783 1888 None lost or destroyed.	751 Warwick Road, Solihull, West Midlands B91 3DQ		Adoption/ Fostering Officer
The Church Society				Colloquial name for Church Adoption Society or the Church of England Children's Society	
Cleveland Moral Welfare Association	Never a registered adoption agency	Was a very active referring agency		Adoptions mainly Durham Family Welfare who hold records, of York Adoption Society	
Clifton Catholic Children's Society				Now Catholic Children's Society (Diocese of Clifton)	
Clifton Catholic Rescue Society	1906–61			Now Catholic Children's Society (Diocese of Clifton)	

Current
voluntary agencies

Name of Agency	Registered	Records: Location/ Availability	Former Address(es)	Notes	Enquiries to
Coram Family Adoption Service (Previously Thomas Coram Foundation for Children)	Founded 1739. Registered 1971. (A number of children adopted by parents before agency registered, the first probably in 1932)	At agency's office, 49 Mecklenburg Square, London WC1N 2QA. Fax 020 7520 0301. None lost or destroyed. No records of admission to Mother and Baby home.	40 Brunswick Square, London WC1 1AZ		Head of Adoption Services
Council for Christian Care (Devon) Inc				Now Families for Children Adoption Agency (Exeter)	
Crusade of Rescue				Now Catholic Children's Society (Westminster)	
Diocesan Council for Family and Social Welfare	1963–77			Now Families for Children Adoption Agency (Exeter)	
Dr Barnado's				Now known as Barnardo's	
Doncaster Adoption and Family Welfare Society Ltd	1946	At society's offices, Jubilee House, 1 Jubilee Road, Wheatley, Doncaster DN1 2UE. None lost or destroyed.	In Doncaster: Church House, 13 Thorne Road, (1946 – April 1963); 40 Netherhall Road; 25 Highfield Road (Moved 1990)		Head of Agency
Doncaster and District Adoption Society	1946–74			Now Doncaster Adoption and Family Welfare Society Ltd	
Durham Diocesan Adoption Society				Now Durham Family Welfare	
Durham Diocesan Family Welfare Adoption Society				Now Durham Family Welfare	
Durham Diocesan Family Welfare Council				Now Durham Family Welfare	
Durham Family Welfare	1959 (The Deanery Adoption Societies' placements go back to 1942)	At agency's office, Agricultural House, Stonebridge, Durham DH1 3RY. Fax: 0191 386 4940. Files and index cards for all Deanery placements since 1950 and cards and some case notes for adoption from 1930–1950.	In Durham: The Chapter Office (1959–61), Hallgarth House (1961–71) and 81 Claypath (1971–73). Also had offices in Bishop Auckland, Lanchester, Darlington, Gateshead, Hartlepool and Horton le Spring		Co-ordinator Adoption Mediation
Durham Diocesan Moral Welfare Association				Now Durham Family Welfare	

Name of Agency	Registered	Records: Location/ Availability	Former Address(es)	Notes	Enquiries to
Durham and Easington Moral Welfare Association	1939–64			Now Durham Family Welfare	
The East Anglia and Family Care Association	1884			Now Adopt Anglia and part of Coram Family Adoption Service	
Exeter Diocesan Association for the Care of Girls			32 Bartholomew Street East, Exeter	Now Families for Children Adoption Agency	
Exeter Diocesan Board for Christian Care and Plymouth Diocesan Catholic Children's Society	1954			Now Families for Children Adoption Agency	
Exeter Diocesan Council for Family and Social Work	1963–77			Now Families for Children Adoption Agency	
Exeter Diocesan Council for Moral Welfare Work	1942–63			Now Families for Children Adoption Agency	
Families for Children Adoption Agency. Joint venture with Plymouth Diocesan Catholic Children's Society www.cosmic.org. uk/christiancare	1954	At agency's office, 96 Old Tiverton Road, Exeter EX4 6LD. Fax: 01392 427237. None lost or destroyed since 1954. Holds Plymouth Diocesan records since 1948.	In Exeter: 20 Alphington Road; 32 Batholomew Road East; 8 Richmond Road (1956, 1958); Pennsylvania Road (1960, 1961); St Olave's Church House, Mary Arches Street (1961–72)	Has a copy of a national register of Catholic children sent to Australia in the 1950s	The Adoption Director
Family Welfare Council (Durham)	1967			Now Durham Family Welfare	
Father Hudson's Home Adoption Society				Now Father Hudson's Society	
Father Hudson's Home for Homeless, Abandoned and Suffering Children				Now Father Hudson's Society	

Name of Agency	Registered	Records: Location/ Availability	Former Address(es)	Notes	Enquiries to
Father Hudson's Society Covers the counties of Warwickshire, Oxfordshire, Staffordshire, West Midlands and Worcestershire	Adoptions arranged from 1921, registered under the Adoption of Children (Regulation) Act 1939	At agency's H.Q. Coventry Road, Coleshill, Birmingham B46 3EB. Fax: 01675 467 335 None lost or destroyed.	St George's House, Coventry Road, Coleshill, Birmingham	Previously incorporated Birmingham Catholic Maternity and Child Welfare Council	The Director (Adoption Department)
The Foundling Hospital	1739–1954			Now Coram Family Adoption Service	
Hexham and Newcastle Diocesan Rescue Society	1945			Now St Cuthburts Care	
Independent Adoption Service	1983	At agency's office, 121–3 Camberwell Road, London SE5 0HB Fax: 020 7277 1668. None lost or destroyed.	23 Baalbec Road, London N5; 55 Dawes St, London SE17 (1965–66); 69 Chaucer Road, London SE24 (1966–69); 160 Peckham Rye, London SE22 (1970–84);		The Director or Deputy Director
Independent Adoption Society	1970–83		160 Peckham Rye, London SE22 (1970–84)	Now Independent Adoption Service	
Jarrow Deanery Adoption Society	1941–77		29 King Street, South Shields	Now Durham Family Welfare who hold records	
Jarrow Deanery Moral Welfare Association	1941–77			Now Durham Family Welfare who hold records	
Jewish Board of Guardians		Possibly with Norwood Jewish Adoption Society		Not an adoption agency but Jewish children may have been placed through them	
Jewish Welfare Board		Possibly with Norwood Jewish Adoption Society		Not an adoption agency, but Jewish children may have been placed through them	
Lancaster Diocesan Catholic Child Welfare Society				Now Catholic Caring Services (Diocese of Lancaster)	
Lancaster Diocesan Catholic Children's Society Ltd				Now Catholic Caring Services (Diocese of Lancaster)	
Lancaster Diocesan Protection and Rescue Society				Now Catholic Caring Services (Diocese of Lancaster)	

Name of Agency	Registered	Records: Location/ Availability	Former Address(es)	Notes	Enquiries to
Lancaster, Morecambe and District Association for Family Social Work	1970–73/4			Now Blackburn Diocesan Adoption Agency	
Lancaster, Morecombe and District Moral Welfare Association	1948–73	Files from 1953	7 Queen Street, Lancaster	Now Blackburn Diocesan Adoption Agency	
Leeds Diocesan Rescue and Child Welfare Society				Now Catholic Care (Diocese of Leeds)	
Leeds Diocesan Rescue, Protection and Child Welfare Society				Now Catholic Care (Diocese of Leeds)	
Liverpool Catholic Children's Protection Society	1926–72			Now The Nugent Care Society	
Liverpool Catholic Social Services				Now The Nugent Care Society	
Manchester Adoption Society	1965	At Society's office, 47 Bury New Road, Sedgley Park, Manchester M25 9JY Fax: 0161 773 2802	27 Blackfriar's Road, Salford		The Secretary
Manchester Diocesan Adoption Society				Now Manchester Adoption Society	
Mansfield Moral Welfare Association	1960 Not a registered adoption society			Now Southwell Diocesan Council for Family Care	
National Adoption Society (not to be confused with entry in Chapter 3)	1916–31			Now Childlink	
National Children's Home				Now NCH	
NCH Action for Children				Now NCH	
NCH	1873 (first placement for adoption)	Database at agency's headquarters, 85 Highbury Park, London N5 1UD. None lost or destroyed.		Adoption Projects in Leeds, Birmingham, Bristol & Horsham	General Records Administrator H.Q.

Current voluntary agencies

Name of Agency	Registered	Records: Location/ Availability	Former Address(es)	Notes	Enquiries to
National Children's Home & Orphanage	1873–1965			Now NCH	
Newark Moral Welfare Association	1912–1980			Now Southwell Diocesan Council for Family Care	
Northampton Diocesan Catholic Child Protection and Welfare Society				Now St Francis Children's Society	
North Devon Association for the Help and Protection of Girls	1922–33			Now Families for Children Adoption Agency	
North Devon Association for Moral Welfare	1934			Now Families for Children Adoption Agency	
North Devon Preventative and Rescue Work Association	1914–21			Now Families for Children Adoption Agency	
Norwood Jewish Adoption Society	1990	At agency's office, Broadway House, 80 The Broadway, Stanmore HA7 4HB Fax: 020 8420 6859	221 Golders Green Road, London NW11. Norwood House, Harmony Way, London NW4. Norwood Orphanage and Homes	Records of any Jewish child placed for adoption may be in the archives. Records go back over 50 years.	Head of Placement Services, Headquarters.
Nottingham Catholic Children's Society				Now Catholic Children's Society (Diocese of Nottingham)	
Nottingham Roman Catholic Diocesan Rescue Society	1946/7–62			Now Catholic Children's Society (Diocese of Nottingham)	
The Nugent Care Society Diocese covers Merseyside (excluding Wirral) SW Lancashire, parts of Cheshire and Greater Manchester and the Isle of Man	Placements from 1926 (legal); previously *de facto* adoptions were arranged	At The Children's Fieldwork Services Team, Blackbrook House, Blackbrook Road, St Helen's WA11 9RJ. Fax: 0151 709 0695. None lost or destroyed.	Liverpool: Shaw Street, 150 Brownlow Hill, Liverpool L3 5RF		The Director
Nursing Services Association				Now Families for Children Adoption Association	
Oxford Diocesan Council for Moral Welfare	1953–67			Now Parents and Children Together (PACT)	

Name of Agency	Registered	Records: Location/ Availability	Former Address(es)	Notes	Enquiries to
Oxford Diocesan Council for Social Work Inc	1953			Now Parents and Children Together (PACT)	
Parents and Children Together (PACT)	1953	At agency's office, 7 Southern Court, South Street, Reading RG1 4QS. None lost or destroyed.	88 Aldgate Street, Oxford; 7 Brock Lane, Maidenhead; Pond Cottage, Shurlock Row, Twyford; 48 Bath Road, Reading RG1 6PQ	Hold incomplete records of St Michael's Windsor	Post Adoption Social Worker or Adoption Manager
Parents for Children	1976	41 Southgate Road, London N1 3JP Fax: 020 7226 7840	222 Camden High Street, London NW1 8QR		The Director
Plymouth Diocesan Catholic Children's Society	1948	Glenn House, 96 Old Tiverton Road, Exeter EX4 6LD. From 1948 none lost or destroyed.	Fore St, Heavitree, Exeter (1948–60); Queensway Road, Chelston, Torquay and 38 Dorchester Road, Weymouth (1961–68); The Presbytery, Shortlands, Cullompton and The Presbytery, 40 Old Road, Tiverton (1968–76); 14 Palace Gate, Exeter EX1 1JA; Rosary House, 27 Fore Street, Heavitree, Exeter	Working jointly with Families for Children Adoption Agency since 1992 and no longer arranging adoptions	The Adoption Director
Plymouth Roman Catholic Diocesan Children's Rescue Society	1948–71			Now working jointly with Families for Children Adoption Agency	
The Rescue Society				No Catholic Caring Services (Diocese of Lancaster)	
Retford, Bawtry and Tuxford Association of Moral Welfare			Yorkshire Penny Bank Chambers, Market Square, Retford; 55 Chancery Lane, Retford	Now Southwell Diocesan Council for Family Care	
Retford Moral Welfare Association	1914–64			Now Southwell Diocesan Council for Family Care	
St Cuthberts Care (Covers Northumberland, Durham, Tyne and Wear and part of Cleveland) Offices formerly in Darlington and Sunderland now closed.	June 1945	At agency's office, St Cuthberts House, West Road, Newcastle upon Tyne NE15 7PY Fax: 0191 228 0177 None lost or destroyed.	9 Jesmond Park West, Newcastle upon Tyne NE7 7DL	Previous offices in Darlington and Sunderland now closed.	The Directors
St Francis Children's Society (Covers Bedfordshire, Buckinghamshire, Northamptonshire and Slough)	1944	Collis House, Newport Road, Woolstone, Milton Keynes MK15 OAA	37 Brook Green, London W6 7BL; 23 High Street, Shefford, Beds, SG17 5DE; 83 Cambridge Street, London SW1; 15 High Street, Shefford, Beds SG17 5DD; 20A Park Avenue North, Northampton NN3 2HS; 64 Gardenia Avenue, Luton	For those adopted through St Francis Children's Society and now living in the Catholic Diocese of East Anglia, birth records counselling is available with East Anglia Diocesan Children's Society, 4 Mason Road, Swanton, Morley.	The Director

Name of Agency	Registered	Records: Location/ Availability	Former Address(es)	Notes	Enquiries to
(Salford) Catholic Children's Society				Now Catholic Children's Rescue Society (Diocese of Salford) Inc	
Salford Catholic Protection and Rescue Society				Now Catholic Children's Rescue Society (Diocese of Salford) Inc	
The Soldiers', Sailors' and Airmen's Families Association – Forces Help	1982, but operating overseas since 1940s	19 Queen Elizabeth Street, London SE1 2LP Fax: 020 7403 8815	23 and then 27 Queen Anne's Gate, London SW1	SSAFA's adoption placement work is carried out overseas only	Director of Social Work
South Devon Association for the Help and Protection of Girls	1922–33			Now Families for Children Adoption Agency	
South Devon Association for Moral Welfare	1914			Now Families for Children Adoption Agency	
South Devon Preventative and Rescue Work Association	1914–21			Now Families for Children Adoption Agency	
Southwark Catholic Children's Society	Founded 1887		59 Westminster Bridge Road, London SE1	Now Catholic Children's Society (Arundel and Brighton, Portsmouth and Southwark)	
Southwark Catholic Rescue Service	1887–1963		59 Westminster Bridge Road, London SE1	Now Catholic Children's Society (Arundel and Brighton, Portsmouth and Southwark)	
Southwell Diocesan Association for Rescue and Preventative Work	1919			Now Southwell Diocesan Council for Family Care	
Southwell Diocesan Association for Moral Welfare, Newark, Norwell, Southwell, Retford, Bawtry, Tuxford	1933			Now Southwell Diocesan Council for Family Care	
Southwell Diocesan Board for Moral Welfare	1944			Now Southwell Diocesan Council for Family Care	

Name of Agency	Registered	Records: Location/ Availability	Former Address(es)	Notes	Enquiries to
Southwell Diocesan Council for Family Care	1977	At agency's office, Warren House, 2 Pelham Court, Pelham Road, Nottingham NG5 1AP Fax: 0115 960 8374 None lost or destroyed since 1944.	In Nottingham. Pilgrims, 3 Pepper Street; St Catherine's Church Hall, St Anns, Well Road; Warren House, 1 Plantagenet Street	Covers Nottingham City and Nottinghamshire County local authority areas.	The Adoption Officer
Southwell Diocesan Council for Moral Welfare	1944			Now Southwell Diocesan Council for Family Care	
Southwell Diocesan Penitentiary Association	1915			Now Southwell Diocesan Council for Family Care	
Stockton and District Branch of Durham Diocesan Moral Welfare Association			Clara Harrison House, Hartington Road, Stockton-on-Tees	Now Durham Family Welfare which holds records	
Stockton-on-Tees Deanery Adoption Society	1944–60		Stockton-on-Tees: 27 Harrington Road; 11 Finkle Street	Now Durham Family Welfare which holds records	
Sunderland Deanery Adoption Society			33 Norfolk Street, Sunderland	Now Durham Family Welfare which holds the records	
Sunderland Social Services Welfare Committee			33 Norfolk Street, Sunderland	Now Durham Family Welfare which holds records	
Thomas Coram Foundation for Children				Now Coram Family Adoption Service	
Trustees of Father Hudson's Homes				Now Father Hudson's Society	
Waifs and Strays	1881			Now Children's Society	
Worksop Moral Welfare Society	1915–85 (Not registered adoption agency)			Now Southwell Diocesan Council for Family Care	

WALES

Barnardo's Derwen Project		11–15 Columbus Walk, Atlantic Wharf, Cardiff CF10 5BZ Fax: 029 2043 6201			The Project Leader

Current voluntary agencies

Name of Agency	Registered	Records: Location/ Availability	Former Address(es)	Notes	Enquiries to
Barnado's New Families Project		Ty're Binwydden, Clayton Road, Mold CH71 1ST Fax: 029 2043 6200			The Project Leader
Cardiff Archdiocesan Rescue and Moral Welfare Society	1943–54			Now Catholic Children and Family Care Society (Wales)	
Cardiff Catholic Rescue Society				Now Catholic Children and Family Care Society (Wales)	
Catholic Children and Family Care Society (Wales)	1942	Bishop Brown House, Durham Street, Grangetown, Cardiff CF11 6PB Fax: 01292 394344 None lost or destroyed.	In Cardiff: 24 Newport Road; 30 Bute Terrace (until 1954); 17 Broad Street (until 1977); 43 Cathedral Road; 38 Charles Street; Westbourne Crescent	Covers the Archdiocese of Cardiff and the Dioceses of Wrexham and Menevia, i.e. the whole of Wales and Herefordshire	The Administrator
Catholic Children's Society (Cardiff)	1979–81			Now Catholic Children and Family Care Society (Wales)	
Catholic Children's Society (Wales)	1942			Amalgamation of Catholic Children's Society (Wales) and Menevia Family Social Service, April 1981. Now Catholic Children and Family Care Society (Wales)	
Catholic Rescue Society (Cardiff)	1954–79			Now Catholic Children and Family Care Society (Wales)	
Menevia Diocesan Rescue Society	1961–67			Now Catholic Children and Family Care Society (Wales)	
Menevia Family Social Service	1961–81		Bishop's House, Sentley Road, Wrexham, Clwyd LL13 7EW	Now Catholic Children and Family Care Society (Wales)	

SCOTLAND

Since the original Adoption Act of 1930, people adopted in Scotland and who are over the age of 17 have been able to see their original birth records. A voluntary help service is available through Birthlink, Family Care, 21 Castle Street, Edinburgh EH2 3DN.

Name of Agency	Registered	Records: Location/ Availability	Former Address(es)	Notes	Enquiries to
Barnado's Family Placement Service		At agency's office, 6 Torphichen Street, Edinburgh, EH3 8JQ		Hold the records of all the Barnardo's Projects in Scotland	The Project Leader
(Edinburgh) Catholic Social Service Centre	1926			Now St Andrew's Children's Society Ltd	

Name of Agency	Registered	Records: Location/ Availability	Former Address(es)	Notes	Enquiries to
Family Care	1955 (Organisation started 1911. First adoptions arranged 1952)	At agency's office, 2l Castle Street, Edinburgh EH2 3DN. None lost or destroyed	37 Frederick Street, Edinburgh (until 1995); Margaret Cottage Children's Home, Juniper Green (until 1960); Edzell Lodge Children's Home, Newbattle Terrace, Edinburgh (until 1984)		Duty Social Worker
Guild of Service	1941–80			Now Family Care	
Guild of Service for Women	1941–64			Now Family Care	
National Children Adoption Association and the Mothers' and Infants' Care Committee				Now Scottish Adoption Association Ltd	
National Vigilance Association of Scotland (Eastern Division). Not to be confused with National Vigilance Association.	1911–41		37 Frederick Street, Edinburgh	Now Family Care	
St Andrew's Children Society Ltd	1926	Gillis Centre, 113 Whitehouse Loan, Edinburgh EH9 1BB. No records before 1940.	In Edinburgh: India Buildings, Victoria Place; 65 York Place; 5 Brandon Street; Bonnington Bank House, 205 Ferry Road; 106 Whitehouse Loan	Historical notes on the Society are on file	Duty Social Worker or The Director
St Margaret of Scotland Adoption Society				Now St Margaret's Children and Family Care Society	
St Margaret's Children and Family Care Society	1955	At agency's office, 274 Bath Street, Glasgow G2 4JR Fax: 0141 332 8393. None lost or destroyed.	19 Waterloo Street, Glasgow (1955–61); 29 Waterloo Street, Glasgow		The Director
Scottish Adoption Association Ltd	Placements from 1919	At agency's office, 2 Commercial Street, Leith, Edinburgh EH6 6JA Fax: 0131 553 6422	In Edinburgh: c/o Child Welfare Department, Johnston Terrace; 2 Coates Crescent; 69 Dublin Street; 34 Bernard Street	Also hold the records for: City of Edinburgh Council, East Lothian Council, Midlothian Council, West Lothian Council and their predecessors. Also The Church of Scotland Committee on Social Responsibility (late 1940s to 1980); The Scottish Episcopal Church Adoption Society (1959–78)	The Director of Adoption Services

Current voluntary agencies

Name of Agency	Registered	Records: Location/ Availability	Former Address(es)	Notes	Enquiries to
Scottish Adoption & Advice Service		Barnardo's, 16 Sandyford Place, Glasgow G3 7ND Tel: 0141 339 0772	Not a placing agency but provides a counselling service throughout Scotland		Project Leader
Scottish Association for the Adoption of Children	1944–77			Now Scottish Adoption Association Ltd	
Scottish Branch of the National Own Adoption Association and the Mothers' and Infants' Care Committee	1923–36			Now Scottish Adoption Association Ltd	
Scottish Children Adoption Association	1937–43			Now Scottish Adoption Association Ltd	

NORTHERN IRELAND

Name of Agency	Registered	Records: Location/ Availability	Former Address(es)	Notes	Enquiries to
Catholic Family Care Society (Northern Ireland)				Now Family Care Society	
Catholic Family Welfare Adoption Society				Now Family Care Society	
The Church of Ireland Adoption Society www.cofiadopt.org.uk	1950	Church of Ireland House, 61–67 Donegall Street, Belfast BT1 2QH Fax: 028 9032 1756	In Belfast: 12 Talbot Street; 10 May Street		BSR Manager (Board for Social Responsibility)
Church of Ireland Moral Welfare Association	1940–50		Clarence Place, Donegal Square East, Belfast	Now the Church of Ireland Adoption Society	
Down and Connor Catholic Family Welfare Society				Now Family Care Society	
Family Care Society	1990	At Society's Offices, 511 Ormeau Road, Belfast BT7 3GS Fax: 01232 649 849; 1a Miller Street, Derry BT48 6SU Fax: 01504 372 611	In Belfast: 48 Falls Road, 139 Glen Road (1972–76) In Derry: 164 Bishop Street	Agency formed by amalgamation of Catholic Family Welfare Adoption Society and Sisters of Nazareth Adoption Society and holds their records	Chief Officer
Sisters of Nazareth Adoption Society			164 Bishop Street, Derry BT48 6UJ	Now Family Care Society	

Name of Agency	Registered	Records: Location/ Availability	Former Address(es)	Notes	Enquiries to

ISLE OF MAN

The Isle of Man 1984 Adoption Act, Section 39 made it possible for people adopted there to obtain information about their origins at the age of 18. Counselling is obligatory for people adopted before the Act and available for those adopted after it. The 1992 Statute Law Revision Act made it possible for them to be counselled by an appropriate agency outside the Island.

Name of Agency	Registered	Records: Location/ Availability	Former Address(es)	Notes	Enquiries to
Diocesan Council for Social Moral and Religious Service				Now Manx Churches Adoption and Welfare Society	
Manx Churches Adoption and Welfare Society	1940s	At agency's office, 3 Albany Lane, Douglas IM2 3NS Fax: 01624 678 304. Records from 1938. Some may be missing.	5 Albert Street; 11 Circular Road, Douglas.		Principal Social Worker
The Nugent Care Agency. Part of Nugent Care Society (Archdiocese of Liverpool)		At Nugent Care Society, 150 Brownlow Hill, Liverpool L3 5RF	Apartment 1, Windsor Road, Douglas		
The United Council of Christian Care				Now Manx Churches Adoption and Welfare Society	

GUERNSEY

The Adoption Amendment (Guernsey) Law 2000 has been registered but needs commencement legislation before it becomes effective. It will enable any Guernsey-born adopted person to receive a copy of their birth certificate through a birth records counsellor. It will also result in the setting up of a local Adoption Contact Register. Probably further legislation will be needed before Guernsey-born adopted people can be given information contained in agency's files.

JERSEY

The law changed on 1 January 1996 to enable adopted people, born in Jersey, to obtain copies of their original birth certificates. The Superintendent Registrar also maintains a Contact Register. As counselling is required in all cases, initial contact should be made with the Children's Service.

EIRE

Legislation is currently being drafted by the Department of Health and Children in relation to access to birth information, but it is likely to be some time before the legislation is enacted. Meanwhile, agencies are aware of the needs of adopted people and birth relatives for information/contact. They are willing to give non-identifying information and are often very helpful about facilitating contact.

Agencies involved in placing children in foster and adoptive homes are Health Boards and Adoption Societies. Most of the Health Boards delegate their adoption work to adoption agencies. For easy reference they are included in the following list with their addresses.

The Department of Foreign Affairs, Hainault House, 69/71 St Stephen's Green, Dublin 2 may have some information about people who were sent to the USA to be adopted between the late 40s and early 70s. Irish-born adopted people who are citizens of the USA are entitled under the USA Freedom of Information/Privacy Act 1998 to access to their immigration file. They need form G-639 from the Immigration & Naturalisation Service, 425 Eye Street, N.W., Washington DC 20536 USA.

The Adoption Board has information about any child who was adopted in Ireland even if they were born in England. Information about the agency can be given to the adopted person or to a birth relative.

Name of Agency	Areas Covered	Records	Notes	Enquiries to
The Adoption Board, Shelbourne House, Shelbourne Road, Ballsbridge, Dublin 4 Fax: 00 353 1 667 1438		Shelbourne House. Catholic Women's Aid (Very limited) Eire	Not an adoption agency. Will help and advise anyone, anywhere, Irish and foreign, on matters relating to adoption	Senior Social Worker
Barnardo's Adoption Advice Service, National Children's Resource Centre, Christ Church Square, Dublin 8 Fax: 00 353 1 453 0300	Eire		Not an adoption agency. Telephone advice service Tuesdays 2–5 pm, Thursdays 10am-2pm (01) 454 6388	Team Leader
Catholic Protection and Rescue Society of Ireland			Now Cunamh	
Clann, Western Regional Adoption Service Merlin Park Hospital, Galway Fax: 00 353 91 7 55 632	Galway, Mayo Roscommon	Headquarters. Has records of St Nichols Adoption Society	Domestic and overseas adoption: search and reunion; Support groups for all parties to adoption	Senior Social Worker
Cork and Ross Family Centre (Incorporating St Anne's Adoption Society), 34 Paul Street, Cork Fax: 00 353 21 27 0 932	Cork: Ross	Headquarters	Support services for birth mothers, adopted people and their families. Post adoption services, tracing.	Senior Social Worker

Name of Agency	Areas Covered	Records	Notes	Enquiries to
Cunamh CPRSI House, 30 South Anne Street, Dublin 2 Fax: 00 353 1 677 0235		Headquarters	Adoption and fostering, tracing and other services.	Senior Social Worker
Eastern Health Board 1st Floor, Park House, North Circular Road, Dublin 7	Kildare, Wicklow, Dublin	All records from 1957 in Park House. Also limited records of children placed under 1908/56 Children at Nurse Act and amendments	Disbanded as an entity on 1 March 2000. Replaced by 3 Health Authorities: East Coast Area Health Board, Western Area Health Board and Northern Area Health Board. Fostering and adoption service administered centrally by Northern area. Adoptions continue to be arranged through St Louise Adoption Society and PACT.	Tracing Service, Child Care Service, Park House
Kerry Adoption & Fostering Team, 6 Denny Street, Tralee, Co Kerry	Cork, Kerry	Headquarters		Senior Social Worker
Limerick Catholic Adoption Society, Unit 3, St Camillus Hospital, Shelbourne Road, Limerick				Senior Social Worker
Midland Health Board Health Centre, Arden Road, Tullamore, Co Offaly	Laois, Longford, Offaly: Westmeath	Headquarters		Senior Social Worker
Mid-Western Health Board	Clare, Limerick, N Tipperary (N Riding)	Mid Western Health Board, Glenbevan Upper Mayorstone, Limerick Fax: 061 321 144	Adoptions arranged through St Catherine's Adoption Society	Social Work Team Leader
North Eastern Health Board St Marys, Dublin Road, Dorogheda, Co Louth	Cavan, Louth, Meath, Monaghan	Has records of St Clare's Adoption Society and information about Ard Mhuire Good Shepherd Convent, Dunboyne, Co Meath		Senior Social Worker
Northern Area Health Board Child Care Services, Park House, North Circular Road, Dublin 7	Covers adoption and fostering throughout area of Eastern Health Board	Park House		Tracing service, Child Care Service, Park House
North Western Health Board, Markievicz House, Barrack Street, Sligo	Donegal Leitrum; Sligo Donegal	Holds records of St Attracta's Adoption Society	Adoptions arranged through St Mura's Adoption Society	Senior Social Worker

voluntary agencies Current

Name of Agency	Areas Covered	Records	Notes	Enquiries to
PACT 15 Belgrave Road Rathmines Dublin 6 Fax: 00 353 1 496 6565	Dublin	Hold records of former Protestant child care organisations. Own records held at Park House.	Part of the Service of Eastern Health Board	Tracing Service, Child Care Service, 1st Floor, Park House, North Circular Road, Dublin 7
Protestant Adoption Society			Now PACT	
St Anne's Adoption Society Family Centre 34 St Paul Street Cork Fax: 00 353 21 270 932			Now incorporated in Cork and Ross Family Centre	The Director
St Catherine's Adoption Society Clarecare Harmony Row Ennis Co Clare Fax: 00 353 65 6841 310	Clare, Limerick, Galway, North Tipperary, part of Offaly	Headquarters		Senior Social Worker
St Louise Adoption Society 1st Floor Park House North Circular Road Dublin 7 Fax: 00 353 1 838 7488	Kildare, Wicklow, Dublin	At Park House	Previous address, 1 James Street, Dublin 8	Tracing Service, Child Care, Park House
St Mura's Adoption Society The Pastoral Centre Letterkenny Co Donegal Fax: 00 353 74 2 8433	Donegal, Sligo, Leitrum	Headquarters	Provides adoption, tracing and counselling services for North Western Health Board Region	Senior Social Worker
SEEK Community Care Centre Cork Road Waterford Fax: 00 353 51 842 811	Waterford, Carlow, Kilkenny, Wexford, S. Tipperary	South Eastern Health Board Community Centre, Cork Road. Holds the records of Challenge St John's and St Kevin's Adoption Societies.	The Regional Adoption Service of the South Eastern Health Board	Senior Social Worker
South Eastern Health Board, Cork Road, Waterford	Waterford, Wexford, Carlow, Kilkenny, S. Tipperary	Headquarters for SEEK, Challenge, St John's and St Kevin's Adoption Societies.	Regional Adoption service provided by SEEK.	Senior Social Worker
Southern Health Board, Adoption Department St Finbarr's Hospital, Douglas Road, Cork Fax: 00 353 21 312 960	Cork, Kerry	Headquarters		Senior Social Worker or Staff Officer

Where to find adoption records 31

3 • Voluntary agencies: previous

Name of Agency	Registered	Records: Location/ Availability	Former Address(es)	Notes	Enquiries to

ENGLAND

Name of Agency	Registered	Records: Location/ Availability	Former Address(es)	Notes	Enquiries to
Ashton-under-Lyne Adoption Society	1949–76	Tameside SSD. None destroyed, odd files missing.	Ashton-under-Lyne: 1 Tatton Street; 101 Old Street		Service Unit Manager Tameside SSD
Avon and North Wiltshire	1920–76	Children's Society HQ. Records: few only before 1955; 1955–76, none lost or destroyed.	Diocesan Church House, 23 Great George Street, Bristol (till 1939); Moral Welfare Association, Lodge Street, Bristol 1 (1939–43); MWA, 20 Park Row, Bristol (1943–66); 70 Pembroke Road, Bristol (1966–76)		Post Adoption and Care Counselling and Research Project, 91 Queens Road, Peckham, London SE15 2EZ Tel: 020 7732 9089
The Baker Street Society				Colloquial name for the National Adoption Society	
The Baptist Society				Colloquial name for the Baptist Union Adoption Society or Spurgeon's Homes	
Baptist Union Adoption Society	1948–70	Camden SSD	4 Southampton Row, London WC1	Became Spurgeon's Homes Adoption Society in 1970	Adoption Counsellor, Children and Families, 115 Wellesley Road, London, NW5 4PA
The Bloomsbury Society				Colloquial name for the Baptist Union Adoption Society or Spurgeon's Homes or the Church Adoption Society	
Bradford Diocesan Family Welfare Council				Became Bradford Diocesan Moral Welfare Council	
Bradford Diocesan Moral Welfare Council	1964–76	Bradford SSD. Mostly on microfilm, only a few missing	Church House, North Parade, Bradford		Unit Manager (Adoption and Fostering) SSD Headquarters
Bristol and Somerset Adoption Society				Became Avon and North Wilts in 1974	
Bristol Diocesan Moral Welfare Association	1920–62	Children's Society. Few early records available before 1955.	1 Lower Park Road; 20 Lower Park Road, Bristol 1	Amalgamated with Bristol and Somerset Adoption Society	Post Adoption and Care Counselling and Research Project, 91 Queens Road, Peckham, London SE15 2EZ Tel: 020 7732 9089

Name of Agency	Registered	Records: Location/ Availability	Former Address(es)	Notes	Enquiries to
Bristol Women's Aid Association		Early records not traced, and probably destroyed. Any records 1955–76 with Children's Society.	c/o Messrs Sibley & Clough, Solicitors, 12 Orchard Street, Bristol 1	May have amalgamated with Bristol and Somerset Adoption Society	
British Adoption Project	1964–69	BAAF, Skyline House, 200 Union Street, London SE1 0LX	Bedford College Annexe, Peto Place, Marylebone Road, London NW1	An experimental project. Part of International Social Service	The Director
Burton-upon-Trent Association for the Protection of Girls	Closed in 1960	Staffordshire SSD (after being lodged with Lichfield Diocesan Association)	53 Union Street, Burton-upon-Trent		Principal Childcare Manager, Family Placement
Carlisle Diocesan Family Welfare Association		Cumbria SSD. Incomplete and only from 1960		Not an adoption agency but worked with Northern Counties Adoption Society	Principal Social Worker (Adoption)
Carlisle Diocesan Society for Moral Welfare				Became Carlisle Diocesan FWA	
Catholic Children's Society (Shrewsbury Diocese) Inc	1963 95	At agency's office. St Paul's House, Farm Field Drive, Beechwood, Preston, Wirral CH43 7ZT None lost or destroyed.	10 Arnside Road, Birkenhead; 7 Park Road, East Birkenhead; 111 Shrewsbury Road, Birkenhead LA42 8SS	In collaboration with Nugent Care Society offer support to children and families involved in adoption prior to 1996. Particularly involved in post adoption support and section 51 counselling. Covers the areas of Cheshire, Halton, Shropshire, South Manchester, Stockport Tameside, Trafford, Warrington, Wirral and Wrekin	
Catholic Child Welfare Society (Diocese of Middlesbrough) Middlesbrough	1952. Now administered by St Cuthberts and Catholic Care Leeds	Catholic Care (Diocese of Leeds), 31 Moor Road, Headingley, Leeds LS6 4BG. None lost or destroyed.	261 Marton Street, Middlesbrough; 4 Oakfield Road, North Ormesby, Middlesbrough, Cleveland TS3 6EN; 110A, Lawrence Street, York Y01 3EB	Used to cover counties of North Humberside, North Yorkshire, City of York and Councils of Middlesbrough, Hartlepool, Stockton on Tees, Redcar and Langbrough	Team Leader (Homefinding Team) Catholic Care
Catholic Moral Welfare Council	1944–77	Catholic Children's Rescue Society (Diocese of Salford)	Gaddum Centre Deansgate, Manchester 3; Bank Buildings, Chapel Street, Salford 3; 2 Anson Road, Manchester	Not an adoption agency	The Secretary
Chelmsford Diocesan Committee for Family Care (Social Care)				Became Family Care	

Name of Agency	Registered	Records: Location/ Availability	Former Address(es)	Notes	Enquiries to
Chelmsford Diocesan Moral Welfare Association	1962			Became Family Care	
Chichester Diocesan Association for Family Social Work. Now Chichester Diocesan Association for Family Support Work	1952–85	East Sussex. None lost or destroyed. Access through East Sussex or Brighton and Hove. Present address: 211 New Church Road, Hove, East Sussex BN3 4ED.	Diocesan Church House, 9 Brunswick Square, Hove until 31 October 1980; 22 Stanford Avenue, Brighton BN1 6DD	Closed as an adoption agency August 1985, but continuing as an organisation. Many placements were made in West Sussex.	Administration Assistant (Adoption) Brighton and Hove Fostering and Adoption Team, East Sussex SSD HQ
Chichester Diocesan Moral Welfare Association	1952–68			Became Chichester Diocesan Association for Family Social Work	
Children – North East	Not an adoption agency. Began work 1891	Limited information available from 1950 onwards. 1 Claremont Street, Newcastle Upon Tyne NE2 4AH.	66 Percy Street, Newcastle-upon-Tyne; Ellison Place, Newcastle-upon-Tyne	Received children into residential care. Some were subsequently adopted but arrange-ments not made by this organisation.	The Director
Children's Aid Society	1946–66	Barnardo's, Cottage No 1, The Village, Barkingside, Ilford, Essex IG6 1BU. Records incomplete. About 425 cases on microfilm.	55 Leigham Court Road, Streatham, London SW16		The Counselling Service
Christian Family Concern	1893–1992	Some early records. Croydon Local Studies and Archives Central Library, Katherine Street, Croydon CR9 1ET; 54 Grove Avenue, London N10. Other records Croydon SSD.	78 Oakley Street, London SE1; 93 Westminster Bridge Road, London SE1; 162 High Road, Wood Green, London N22; Knighton Lodge, Canford Magna, Wimborne, Dorset; 14 South Park Hill Road, Croydon CR2 7YB; 54 Grove Avenue, London N10		The Archivist, Central Library or Service Manager, Adoption, Fostering and Leaving Care, Council Offices, 130 Brighton Road, Purley, Surrey, CR8 4HA
Christian Outreach Adoption Society	1974–88	1 New Street, Leamington Spa CV31 1HP	62 Bus Ridge Lane, Godalming, Surrey; 34 St Mary's Crescent, Leamington Spa, Warwickshire		The Director
Church's Association for Family Welfare				Became Avon and North Wilts	
Cleveland Family Welfare	Not a registered adoption society			Assessed families and placed babies with a variety of registered adoption societies, including Durham, Jarrow, Sunderland, and the Church of England Children's Society	

Previous voluntary agencies

Name of Agency	Registered	Records: Location/ Availability	Former Address(es)	Notes	Enquiries to
Cornwall Social and Moral Welfare Association	1951–66	Cornwall SSD. Some information from 1941. Complete files microfilmed, minute books and miscellaneous papers – about 500 papers.	Morwenna, Lescudjack Terrace, Penzance; Gwendroc, Truro		Team Leader (Adoption and Family Finding Unit)
Derby Diocesan Council for Moral Welfare				Became Derby Diocesan Council for SW Adoption Committee	
Derby Diocesan Council for Social Work Adoption Committee	1964–74	Derby City Council – records before 1964 lost, otherwise none lost or destroyed.	5 College Place, Derby		Assistant Director, Children's Services, Middleton House, 27 St Mary's Gate, Derby DE1 3NV
Diocesan Children's Rescue Society			111 Shrewsbury Road, Birkenhead	Became Catholic's Children's Society (Shrewsbury Diocese) Inc	
Diocese of Portsmouth Catholic Child Welfare Society	1952–77		Peter House, Peter Street, Winchester; 100 Wilton Avenue, Southampton	Merged with Catholic Children's Society (Arundel and Brighton, Portsmouth and Southwark) where records are held	
Diocese of Portsmouth Catholic Social Service Council	1952		29 Jewry Street, Winchester; 18 The Avenue, Southampton	Merged with Catholic Children's Society (Arundel and Brighton, Portsmouth and Southwark) where records are held	
Downguard Ltd				Became York Adoption Society	
Durham and Northumberland Adoption Society				Became Northern Counties Adoption Society	
Ely Diocesan Moral Welfare Association	1920–65	Cambridge SSD	Bateman St, Cambridge; Cluny, Chittering, Cambridge; Bishop Woodford House, Barton Road, Ely		Homefinding, Buttsgrove Centre, 38 Buttsgrove Way, Huntingdon PE18 7LY and Homefinding, 18–20 Signet Court Road, Cambridge CB5 8LA

Name of Agency	Registered	Records: Location/ Availability	Former Address(es)	Notes	Enquiries to
Fairhaven	Closed 1967	Not traced	6 Church Hill, 76 Leam Terrace, Leamington Spa	Run by Leamington and Warwickshire Girl's Shelter Association. Was also a Mother and Baby Home	Worth trying Coventry SSD for individual records.
Family Care	Closed 1982	Essex SSD. Records intact – microfilmed.	40 Argyle Road, Ilford; Durning Hall, Ilford; 71 New London Road; 126 New London Road and 53 New Street, Chelmsford		The Administrator, Adoption Resource Centre, SSD, Eckard House, Eastern Road, Witham CM8
Family Ties	1942–98	Parents for Children, 41 Southgate Road, London N1 3JP. Some records destroyed after 25 years. Others incomplete/intact since 1965.	11 Wilton Place, London SW1 (1969–72); 98A Earls Court Road, London W8 (1972–73); 88 West Hill, London SW15 2UT (1973–1998)	Before 1969 Mrs Phyllis Holman Richards was placing children as a third party in arranging adoptions	The Director, Parents for Children
F B Myer's Children's Home	1920			Became Christian Family Concern	
Four Deaneries Family Welfare Association		N. Yorkshire SSD; records retrievable.	13 Pavilion Street, Scarborough	Not an adoption agency but does have information about some adoptions arranged through local agencies	Adoption Section
Girls' Home			53 Union Street, Burton-upon-Trent	Became Burton-upon-Trent Association for the Protection of Girls	
Gloucester Diocesan Association for Moral Welfare	1935–61		College Chambers, College Court, Gloucester	Became Gloucester Diocesan Council for Social Work	
Gloucester Diocesan Association for Prevention and Rescue Work	1912–35			Became Gloucester Diocesan Council for Social Work	
Gloucester Diocesan Council for Social Work	1948–83	Gloucester SSD. No formal records of placements before 1948. Some case files of natural parents still in existence (though records of parents in Cheltenham area 1948–54 lost or destroyed).	College Green, Gloucester (1926–44); The Cloisters, Gloucester (1944–1954). The organisation had a second office at 18 Imperial Square, Cheltenham (1954–76)		Adoption Panel Administrator, SSD, Block 4 Shire Hall, Westgate Street, Gloucester GL1 2TR
Hamilton House	Closed 1953	Not traced. Thought to be run by Coventry Diocese.	12 Bilton Road, Rugby		Worth trying Coventry SSD for individual records.

Name of Agency	Registered	Records: Location/ Availability	Former Address(es)	Notes	Enquiries to
Harrow and Willesden Ruri-Decanal Association for Moral Welfare		London Metropolitan Archives have House Committee Minutes June 1917–July 1932	4 Peterborough Road, Harrow		Worth trying Barnado's as well as London Metropolitan Archives
Haven for Homeless Little Ones	1912–18			Became Christian Family Care	
The Haven for Moral Welfare		Records destroyed on closure but files of individuals may be with Wakefield SSD.	1–3 Linden Terrace, Pontefract	Not a registered adoption agency but a mother and baby home, from which adoptions may have been arranged.	Adoption Officer, Family Placement Team, Children's Centre, 6 Springfield Grange, Flanshaw, Wakefield WF2 9QT
Homeless Children's Aid and Adoption Society			54 Grove Avenue, Muswell Hill, London N10	Became Christian Family Concern	
Hong Kong Project	1958–1969	Intact. With International Social Service.	70 Denison House, 296 Vauxhall Bridge Road, London SW1; 39 Brixton Road, London SW9 6DD.	Adoption of Children from Hong Kong in collaboration with National Children's Home and Barnardo's.	The Director, International Social Service, 39 Brixton Road, London SW9 6DD.
Hutchinson House Children's Home	1920–24		Buswood, London E11	Part of Homeless Children's Aid and Adoption Society	
International Social Service	Registered Agency for duration of two Projects		70 Denison House, 296 Vauxhall Bridge Road, London SW1; 39 Brixton Road, London SW9 6DD.	Were involved only with the British Adoption and Hong Kong Projects.	
The Knightsbridge				Colloquial name for the National Children Adoption Association	
Lahai-Roi	1949–59 (Approx.)	No separate records. Worth contacting Birmingham SSD about individuals.	42 Park Hill, Moseley, Birmingham 13		Senior Social Worker (Central Resource Exchange)
Lancashire and Cheshire Child Adoption Council	1929–79	Liverpool SSD, from 1943 only. Some missing.	Former addresses all in Liverpool: Bluecoat Chambers, School Lane; 2 Maryland Street; 23 Clarence Street (1935–45); 5 Cases Street (1945–66); 72 Rodney Street (1966–79)	On BAAF files is an interesting short account of the Council's early history	Team Manager Adoption
Leamington and Warwick Girls' Shelter Association	Uncertain	Warneford Hospital, Leamington Spa	Fairhaven, 6 Church Hill, Leamington.	Was an extension to Gay Block Maternity Wing, Warneford Hospital	Hospital Administrator (access may be difficult)

Name of Agency	Registered	Records: Location/ Availability	Former Address(es)	Notes	Enquiries to
Leicester & Leicestershire Adoption Society				Became Leicester Diocesan Board for Social Responsibility	
Leicester Diocesan Board for Social Responsibility	1943–80	Leics SSD. Some records possibly destroyed.	21 Manor Road, Kingsthorpe; 278 East Park Road, Leicester		Team Manager (Adoption), 11 Grey Friars, Leicester LE1 5RB
Leicester Diocesan Board of Social Work	1972			Became Leicester Diocesan Board for Social Responsibility	
Leicester Diocesan Council for Social Work	1965–72		In Leicester: 70 Regent Road (1935–40); 3a West Street (1941–72); 278 East Park Road	Became Leicester Diocesan Board for Social Responsibility	
Leicester Diocesan Moral Welfare Association	1935–64			Became Leicester Diocesan Board for Social Responsibility	
Lichfield Diocesan Association for Family Care	1954–76	Staffordshire SSD; five files with Wolverhampton SSD. Brief records of adoptions from 1952.	Rickerscote House, Stafford; 49 Cedar Way, Walton-on-the-Hill, Stafford; 23 Greengate Street, Stafford		Principal Child Care Manager, Family Placement
Lichfield Diocesan Association for Moral Welfare	1943			Became Lichfield Diocesan Association	
Lincoln Diocesan Association for Moral Welfare	1943			Became Lincoln Diocesan Board for Social Work	
Lincoln Diocesan Board for Social Work	1943–74	Lincolnshire SSD. None lost or destroyed. About 2500 cases.	1 James Street, Lincoln; Jews Court, Steep Hill, Lincoln		Adoption Records Section, SSD
Manchester and District Child Adoption Society	1944–78	Manchester SSD, 25 Rochdale Road, Manchester M9 1DD. None lost or destroyed.	1944–48: work done from home of Secretary, Mr E Scully, 241 Dickinson Road, Manchester 14; 1949–54: from home of Chairman and Secretary, Mrs E Falkner Hill and Miss A K Hill; office in Gaddum House, 16–18 Queen Street, Manchester 2; office at 3 Ridgefield, Manchester M2 6EG, Secretary Mrs T Hedley Bell		Senior Manager, Family Placement, SSD, 25 Rochdale Road, Manchester M9 1DD
Memorial Centre of Help for Babies	1942–72	No trace of records prior to 1958.	South Lodge, Lower Beeding, Horsham, Sussex (1942–)	Became Family Ties	
Middlesbrough Diocesan Resource Society				Became Catholic Child Welfare Society (Diocese of Middlesbrough)	

Name of Agency	Registered	Records: Location/ Availability	Former Address(es)	Notes	Enquiries to
Mission of Hope	1893		In London: 4 Shernhall Street and Vine House, Walthamstow; Castle House, Walton Heath; 93 Grove Lane, SE5; Rokeby, 54 & 132 Leigham Court Road, Streatham (1914–); Birdhurst Lodge, South Park Hill Road, Croydon (1922–)	1979 Merged with Homeless Children's Aid and Adoption Society and F B Meyers Children's Home. Became Mission of Hope for Children's Aid and Adoption	
Mission of Hope for Children's Aid and Adoption	1979		78 Oakley Street, London SW3 and 93 Westminster Bridge Road, London SE1; 162 High Road, Wood Green, London N22; Knighton Lodge, Canford Magna, Wimborne, Dorset; 42 South Park Hill Road, Croydon CR2 7YB; Linden Gate, Clifton, Dover Road, Bristol BS8 4AH	Became Christian Family Concern	
Muswell Hill Society			54 Grove Avenue, London N10	Colloquial name for Homeless Children's Aid and Adoption Society	
National Adoption Society (Not to be confused with entry in Chapter 2)	1917–86 Earliest placements 1917–18. First placements under 1926 Adoption Act in 1927	Brent SSD	In London: 2 Baker Street, W1 (1918–?); 4 Baker Street, W1 (until 1955); 47a Manchester St, W1M 6DJ (until 1979); Hooper Cottage, Kimberley Road, NW6 (until 1986)		The Administrative Secretary, NAS Records Office, Triangle House, 328/330 High Street, Wembley HA9 6AZ
National Children Adoption Association	1917–78	Westminster SSD. First 10,000 files lost in the Second World War.	46 Sydenham Hill, London SE26 (1940); 19 Sloane Street, London SW1; 20 Calverton Road, Stony Stratford, Bucks (1942); Denton Lodge, Wokingham (1943); 71 Knightsbridge, London SW1		The Administrator, Family Placement Service, 33 Tachbrook Street, London SW12 2JR
North East Children's Society				Became Children – North East	
Northern Counties Adoption Society	1943–77	Newcastle-upon-Tyne SSD. Records almost complete.	In Newcastle-upon-Tyne: Mea House, Ellison Place; 24 St Mary's Place; 5 Saville Place; 1 Nixon Street; 34 Dean Street		Administrative Officer (Adoption Unit) Newcastle-upon-Tyne SSD
Nottingham Day Nursery and Children's Homes	Closed 1954	Nottinghamshire Archives, County House, Castle Meadow Road, Nottingham NG2 1AG (Ref. DD1101)	Imperial Road, Beeston, Notts	Not an adoption agency but children may have been adopted from it	Principal Archivist

Name of Agency	Registered	Records: Location/ Availability	Former Address(es)	Notes	Enquiries to
Oldham Adoption Society	1943–82	Oldham SSD. Some records destroyed after 25 years; others incomplete. Intact since 1963.	In Oldham: 11 Clegg Street; 6 Ascroft Street; 3 Bertha Street		Family Placement Team, Children's Central Resources, Marian Walker House, Frederick Street, Oldham OL8 1SW
Oldham Council of Social Services Adoption Committee				Became Oldham Adoption Society	
Phyllis Holman Richards Adoption Society	1942–94			Became Family Ties	
Plymouth and District Association for Girls' Welfare		At closure, records passed to Children's Department but not traced since. Worth trying Devon SSD for individual records.	2 Woodside Place	A mother and baby home from which adoptions may have been arranged	Adoption Service Manager, Adoption Unit, Foxhole, Dartington, Totnes TQ9 6EB
Poor Children's Holiday Association and Rescue Agency, Newcastle-upon-Tyne				Became Children – North East	
The Poor Children's Homes Association and Rescue Agency, Newcastle-upon-Tyne				Became Children – North East	
Portsmouth Catholic Social Services Council	1973–77	Catholic Children's Society, 49 Russell Hill Road, Purley, Surrey CR8 2XB None lost or destroyed.	29 Jewry Street, Winchester, (1952–57); 18 The Avenue, Southampton (1957–62); 100 Wilton Avenue, Southampton SO1 2HD	Became part of Catholic Children's Society (Arundel & Brighton, Portsmouth & Southwark)	The Directors
Portsmouth Diocesan Catholic and Welfare Society				Became part of Catholic's Children's Society (Arundel & Brighton, Portsmouth & Southwark)	
Portsmouth Diocesan Children's Society	1952–73			Became part of Catholic's Children's Society (Arundel & Brighton, Portsmouth & Southwark)	

Previous voluntary agencies

Name of Agency	Registered	Records: Location/ Availability	Former Address(es)	Notes	Enquiries to
Portsmouth Diocesan Council for Moral Welfare	1947–61		29 Jewry Street, Winchester (1952–57); 18 The Avenue, Southampton (1957–62)	Became Portsmouth Diocesan Council for Social Responsibility	
Portsmouth Diocesan Council for Social Responsibility	1947 – Jan 1978	Hampshire SSD but accessed through Adoption Manager, Portsmouth	St David's Road, Southsea (1946–59); Highbury Grove, Cosham (1959–75); 159 Elm Grove, Southsea; All Saints' Church, Commercial Road, Portsmouth		Adoption Manager, Adoption Section, Civic Offices, Guildhall Square, Portsmouth PO1 2EP
Portsmouth Diocesan Council for Social Work			18 Sandport Terrace, Southsea	Became Portsmouth Diocesan Council for Social Responsibility	
Project Vietnam Orphans	1952–73			Became Christian Outreach Adoption Society Ltd	
The Retreat (Run by National Free Church Women's Council)		Some records with London Metropolitan Archives	19 and 35 Ross Road, London SE25	A mother and baby home from which private adoptions may have been arranged	Croydon SSD might have records of some individuals
Royal Society				Colloquial name for National Children Adoption Association	
St Albans Diocesan Association for Girls' Aid	1890–1941			Became St Albans Diocesan Council for Social Responsibility	
St Albans Diocesan Council for Moral Welfare Work	1942–65			Became St Albans Diocesan Council for Social Responsibility	
St Albans Diocesan Council for Social Responsibility	1954–1977	Herts SSD. None lost or destroyed. No early records of placements.	St Albans Abbey Institute, Romelands; 41 Holywell Hill	Before setting up of adoption agency in 1954, social workers arranged their own adoptions locally, often through National Adoption Society, Baptist Union or National Children's Home. Some pre-1957 case notes are available.	Post Adoption Worker Family Placement Team, 120 Victoria Street, St Albans AL1 3TG
St Albans Diocesan Council for Social Welfare				Became St Albans Diocesan Council for Social Work	
St Albans Diocesan Council for Social Work	1966–76			Became St Albans Diocesan Council for Social Responsibility	

Name of Agency	Registered	Records: Location/ Availability	Former Address(es)	Notes	Enquiries to
St Faith's Adoption Society or St Faith's Shelter	(Stems from work for mothers and babies begun 1895.) Registered between 1939 and 1945, first legalised adoptions probably in 1943.	Coventry SSD. Early records destroyed. Difficult to trace files before 1948. Some information held in notebook form from 1927.	Addresses in Coventry: 17 Trafalgar Street (1895); Ardenside, Coudon Road (1904); Holy Trinity Vicarage, St Nicholas Street (1913); Holyhead Road (1917); 41 Chester Street (1919) (first known as St Faith's); Little Park Street; Dudley Lodge, 143 Warwick Road		Administrative Assistant (Family Placement Service), Stoke House, Lloyd Crescent, Wyken, Coventry CV2 5NY
St Gabriel's Adoption Society (Weymouth)	1952–73	Dorchester SSD. None lost or destroyed. 312 cases. Microfilm only. No originals.	In Weymouth: 18 Dorchester Road; Health Centre, Westham Road		Adoption and Fostering Team, Dorchester SSD, Acland Road, Dorchester, Dorset DT1 1SH
St Saviour's Diocesan Maternity Home	1948		21 Manor Road, Kingsthorpe; 103 Harteston Road, Northants	Became Leicester Board for Social Responsibilty	
Sheffield Council of Social Service				Became Sheffield and District Child Adoption Association	
Sheffield and District Child Adoption Association	1943–76	Sheffield SSD. Records before 1951 destroyed.	55 Norfolk Street, Sheffield 1; 57 Upper Hanover Street, Sheffield S3 7RJ		Family Placement Service, Sheffield City Council, 2nd Floor, Castle Market Buildings, Exchange Street, Sheffield S1 2AH
Shrewsbury Diocesan Catholic Children's Society and Family Advice Service			Became Catholic Children's Society (Shrewsbury Diocese) Inc.		
Shrewsbury Diocesan Children's Rescue Society	1948		Became Catholic Children's Society (Shrewsbury Diocese) Inc.		
Spurgeon's Homes Adoption Society	1970–72	Camden SSD	Park Road, and Haddon House, Station Road, Birchington, Kent; 4 Southhampton Row, London WC1		Adoption Counsellor, Children and Families, 115 Wellesley Road, London NW5 4PA
Welcare, Chelmsford	1971			Became Family Care	

Previous voluntary agencies

Name of Agency	Registered	Records: Location/ Availability	Former Address(es)	Notes	Enquiries to
Western National Adoption Society	1941–76	Brent SSD. Some early records destroyed during 1935–45 war.	In Bath: 8 Bennet's Street; 8 Queen's Parade; 1 John Street		The Administrative Secretary, NAS Records Office, Triangle House, 328/ 330 High Street, Wembley HA9 6AZ
West of England Adoption Society				Another name for Western National Adoption Society	
Women's Mission to Women				Became Children's Aid Society	
Worcester Diocesan Association for Family and Social Services	1947–72	Worcestershire CC. None lost or destroyed. About 2000 cases.	12 Severn Terrace, Worcester; 165 Worcester Road, Malvern; 91 Lowsmoor, Worcester	Index with SSD Central Office	Principal Officer (Adoption), The Pines, Bilford Road, Worcester WR3 8PU
Worcester Diocesan Association for Moral Welfare Work				Became Worcester Diocesan Association for Family and Social Services	
Worthing and District Council of Social Service www.guildcare. co.uk	1950–73	Now Guild Care, 1 Aldsworth Parade, Goring Way, Goring-by-Sea, Worthing, West Sussex BN12 4TX	Chatsworth Chambers, Chapel Road, Worthing (before 1957); Worthing Area Guild of Voluntary Service, 7–9 North Street, Worthing		The Chief Executive
York Adoption Society	1943–83	N. Yorkshire SSD	In York: 9 Minster Yard (1943–45); 84 Walmgate (1946–); 64 Walmgate (1947–57); 10 Priory St (1952–66); 29 Marygate (1966–83)		Adoption Section
York Community Council				Became York Adoption Society	

WALES

Name of Agency	Registered	Records: Location/ Availability	Former Address(es)	Notes	Enquiries to
Bangor Diocesan Adoption Society	1960–1984	Arfon Office, SSD Gwynedd Council	The Vicarage, Port Dinorwice, Gwynedd; The Old Vicarage, Waterloo Street, Bangor, Gwynedd LL57 1DS		Adoption Officer, SSD, Gwynedd Council, Penrallt, Caernarfon, Gwynedd LL55 1BN, Fax: 01286 672765
Bangor Diocesan Council for Moral Welfare				Became Bangor Diocesan Adoption Society	

Previous voluntary agencies

Name of Agency	Registered	Records: Location/ Availability	Former Address(es)	Notes	Enquiries to
Bangor Diocesan Council for Social Work				Became Bangor Diocesan Adoption Society	
National Children's Home		Previous records all held at 85 Highbury Park, London N5 1UD. None lost or destroyed.			General Records Administrator, NCH Headquarters RH12 4EU
St David's Adoption Society	1945–73	Carmarthenshire SSD	2 Wellfield Road; 23 Longacre Road; Ty'or Eglwys, Abergwili; St Peter's Church House, North Square; Fronhaul, Llanybyther, Carmarthen		Assistant Director for Children's Services, Adoption Archive, Department of Social Care and Housing, 3–5 Spilman Street, Carmarthen SA31 1LE, Fax: 01267 228908
St David's Diocesan Moral Welfare Committee				Became St David's Adoption Society	
Swansea and Brecon Diocesan Council for Social Work	1959–79	Swansea SSD. Some lost or destroyed.	The Vicarage, Llanfaes, Brecon, Powys; 57 Sketty Road, Uplands, Swansea; 20 John Street and 101 Walter Road, Oystermouth, Swansea		The Adoption Officer, Cockett House, Cockett Road, Cockett, Swansea SA2 0FJ
Swansea and Brecon Diocesan Moral Welfare Association				Became Swansea and Brecon Diocesan Council for Social Work	

SCOTLAND

Name of Agency	Registered	Records: Location/ Availability	Former Address(es)	Notes	Enquiries to
Aberdeen Association of Social Service				Became Voluntary Service, Aberdeen	
Barnardo's New Families Project	1976–84	Barnado's Family Placement Service, 6 Torphichen Street, Edinburgh EH3 8JQ	227 Byers Road, Glasgow; 235 Costorphine Road, Glasgow		Project Leader
Church of Scotland Committee on Social and Moral Welfare	1963–80			Became Church of Scotland Committee on Social Responsibility	

Previous voluntary agencies

Name of Agency	Registered	Records: Location/ Availability	Former Address(es)	Notes	Enquiries to
Church of Scotland Committee on Social Responsibility	1951–80	Scottish Adoption Association. Records available from 1943.	Adoption Section, Committee on Social Service (to 1963) and Committee on Social and Moral Welfare (1963–80), 121 George Street, Edinburgh EH2 4YN		Scottish Adoption Association, 2 Commercial Street, Leith, Edinburgh EH6 6JA, Fax: 0131 553 6422 or Planning and Commissioning Manager, City Council, Shrubhill House, 7 Shrub Place, Edinburgh EH7 4PD
Church of Scotland Committee on Social Service	Up to 1963			Became Church of Scotland Committee on Social Responsibility	
Dundee Association for Social Service	1971–79	Dundee City Council. None lost or destroyed.	Castlehill House, 1 High Street, Dundee		Senior Officer, Adoption and Fostering SWD, 6 Kirton Road, Dundee DD3 0B2
Episcopal Church in Scotland, Social Services Board				Became Scottish Episcopal Church Adoption Society	
Melville House Adoption Society	1957–70	Dundee City Council	Melville House, Perth (1909); 129 Scott Street, Perth		Senior Officer, Adoption and Fostering SWD, 6 Kirton Road, Dundee DD3 0B2
National Vigilance Association *Not to be confused with National Vigilance Association of Scotland (below)*	Closed mid 1970s	Records destroyed on closure, but Glasgow may have supervision records of children placed within Glasgow area.			Families for Children, 115 Wellington St, Glasgow G2 2XT
National Vigilance Association of Scotland				Became Melville House (Not to be confused with National Vigilance Association)	
Perth and Dundee Association of Social Service		Dundee City Council			Senior Officer, Adoption and Fostering SWD, 6 Kirton Road, Dundee DD3 0B2

Name of Agency	Registered	Records: Location/ Availability	Former Address(es)	Notes	Enquiries to
Scottish Episcopal Church Adoption Society	1959–78	Scottish Adoption Association. None lost or destroyed.	In Edinburgh: 21 Grosvenor Crescent, 13 Drumsheugh Gardens (until 1970)		Scottish Adoption Association, 2 Commercial Street, Leith, Edinburgh EH6 6JA, Fax: 0131 553 6422
Voluntary Service, Aberdeen	1963–84	Aberdeenshire SWD			Principal Planning Officer (Children's Services), Woodhill House, Westburn Road, Aberden AB16 5GB

EIRE

Name of Agency	Registered	Records: Location/ Availability	Former Address(es)	Notes	Enquiries to
Challenge Adoption Society		SEEK 32 The Mall, Waterford	Sion House, Waterford Road, Kilkenny		Senior Social Worker
Catholic Women's Aid Society		Held by : Sacred Heart Convent, Blackrock, Cork and some (very limited) by the Adoption Board Shelbourne House, Shelbourne Road, Ballsbridge, Dublin 4	14 Brown Street Cork		Senior Social Worker
Holles Street Hospital Adoption Agency		Adoption Board, Shelbourne House, Shelbourne Road, Ballsbridge, Dublin 4, Fax: 00 353 1 667 1438	Dublin		Senior Social Worker
Limerick Catholic Adoption Society		De-registered 30/11/99. The Mid-Western Health Board, Glenbevan, Upper Mayorstone, Limerick, Fax: 00 353 6 132 1144	Unit 3, St Camillius Hospital, Shelbourne Road, Limerick, Glenbevan House, Upper Mayorstone, Limerick		Social Work, Team Leader
Ossory Adoption Society				Became Challenge Adoption Society	
Rotunda Girls Aid Society (RGAS)		With Society at 1a Cathedral Street, Dublin 1		Provides post-adoption service to adopters and a search and reunion service.	The Secretary
Sacred Heart Adoption Society		Records with Sacred Heart Adoption Society, Blackrock, Cork Fax: 00 353 2 135 9395	Castlepollard, Co Westmeath		Senior Social Worker

Previous voluntary agencies

Name of Agency	Registered	Records: Location/ Availability	Former Address(es)	Notes	Enquiries to
Sacred Heart Adoption Society		Sacred Heart Convent, Blackrock, Cork Fax: 00 353 2 135 9395	Bessboro	Some children were sent abroad for adoption. Hold records of Sean Ross Abbey, Roscrea, Co Tipperary and Castlepollard, Co Westmeath. Continue to provide a trace and reunion service.	Senior Social Worker
St Attracta's Adoption Society		North Western Health Board, Markieviez House, Barrack Street, Sligo	St Mary's, Sligo Summerhill Athlone	Provides a post adoption service to adopters and a search and reunion service.	Senior Social Worker
St Brigid's Adoption Service		With agency, Holy Faith Convent, 16 The Coombe, Dublin 8	46 Eccles Street, Dublin, 68 Iona Road, Glasnevin	No longer placing children for adoption but provides a search and reunion service and a post adoption service to adopters.	Social Worker or Sister in charge
St Clare's Adoption Society		Child and Family Centre, North Eastern Health Board, Dublin Road, Drogheda, Co Louth Fax: 00 353 413 3067	St Michael's Presbytery, Castlepollard, Co Westmeath, Stamullen, Co Meath		Senior Social Worker
St John's Adoption Society		SEEK 32 The Mall Waterford Fax: 00 353 5 187 8574	Cathedral Presbytery, 3 George's Street, Waterford		Senior Social Worker
St Kevin's Adoption Society		SEEK 32 The Mall Waterford Fax: 00 353 5 187 8574	St Joseph's Hospital, Dungarvan, Co Waterford		Senior Social Worker
St Mary's Adoption Society		Kerry Adoption and Fostering Service, Southern Health Board, 18-20 Denny Street, Tralee, Co Kerry Fax: 00 353 66 24515	20 Denny Street, Tralee, Co Kerry		Senior Social Worker, Kerry Adoption and Fostering Team, 6 Denny Street, Tralee, Co Kerry
St Nicholas' Adoption Society		Clann Western Regional Adoption Service, Merlin Park Hospital, Galway Fax: 00 353 91 755 632	Ross House Victoria Place Galway		Senior Social Worker
St Patrick's Guild, 82 Haddington Road, Dublin 4 Fax: 00 353 1 668 6234		Headquarters of agency	Middle Abbey Street, Dublin (until approx. late 60's)	Provides search / reunion services for adoptees and birth parents. Post adoption service to adopters.	

Name of Agency	Registered	Records: Location/ Availability	Former Address(es)	Notes	Enquiries to
St Rita's Sandford Road, Ranelagh, Dublin 6		Limited information with Public Health Dept, Regional Health Authority, Eastern Health Board, Dr Steven's Hospital, Dublin 8		Not an adoption agency. A nursing home privately run by a family named Keating. In some cases, children were placed with American service families and others, often having been registered in the names of their adopting parents.	Information obtainable by social workers only through the Adoption Board, Dublin or Barnardo's, Dublin
St Theresa's Adoption Society		Very limited records. Adoption Board, Shelbourne House, Shelbourne Road, Ballsbridge, Dublin 4 Fax: 00 353 1 667 1438	Carmelite Priory, 56 Aungier Street, Dublin 2 ; Whitefriar Street, Dublin		Senior Social Worker
Sean Ross Abbey		Sacred Heart Adoption Society, Blackrock, Cork Fax: 00 353 21 359 395	Roscrea, Co Tipperary		Senior Social Worker Fax: 00 353 21 359 395

4 • Homes: maternity, mother-and-baby, shelter

"Adoptions" were arranged before the first Adoption Act in 1926 by existing adoption agencies (sometimes by Indentures) and by Poor Law Guardians who had a responsibility for destitute children. They were also arranged by professional people such as nurses or doctors, and by private arrangements between individuals. In a few cases, children were registered at birth as the children of the adopting family. Some children were sent abroad.

From the second half of the 19th century onwards, homes where pregnant women could receive help, and from which children could be adopted, were set up by a wide variety of (mainly Christian) organisations, and by many concerned individuals. Although the latter often had affiliations with established organisations, such as Churches or Dioceses, they could be independent trusts or ad hoc bodies with local management committees.

Moral Welfare workers (later known as WelCare workers) often had "outside cases" of women living in the community. They also had responsibility for mothers in a residential home to which they normally went for six weeks before, and six weeks after, the babies' births because a birth mother's consent to adoption was not legal for the first six weeks, and workers frequently had a group of foster mothers whom they used regularly. BAAF has a list of some of those used by London workers in the 1950s and 60s. Some workers kept scanty records. Others kept meticulous registers, reports to case committees (sometimes giving first names only) and, in addition, kept individual case papers. This was more frequent in the post-Second World War years. The homes were used by many different social workers, often quite a distance away, and the main records would be kept by them. Confidentiality was very strict indeed, so that when Moral Welfare workers retired, or a home was closed, papers could be destroyed, or retained by the individual worker and subsequently lost. A number of the workers are listed by name in chapter 5.

When still extant, records are usually with social services/ social work departments, county or borough archivists, the Social Responsibility Officer at the Church of England Diocesan Board for Social Responsibility or the Catholic Diocesan Children's Society. Details of all the Boards for Social Responsibility in England are contained in the Directory available from Church House. Details of Catholic Dioceses are contained in the Catholic Directory, available from the Catholic Child Welfare Council (addresses in Chapter 9). The registers are not always with the case papers, and archivists quite often have administrative records with no details about individuals.

An additional complication is that deaneries (a sub-unit of a diocese) and dioceses do not coincide with county boundaries, and London deaneries were not coterminous with boroughs until 1965. Thus, for example, Southwark WelCare was founded in April 1894 as the Rochester Diocesan Association for the Care of Friendless Girls. The present Diocese of Southwark then formed part of the Diocese of Rochester. It now covers all the London boroughs south of the river, and many of its early records are with the London Metropolitan Archives. Some boroughs still have their own WelCare offices. Similarly, the London Diocesan Board for Social Responsibility covers all the London boroughs north of the river, and although some individual boroughs still have their own offices, all pre-1980 records have been centralised, and are held by Barnado's.

Quite often, babies were christened while in the home, so minimal information could still be available in the local church register. BAAF has a little additional information about children's homes, foster mothers in London, and the history of some voluntary organisations. If the area in which the adoption order was made is known, it is always worth asking the local social services department if they have records.

At one time, Guardian *ad litem* reports for the court being asked to make an adoption order were prepared by Education Officers responsible to the local County Council. If the child was in the care of that council and the Education Officers were therefore regarded as interested parties, the Guardian *ad litem* report might be prepared by a probation officer. The Probation Service keeps its records for 10 years only. There is no doubt that many records were lost, particularly when systems changed in 1948 and 1971. Also, when the county and borough boundaries changed in 1974, not all records were transferred to the new social services/social work departments. Great care of records was taken during the boundary changes of 1996–8, but some records may be in unexpected places.

In the following sections, when the address of the archivist or other record-holding organisation is given under the area heading, it is not repeated in that section. If the specific location or absence of records is not given under the heading "Records", the originating or using organisation has them as far as is known.

Normally all records held by archivists should be accessed through an adoption counsellor as there is often an embargo of many years on confidential information held by them.

Area	Name and Address	Run or used by	Records

ENGLAND

BATH & NORTH EAST SOMERSET Part of Avon until 1 April 1996

Area	Name and Address	Run or used by	Records
Bath	Hillview, 12 Walcot Parade, Bath (1920-56)	Bath Vigilance Association	Extremely scanty records with City Archivist, Guildhall, Bath BA1 5AW
	St Joseph's, Corston, Bath (previously St Joseph's, Lambeth)	Roman Catholic (Diocese of Southwark)	Probably Catholic Children's Society (Arundel and Brighton, Portsmouth and Southwark)

BEDFORDSHIRE

Area	Name and Address	Run or used by	Records
Bedford	Bedford and County Girls' Home, 1 Hillrise, Park Road North, Bedford	St Albans Diocesan Council for Social Responsibility	
	Hillrise (M&B), 1 Hillrise, Park Road North, Bedford (1931–58)	Bedford and District Churches Housing Association Ltd; C of E Diocese (St Albans)	Herts SSD hold some records from North Bedfordshire which sometimes have information about individuals who had been in Hillrise.
	Holt House (M&B), 178 Hurst Grove, Bedford (1961–68)	St Albans Diocesan Council for Social Responsibility; C of E Diocese (St Albans)	

BLACKBURN

Part of Lancashire until 1 April 1998
The County Archivist, Lancashire Record Office, Bow Lane, Preston, Lancs PR1 2RE holds records of Blackburn Diocesan Moral Welfare Council & Leyland Deanery M.W. Association.

Area	Name and Address	Run or used by	Records
Blackburn	The Grange (M&B), Wilpshire, Blackburn (Closed)	Manchester and District Child Adoption Society	County Archivist as above
	Springfield House, 133 Preston New Road, Blackburn (closed 1959)	Blackburn Diocesan Adoption Agency	County Archivist as above
	Viewfield (M&B), off Manor Road, Blackburn Closed about 1946 Replaced by The Grange	Blackburn Adoption Agency	County Archivist as above

BLACKPOOL

Part of Lancashire until 1 April 1998

Area	Name and Address	Run or used by	Records
Blackpool	Fylde House (M&B), 141 Hornby Road, Blackpool	Ashton-under-Lyne Adoption Society; Blackburn Diocesan Adoption Agency	County Archivist, Lancashire Record Office, Bow Lane, Preston, Lancs PR1 2RE

BOURNEMOUTH

Part of Dorset until 1 April 1997

Area	Name and Address	Run or used by	Records
Bournemouth	Free Church Maternity Home, 3 and 11 St Alban's Avenue, Bournemouth and 46 Foxholes Road, Bournemouth (closed 1969)	Bournemouth Free Church Council; National Free Church Women's Council; Mission of Hope for Children's Aid and Adoption (from 1945)	Some records with Hampshire SSD; possibly some with Mission of Hope Records; London Metropolitan Archives has some records of the Free Church Women's Council
	St Thomas's Lodge (M&B), 12 Charminster Road, Bournemouth (1964–71)	Bournemouth Deanery Council for Moral Welfare; C of E Diocese (Winchester)	Any available records with Hampshire SSD

Homes and Shelters

Area	Name and Address	Run or used by	Records
BRIGHTON & HOVE	Part of East Sussex until 1 April 1997		
	Chichester Diocesan Association for Family Social Work (now Chichester Diocesan Association for Family Support Work) was responsible for most of the C of E Diocese (Chichester) Homes in East & West Sussex, Brighton & Hove. Casework files were destroyed after 10 years. The records of any adoptions arranged by the Society are with East Sussex SSD.		
Brighton	Albion Hill House, 11 Finsbury Road, Brighton	Church Army	Not traced. Worth trying East & West Sussex SSD as above.
	Bevan House (MH), Finsbury Road, Brighton	Church Army	Not traced. Worth trying East & West Sussex SSD as above.
	Garton House (M&B), 22 Stanford Avenue, Brighton (closed)	Chichester Diocesan Association for Family Social Work	Lewes SSD (Archives)
	Marie Vickers House, Finsbury Road, Brighton	Church Army	Not traced. Worth trying as above.
Hove	Day Servants' Hostel, 21 Seafield Road, Hove	Affiliated to National Council for One Parent Families	Not traced. Worth trying East Sussex SSD as above.
Ovingdean	St Mary's, Ovingdean, Nr Rottingdean	C of E Diocese (Chichester)	Worth trying East Sussex SSD as above.
BRISTOL	Part of Avon until 1 April 1996 The records of Bristol M.W. Association are held by the Children's Society.		
Bristol	Bristol Maternity Hospital	See Southwell House below	Senior Archivist, Bristol Record Office, 'B' Bond Warehouse, Smeaton Road, Bristol BS1 6XN
	Elizabeth Bishop House Nursery, Bristol	Barnardo's	
	Elm House Shelter, 10 Whatley Road, 11 Victoria Walk and 246 York Road, Cotham, Bristol (closed 1972)	C of E Diocese (Bristol); Avon and North Wiltshire	
	Grove House, Grove Road, Clifton, Bristol and 148 Redland Road, Bristol (closed 1947)	C of E Diocese (Bristol); Avon and North Wiltshire	
	Grosvenor House, 89 Ashley Road, Bristol (1921–29)	Salvation Army	
	The Mother and Baby Home, 11/13 Snowdon Road, Fishponds, Bristol	Bristol Social Services	
	Mount Hope, 10 Ashley Hill, Bristol 6 (closed1968)	Salvation Army	
	Muller's Children's Home, Ashley Down and then 7 Cotham Park	Adoptions arranged mainly through the local authority & Children's Depts & Thomas Coram Foundation (now Coram Family).	

Area	Name and Address	Run or used by	Records
	Nazareth House, Stoke Bishop, Bristol 9	Clifton Catholic Children's Society	Agency or Nazareth House Archives, Nazareth House, Hammersmith Road, London W6 8DB
	St John's Home (M&B), 29 Ashley Road, Bristol 6 (1880–87) and 13–15 Wellington Park, Bristol (1907–37)	Avon and North Wiltshire	Some records with Senior Archivist, Bristol Record Office, as above
	St Raphael's (M&B) Home, Hill End Road, Bristol	Clifton Catholic Children's Society; Portsmouth Catholic Social Service Council; Good Shepherd Sisterhood	
	Southwell House, Southwell Street, Kingsdown, Bristol. Later became Bristol Maternity Hospital.	By Committee	Senior Archivist as above, 1901–24 (ref:37006) and possibly some with London Metropolitan Archives.
	Whiteladies Road, Bristol	Barnardo's	
BUCKINGHAMSHIRE	Bucks SSD have 4 registers of foster parents and fostered children 1923–49 and many individual and Guardian *ad litem* reports.		
	Bucks CC Record Office, County Hall, Aylesbury, HP20 1UU, also has a 1939–43 register of people admitted to maternity homes under the 1918 Mother and Child Welfare Act. They include Putnam House, The Royal Bucks Hospital and hospitals at Bedford, Hillingdon, High Wycombe, Northampton, Reading and Slough and West Herts.		
	It is known that pre-1967 Oxford Diocesan Records were destroyed. Adoptions were usually arranged through the Children's Society or Father Hudson's Homes.		
Amersham	Shardeloes House (Emergency Maternity Hospital)	Used by Queen Charlotte's and other hospitals 1939–45. Births registered in Beaconsfield	Some Queen Charlotte's records with London Metropolitan Archives.
Aylesbury	Aylesbury MH, 33 Bicester Road, Aylesbury	Affiliated to National Council for One Parent Families	Not traced but worth trying Bucks & Oxford SSD & PACT for records of individuals.
	The Gables (NH), Wendover Road, Aylesbury	Privately run by Mrs Stride who arranged a number of adoptions, mainly within Berkshire	Not traced but worth trying Bucks & Oxford SSD & PACT for records of individuals.
	Putnam House (M&B), Buckingham Street, Aylesbury (closed 1929)	C of E Diocese (Oxford)	Some records with Bucks Record Office
	Tindall Hospital	Used 1939–45 by St George's Hospital, London	St George's have no records. Worth trying as above.
Farnham Common	Colinswood		Not traced. Worth trying as above.
High Wycombe	The Grange (M&B), 56 Amersham Hill, High Wycombe	C of E Diocese (Oxford)	Not traced. As above.
	Royal Female Orphanage, Beddington, London Road (closed 1965)	Associated with National Orphans' Home and Ham Common	The Historian, Richmond Public Library, Little Green, Richmond, Surrey TW9 1QJ

Area	Name and Address	Run or used by	Records
Tyringham & Filgrave	Tyringham House, Nr Newport Pagnell	Used by British Lying-In Hospital for Women, Woolwich 1939–45 and possibly known post-war as the British Hospital for Mothers & Babies, Woolwich	London Metropolitan Archives have records of the Lying in Hospital, Woolwich.
Waddesdon	Waddesdon Manor	Used by Croydon Public Assistance Committee and a Jewish rescue organisation	Not traced. Possibly some individual records with Norwood Child Care.
Wendover	Winterton House (open in 1953)		Not traced. Worth trying Bucks & Oxford SSD & PACT.

CAMBRIDGESHIRE	Some Cambridgeshire adoption records are held by Peterborough Diocesan Family Care, 222 Dogsthorpe road, Peterborough PE1 3PB		
Cambridge	Cambridge Shelter for Girls, 14 Downing Street (1920–21), 13 Hertford Street (1922/23 to 1924/25), 6 Glisson Road (1925/26 to 1926/27)	C of E Diocese (Ely)	Not traced. Worth trying above & Adopt Anglia as well as Social Services for named individuals.
	Ely Diocesan Home, 48 Bateman Street, Cambridge (closed early 70s).	C of E Diocese (Ely); Cambridge Association for Social Welfare	Ely Diocesan Committee for Family and Social Welfare, Bishop Woodford House, Barton Road, Ely, Cambs CB7 4DX has scanty records. No files. Adoption case minutes 1954–61. Some books 1920–70. Adopt Anglia have records of children adopted through them, particularly 1966–70.

CHESHIRE	The County Archivist, Chester Record Office & Chester Diocesan Record Office, Duke Street, Chester, Cheshire CH1 1RL has:		
	Records from 1955 of Chester Diocesan Adoption Society;		
	Some records of the Moral Welfare Associations of Chester, Macclesfield, Congleton & District & Wallasey;		
	A number of adoption records from 1927 from the areas of Bucklow, Eddisbury, Macclesfield, Northwich, Prestbury, Warrington, Warrington County & Winsford;		
	Specific records of only one M&B home. Where the C of E Chester Diocese was involved it would always be worth an approach to the Record Office through the Social Services. Only the Adoption Society should be approached direct.		
Chester	House of Mercy, from 1921–74 known as St Bridget's (M&B), 15 Lache Lane, Chester	C of E Diocese (Chester); Chester Diocesan Adoption Society; Leicester Diocesan Board for SR	County Archivist as above. Day to day diary notes only with the Archive Sister: Community of St Mary the Virgin, St Mary's Convent, Wantage, Oxfordshire OX23 9DJ
	House of Shelter, 4 Vicar's Lane, Chester	C of E Diocese (Chester)	Worth approach to Chester SSD and County Archivist re: individuals.
Crewe	St Hilda's (M&B), 28 Stalybridge Road and 71 West Street, Crewe (1925–36/37)	Chester Diocesan Adoption Society; C of E Diocese (Chester)	
Frodsham	Springside Nursery, Frodsham, Nr Warrington (closed)	National Children's Home	

Area	Name and Address	Run or used by	Records
Handforth	Knowle House (M&B), Sagars Road, Handforth	Manchester Health Committee	Manchester SSD 1948–69. Limited records.
Macclesfield	Pallotti Hall, Nr Macclesfield	Congregation of Sisters; The Pallotine Missionary Sisters; Catholic Children's Rescue Society (Salford); Liverpool Catholic Social Services; and other agencies	

CORNWALL

Area	Name and Address	Run or used by	Records
Penzance	Morwenna, Lescudjack Terrace, Penzance	Penwith Association for Girls' Welfare; Cornwall Social and MW Association	Probably with SSD
	1 and 7 Penare Road (Shelter) moved to Morwenna	C of E Diocese (Truro)	Not traced but worth approach to Cornwall SSD about individuals.
Redruth	Mount Prospect (MH), Redruth (closed 1920s)	C of E Diocese (Truro)	Possibly with Cornwall SSD
St Agnes	Rosemundy Home, St Agnes (closed)	C of E Diocese (Truro)	Possibly Cornwall SSD and some may be at County Records Office, County Hall, Station Road, Truro

CUMBRIA

All adoption records previously held by the Diocese now with SSD.

Area	Name and Address	Run or used by	Records
Arnside	Sunny Bank Orphanage	Mrs Constance Whishaw, an individual who is said to have arranged many adoptions.	One orphanage given to the Children's Society so worth contacting them about named individuals.
Barrow-in-Furness	Hope House (M&B), Friars Lane and 216 Storey Square, Barrow-in-Furness	C of E Diocese (Carlisle)	Not traced but worth trying SSD.
Carlisle	Coledale Hall (M&B), 94 Newtown Road, Carlisle (closed); 25 Myddleton Street, Carlisle (previously known as St Mary's Home)	C of E Diocese (Carlisle)	Cumbria SSD from 1960
	St Mary's Home: see Coledale Hall above		
Kendal	Brettargh Holt: see Sacred Heart Convent		
	Sacred Heart Convent (M&B), Brettargh Holt, Kendal (closed about 1969/70) (previously known as Brettargh Holt)	Hexham and Newcastle Diocesan Rescue Society; Shrewsbury Diocesan Children's Rescue Society; Lancaster Diocesan Protection and Rescue Society; Catholic Children's Rescue Society (Diocese of Salford) Inc.	
	St Monica's (M&B), 8 Dalton Drive, Sedburgh Road, Kendal	C of E Diocese (Carlisle)	Cumbria SSD from 1960

Area	Name and Address	Run or used by	Records
Workington	8 Dora Crescent, Workington	C of E Diocese (Carlisle)	Records not traced but individual records may be with Cumbria SSD
DARLINGTON	(Part of Durham until 1 April 1997)		
Darlington	St Agnes (M&B), 45 Duke Street, Darlington (closed)	Durham Diocesan Family Welfare Council	
DERBY CITY	(Part of Derbyshire until 1 April 1997)		
	Derby City have the records of Derby Diocesan Council for SW Adoption Committee		
Derby	Morley Maws (Nursery), Nr Derby	Barnardo's	
	10 Vernor Street (M&B) (closed) (Previously 55 Gerrard Street)	C of E Diocese (Derby)	SSD may have information
DERBYSHIRE			
Borrowash	Borrowash House (colloquial name for St Joseph's)		
	St Joseph's Nursery, Borrowash House, Borrowash (1946/47–51)	Nottingham Catholic Children's Society which covers the whole of RC Diocese of Nottingham	
	St Joseph's (M&B), Borrowash House, Borrowash (1951–75). Has now reopened.	Nottingham Catholic Children's Society	
Chesterfield	Magdalen House, 2 Cromwell Road, Chesterfield	C of E Diocese	SSD may have information
DEVON	The County Archivist, Devon Record Office, Castle Street, Exeter EX4 3PU holds the records of the C of E Diocese (Exeter) but they may not contain much that relates to adoption. Access should normally be through an adoption counsellor.		
Bovey Tracey	House of Mercy 1863 still operating in 1935	C of E Diocese (Exeter)	Not traced. Worth an approach to County Archivist.
Bradninch	Dunmore House, Bradninch. Evacuated in 1940 from Abbotsfield, Plymouth. Returned to Plymouth in 1961.	Salvation Army	
Exeter	Exmouth House, Exeter (1963–)	C of E Diocese (Exeter)	Not traced. For individuals' records try Council for Christian Care & SSD
	St Elizabeth's Home, Melbourne House, Friars Walk, Exeter. 1879 – still operating 1935	C of E Diocese (Exeter)	As above
	St Elizabeth's Home, 26 Bartholomew Street West, The Muit, Exeter. Founded 1919. The two Homes above may be the same but at different addresses.	C of E Diocese (Exeter)	As above

Area	Name and Address	Run or used by	Records
	St Mary's Home, 25 Mary Arches Street, Exeter. 1917 – still operating 1935. Took medical cases through local authorities.	C of E Diocese (Exeter)	Not separately traced. Worth an approach to SSD & Council for Christian Care.
	St Nicholas (M&B), 20 Alphington Road, Exeter (closed). Was previously a babies' home called Dunraven	Council for Christian Care	
	St Olave's (M&B), 32 Bartholomew Street, Exeter (closed)	Council for Christian Care; Exeter Diocesan Association for the Care of Girls (originally a religious community)	Some records with County Archivist as above. Some with Hampshire SSD who hold the records of Winchester Board for Social Resonsibility.
	14 Marlborough Road, Exeter	C of E Diocese (Exeter)	Not traced. Worth an approach to SSD & Council for Christian Care.
Teignmouth	Regia House (1946–48)	WRVS	No records. Adoptions through National Children Adoption Association, Mission of Hope, Church of England Children's Society or Western National Adoption Society
Yelverton	Nazareth House, Yelverton	Plymouth Diocesan Catholic Children's Society	Agency & Nazareth House Archives, Nazareth House, Hammersmith Road, London W6 8DE
	St Vincent's Orphanage	The Sisters of Charity of St Vincent de Paul	Provincial Archivist, Sisters of St Vincent de Paul, Provincial House, The Ridgeway, London NW7 1EH
DORSET			
Weymouth	St Gabriel's (M&B), 6 Abbotsbury Road and 18 Dorchester Road, Weymouth (closed)	C of E Diocese (Salisbury)	Some records with Hampshire SSD & records of St Gabriel's Adoption Society with Dorset SSD.
DURHAM			
Bishop Auckland	St Monica's Home, Bishop Auckland (closed 1946)	Durham Diocesan Family Welfare Council	Agency has 2 registers & records of any adoptions they arranged, as has SSD.
Crook	Smelt House (M&B), Howden-le-Wear, Crook	Durham SSD, Durham Diocesan Family Welfare Council	No separate records traced but both agencies may have adoption records.
Durham	Ramside (M&B), Belmont, Durham (closed 1954)	C of E Diocese (Durham); Durham Diocesan Family Welfare Council	Worth an approach to agency and SSD about individuals.
	St Catherine's, 25 Allergate, Durham (closed 1938)	C of E Diocese (Durham)	Not traced, mainly a shelter. Worth an approach as above.

Area	Name and Address	Run or used by	Records
	St Mary's, Kepier Terrace, Durham City (approx. 1952–60)	Durham Diocesan Family Welfare Council	No records but worth an approach as above.
	Sydney House, The Peth, Durham. Mainly a shelter.	Durham Diocesan Family Welfare Council	The County Archivist, Durham Record Office, County Hall, Durham DH1 5UL has committee meeting minute book 1921–49 (D/DDFW51). Access only through an adoption counsellor.
EAST SUSSEX	Chichester Diocesan Association for Family Social Work (now Chichester Diocesan Association for Family Support Work) was responsible for most of the C of E Diocese (Chichester) Homes in East Sussex, Brighton & Hove. Casework files were destroyed after 10 years. The records of any adoptions arranged by the Society are with East Sussex SSD.		
Barcombe	Barcombe Place Nursery	Barnardo's	
Crowborough	Melbourne House (closed)	C of E Diocese (Chichester)	As in preface above.
Eastbourne	The Bell Hostel, 12 Salehurst Road, Eastbourne (demolished)	Chichester Diocesan Association for Family Social Work	As in preface above.
	St George's, 2 Salehurst Road, Eastbourne	Chichester Diocesan Association for Family Social Work	As in preface above.
Hastings	Hastings House, 9 Bohemia Road, Hastings (closed)	Chichester Diocesan Association for Family Social Work	As in preface above.
Lewes	Gateway House, East Street, Lewes (closed 1929)	C of E Diocese (Chichester)	As in preface above.
Rotherfield	Burwood, Rotherfield (previously known as Devon Nook, Chiswick)	Westminster Archdiocese	Not traced, but worth checking with Catholic Children's Societies (Westminster and Arundel and Brighton, Portsmouth and Southwark)
St Leonard's	St Monica, 9 Bohemia Road, St Leonard's	C of E Diocese (Chichester)	As in preface above.
Seaford	Seaford House, 1 Prospect Villas, 60 Claremont Road, Seaford (now Staples House, Flatlet House)	C of E Diocese (Chichester)	As in preface above.
EAST RIDING	Part of Humberside until 1 April 1996		
Bridlington	The Avenue Hospital, Westgate	E Riding (Yorks) CC	N Yorkshire County Record Office, County Hall, Northallerton DL7 8AD
ESSEX	Records of WelCare work in Basildon, Ilford, East and West Ham, Southend, Forest Gate and Whipps Cross Hospital are with County Archivist, Essex Record Office, Wharf Road, Chelmsford CM2 6YT. So too are Adoption Registers for Saffron Walden Division 1929–47; Orsett Division 1934–59; Harlow Division 1960–69. They also have minute books of proceedings of the Adoption Committee in Chelmsford Division 1928–58. All enquiries *must* be made through an adoption counsellor. Adoption records of people known to Chelmsford Diocesan Committee but not placed by them are with Barnado's.		
Brentwood	Sunnedon House, 75 Warley Hill, Brentwood (1960–)	Chelmsford Diocesan Committee for Family Care, C of E Diocese (Chelmsford)	Essex County Archivist (see above)

Area	Name and Address	Run or used by	Records
Buckhurst Hill	Ardmore, 136 High Road, Buckhurst Hill (also Coggeshall)	Essex CC	Not traced but worth trying Essex SSD.
	Astral House, Buckhurst Hill	Society for the Rescue of Young Women and Children	Not traced but worth trying Essex SSD.
Chelmsford	Bartletts, Tavistock House, 201 New London Road, Chelmsford	Chelmsford Diocesan Committee for Family Care	Essex County Archivist (see above)
Coggeshall	Sunnedon House (closed 1959): name transferred to Brentwood		Brief details 1926–59 when council papers destroyed: Essex County Archivist (see above)
Colchester	Hostel of the Good Shepherd, 87 East Hill, Colchester (now Cambridge Lodge)	Chelmsford Diocesan Committee for Family Care	County Archivist as above.
Epping	Loretto Convent (M&B), Theydon Road, Epping (transferred from St Nicholas House, Highbury, 1982)	Franciscan Missionaries of Divine Motherhood; Crusade of Rescue	Any records likely to be with Catholic Children's Society (Westminster).
Great Bentley	The Hall, Great Bentley	Mission of Hope for Children's Aid and Adoption	
	The Old Mill House, Great Bentley	Mission of Hope for Children's Aid and Adoption	
Great Easton	Great Easton, Dunmow (MH) (1920–24)	C of E Diocese (Chelmsford)	Not traced but worth contacting Essex SSD.
Great Maplestead	House of Mercy, Great Maplestead, Halstead; became St Mary's in 1929	C of E Diocese (Chelmsford)	County Archivist has admission registers 1880–1993. Ref D/C/A.c-6/5. Some records with Children's Society.
Hockley	Clements Hall	Private house owned by Mrs Hawkesley	Not traced. Worth trying SSD for individuals.
Kelvedon	Farm Hill Nursery, Kelvedon	Barnardo's	
Loughton	St. Faith's (M&B), 38 Station Road and 117 Queen's Road, Loughton	Chelmsford Diocesan Committee for Family Care	County Archivist as above
GLOUCESTER	The County Archivist, County Record Office, Clarence Row, Alvin Street, Gloucester, GL1 3DW has Parish, Census, Diocesan, Courts, Hospitals and Poor Law records as well as some Wills and records of Societies.		
Cheltenham	Cheltenham Female Refuge (later the North Parade Home for Girls) 1846–1933/4		County Archivist (see above)
	Nazareth House, Bath Road, Cheltenham	Clifton Catholic Children's Society	Agency & Nazareth House Archives, Nazareth House, Hammersmith Road, London W6 8DE
	St Catherine's House for Friendless Girls, 28 Cambray and 21 Pittville Lawn, Cheltenham (closed 1969)	Gloucester Diocesan Council for Social Work	Individual records likely to be with Gloucester SSD

Area	Name and Address	Run or used by	Records
Ebley	Ebley House (Nursery), 235 Westward Road, Ebley, Nr Stroud (closed)	National Children's Home	
Gloucester	Picton House, Wellington Parade, Gloucester (previously know as Magdalen Asylum)	Gloucester Diocesan Council for SW; C of E Diocese (Gloucester);	No records of home but individual adoption records with Gloucester SSD
	St Lucy's Home & Children's Hospital	Reports and correspondence of the 19th & 20th centuries	County Archivist as above (D 177. Boxes 17–19)
Stroud	St Mary's Lodge, 16 Alexandra Road, Gloucester (pre-1949)	Gloucester Diocesan Council for Social Work	As previous entry above
	House of Mercy, Bussage, Stroud	C of E Diocese (Gloucester)	Some historical papers with County Archivist (see above). Individual records may be with SSD.
Temple Guiting	c/o Mrs Stacey, Temple Guiting (evacuated from Connaught House, Harlesden, London NW10)	National Adoption Society	
HALTON	Part of Cheshire until 1 April 1998		
Widnes	Nazareth House, Ditton, Widnes (closed 1960)	Liverpool Catholic Social Service	Agency & Nazareth House Archives, Nazareth House, Hammersmith Road, London W6 8DE
HAMPSHIRE	Hampshire SS hold the records of Winchester & Portsmouth Diocesan Councils for Social Responsibility which had very incomplete records for people who lived in most parts of Hants between 1963 and 1973 (to 1978 for Bournemouth). They also have some for the Channel Islands.		
Aldershot	St Agnes Lodge, Grosvenor Road, Aldershot (1883–1961)	C of E Diocese (Guildford)	Surrey History Centre, 130 Goldsworth Road, Woking GU21 1ND and Hants SSD
Alton	St Mary's, Alton (1920–)	C of E Diocese (Winchester)	The Archive Sister, The Community of St Mary the Virgin, St Mary's Convent, Challow, Wantage OX12 9DJ has registers but it is unlikely that the women there were pregnant.
Alverstoke	Anglesey Lodge (Nursery), Stokesmead, Clayhall Road, Alverstoke, Gosport	National Children's Home	
Basingstoke	House of Mercy, Basingstoke (1920–27)	Sisters of the Transfiguration, Wingrove, nr Aylesbury	Not traced but worth checking Hants SSD for individuals.
Petersfield	St Agnes Home, Petersfield (closed 1923).	Bordon Camp Mission until 1923. Haslemere & District M.W. Association	General information with The County Archivist, Surrey History Centre, 130 Goldsworth Road, Woking, Surrey, GU21 1ND.

Area	Name and Address	Run or used by	Records
Sherfield	Nazareth House, Sherfield	Portsmouth Catholic Social Service Council	Agency & Nazareth House Archives, Nazareth House, Hammersmith Road, London W6 8DE.
Winchester	St Bartholomews, 1 North Walls, Winchester (closed)	C of E Diocese (Winchester)	Hants SSD
	55 Eastgate Street, Winchester	C of E Diocese (Winchester)	Not traced but worth trying Hants SSD for individuals.
Yately	The Haven, Vigo Lane, Nr Camberley	Baptist Union	Agency (Camden SSD) & Hants SSD

HEREFORD

(Part of Hereford & Worcester until 1 April 1998)

The Record Office, Herefordshire District Council, The Old Barracks, Harold Street, Hereford, HR1 2QX holds the records of the C of E Diocese (Hereford).

Area	Name and Address	Run or used by	Records
Hereford	The Haven, 13 Nicholas Street, 12 Bridge Street and Barton Street, Hereford	C of E Diocese (Hereford)	Limited records with Record Office Manager.
	St Martin's, Walnut Tree Avenue, Hereford (closed)	C of E Diocese (Hereford); Church Army	As above

HERTFORDSHIRE

Hertfordshire Archives & Local Studies, County Hall, Hertford SG13 8EJ holds records for a large proportion of the establishments that have been run by the County Council and others. They have details of children's homes, bursaries, surviving records of the pre 1930 Boards of Guardians and of their successors, some records relating to children adopted and taken into care from 1930 onwards. They hold the minutes of the Maternity & Child Welfare Committee for 1947–48 (ref HCC 31/12) which include references to residents at Campions, Shenley & Russells, Watford.

During the 1939–45 war, a number of maternity homes and hostels were set up by the Hertfordshire County Council because of the large numbers of evacuees there. Panshanger (the house of Lady Desborough) was one of these. It appears to have been used for ante and post natal care and possibly a nursery school. Miss Keating was Matron in 1943. The Archivist holds no records and it seems almost certain that none survived.

Area	Name and Address	Run or used by	Records
Berkhamsted	Cross Roads Club	Run by Committee financially aided by Thomas Coram Foundation (now Coram Family) which was not otherwise involved.	Not traced. Some general records of Thomas Coram with Hertfordshire County Record Office, as above. Many births at Queen Charlotte's Hospital whose records are held by the London Metropolitan Archives.
Bishop Stortford	St Gabriel, 41 Dane Street, Bishop Stortford	C of E Diocese (St Albans)	Individual records: Hertfordshire SSD
Cheshunt	Hope House (M&B), 1 High Street, Cheshunt (closed)	C of E Diocese (St Albans)	Hertfordshire SSD
Hadley Wood	Covenden (M&B) Beech Hill, Hadley Wood 1918–64 and then in Hampstead.	C of E Diocese (London) Independent Trust	The Senior Archivist, Camden Local Studies & Archives Centre, 32–38 Theobald's Road, London WC1X 8PA; some at London Metropolitan Archives.
Hemel Hempstead	St Mary and the Angels' war-time evacuation from Stamford Hill	Community of St Mary the Virgin, Wantage	Archives Sister, Community of St Mary the Virgin, St Mary's Convent, Challow, Wantage OX12 9DJ. Possibly some with London Metropolitan Archives.

Area	Name and Address	Run or used by	Records
Hertford	33 Fanshawe Street, Bengeo, Hertford	C of E Diocese (St Albans)	Hertfordshire SSD
Hitchin	39 Walsworth Road, Hitchin	C of E Diocese (St Albans)	Hertfordshire SSD
Lemsford	Cross Roads Club, Lemsford (1936–) (later Cross Roads Club, London, Camden, Westminster and Barnet)	Thomas Coram Foundation for Children (administration only)	Not traced (as above entry for Cross Roads Club, Berkhamsted)
St Albans	St Barnabas, 27 Sandpit Lane, St Albans	C of E Diocese (St Albans)	Hertfordshire SSD
Shenley	Campions, Green Street, Shenley (1948–54)	Hertfordshire CC	Not traced; when closed, girls went to a private maternity home, St Olive's, which was in St Albans and closed in 1957. Worth contacting Hertfordshire SSD
Watford	Russells (1946/7–48)	Hertfordshire CC	As above entry
ISLE OF WIGHT	Part of Hampshire until 1 April 1995 when it became a unitary council.		
Newport	The Hostel, 4 High Street, Newport: possibly moved to Mount House, 18 Staplers Road (closed 1960)	C of E Diocese (Portsmouth)	Any available records with Hants SS through Isle of Wight SSD.
Ryde	Orchardleigh (M&B), 86 Pelhurst Road, Ryde (closed by 1935)	C of E Diocese (Portsmouth)	As above.
KENT	Poor Law Records sometimes available through SSD, Education Department Adoption Records destroyed in 1948. Kent SSD has records of Canterbury & Rochester Boards for Social Responsibility.		
Ashford	The Lodge, 243 Faversham Road, Kennington, Ashford	C of E Diocese (Canterbury)	Some records with Kent SSD
Faversham	46 Newton Road, Faversham	C of E Diocese (Canterbury)	Not separately traced but Kent SSD may have records of individuals.
Folkestone	St Agnes House, 49 Coolinge Road Folkestone	C of E Diocese (Canterbury)	As above
Gravesend	Kendal (M&B), 12 The Grove and 46 Pelham Road, Gravesend	C of E Diocese (Thameside Branch of Rochester)	As above
	St Mary's Nursery, Gravesend	Southwark Catholic Children's Society	
Hawkhurst	Babies Castle Nursery, Hawkhurst	Barnardo's	
Maidstone	St Faith's (M&B), Bearsted, Maidstone (closed), 1 Lower Fort Road, Maidstone and 7 Bedford Place, Maidstone	C of E Diocese (Canterbury)	Kent SSD
Ramsgate	Braeside, Margate Road, Ramsgate	C of E Diocese (Canterbury)	Kent SSD

Area	Name and Address	Run or used by	Records
Sevenoaks	Berwick House, 32 Dartford Road, Sevenoaks (1966–) (Bedsits)	C of E Diocese (Rochester); Sevenoaks District Council	Kent SSD
Stone	St Mary's, Watling Street, Stone, Dartford	C of E Diocese (Rochester)	Not traced but Kent SSD may have records of individuals.
Tunbridge Wells	13 Broadwater Down, Tunbridge Wells	Kent CC	Not traced but worth trying Kent SSD
	Heatherlands, 184 Forest Road, Tunbridge Wells (closed)	C of E Diocese (Rochester)	Kent SSD
	St Christopher's, Tunbridge Wells	Barnardo's	
	36 Upper Grosvenor Road, Tunbridge Wells		Not traced but worth trying Kent SSD for individuals.

KINGSTON-UPON-HULL

Part of Humberside until 1 April 1996

Many confinements in this area took place at the Maternity Hospital, Hedon Road, Hull.

Area	Name and Address	Run or used by	Records
Kingston-upon-Hull	78 Beverley Road, Hull	C of E Diocese (York)	Not traced
	Linnaeus House, 14 Linnaeus Street, Hull (now Humberside Family Welfare Centre) (still open)	York Diocesan Council for Social Responsibility	No early records but those of individuals may be with agencies
	Sutton House (M&B), Sutton upon Hull (closed 1962)	C of E Diocese (York); York Adoption Society	Home records not traced but worth contacting agency & SSD

LANCASHIRE

Area	Name and Address	Run or used by	Records
Burnley	The House of Help, Burnley and Nelson Area, Bankfield, Todmorden Road, Burnley (closed)	Blackburn Diocesan Adoption Agency	County Archivist, Lancashire Record Office, Bow Lane, Preston, Lancs PR1 2RE
Lancaster	The Girls' Hostel (M&B), 7 Queen Street, Lancaster	Blackburn Diocesan Adoption Agency	County Archivist as above
	Nazareth House, Ashton Road, Lancaster	Lancaster Diocesan Protection and Rescue Society	Nazareth House Archives, Nazareth House, Hammersmith Road, London W6 8DE
Preston	2 Golden Square, Preston	Blackburn Diocesan Board for Social Responsibility	County Archivist as above
	Parkinson House, 68 West Cliff, Preston	Blackburn Diocesan Board for Social Responsibility	As above

LEICESTERSHIRE

Area	Name and Address	Run or used by	Records
Kirby Muxloe	Carmel Children's Home, Kirby Muxloe	Nottingham Catholic Children's Society	
Leicester	St Mary's, Ashleigh Road, Leicester (until 1946). Moved to 33a West Street (1946 – early '70s) and then 278 East Park Road (closed 1980)	C of E Diocese (Leicester); Run in conjunction with Leicester Royal Infirmary	Adoption records with Leicester SSD. Other records not traced.

Area	Name and Address	Run or used by	Records
LINCOLNSHIRE			
Great Grimsby	Hope House (M&B), 145 Victoria Street, 44 Heneage Road and 8 Prince's Avenue, Great Grimsby (closed 1968)	C of E Diocese (Lincoln)	Lincolnshire SSD
Lincoln	The Quarry (MH), Wragby Road, Lincoln	C of E Diocese (Lincoln)	Lincolnshire SSD
	St Swithin's, Free School Lane, Lincoln (closed)	C of E Diocese (Lincoln)	Lincolnshire SSD

LONDON

In 1965 the London County Council (LCC) and the Middlesex County Council (MCC) joined to become the Greater London Council (GLC). Many existing borough boundaries were changed, and a number of new boroughs were incorporated from parts of Essex, Hertfordshire, Kent and Surrey. The changes are indicated under the appropriate headings.

Many of the records of the London Diocesan Board for Social Responsibility (which covers all boroughs north of the Thames) up to 1992 are held by Barnardo's. Many records of Southwark Diocesan Council for WelCare (which covers boroughs south of the Thames) are held by London Metropolitan Archives. For all London boroughs it is worth checking for individuals with Barnardo's, London Metropolitan Archives, the local Social Services, any local Diocesan CARIS (previously WelCare) Offices as well as national agencies.

London Metropolitan Archives holds records of the London Guardians; the Poor Law District Schools and numerous children's homes until 1930. It also has records of children in the care of the London and Middlesex County Councils from 1927–65 and their adoptions; the records of the Juvenile Courts from 1927 to the early 1970s; limited records of Juvenile Courts in the Brentford and Spelthorne Sessions; Schools registers from the 1870s through the various administrative changes to 1990. It has records of a number of M&B Homes but with a few exceptions they are mainly administrative. Additionally it holds the records of some Hospitals, notably Queen Charlotte's registers of births 1886–1985 and St Thomas's.

Initial enquiries can be made by telephone. They should be followed up by a letter to the Senior Archivist, Access and Enquiries section.

Barnet

Parts of Barnet/Southgate were in Hertfordshire until 1965. So it is always worth trying Hertfordshire SSD for individuals.

Area	Name and Address	Run or used by	Records
	Crathorne, Oak Lane, East Finchley (1926–33)	Church Army	Not traced, but worth checking as above
	Cross Road Club, Oakdene, 33 Lyonsdown Road, New Barnet (closed 1959, see Westminster and Hertfordshire)	Thomas Coram Foundation (administration only) (now Coram Family)	Not traced. Worth checking for individuals as above. BAAF has history.
	London Diocesan Hostel, Guildford House (M&B). Moved to Storth Oaks	C of E Diocese (London) Crusade of Rescue	Barnet SSD. One special book about the first 2 years with Barnardo's.
	Nazareth House, 162 East End Road, N2	Crusade of Rescue	Nazareth House Archives, Nazareth House, Hammersmith Road, London W6 8DE & Catholic Children's Society (Westminster) if child placed by them.
	St Helena (Convalescent), Thorverton Road, NW2	C of E Diocese (London)	London Metropolitan Archives has Admission & Discharge Registers (Oct 1933-Aug 1953)
	St Vincents Provincial House, The Ridgeway, London NW7	Crusade of Rescue	St Vincents and Catholic Children's Society (Westminster) if child placed by them

Area	Name and Address	Run or used by	Records
	Storth Oaks, 1 Downage, Hendon, NW4	Barnet SSD	
Bexley	Part of Kent until 1965		
	Oakhurst (M&B), Lesney Park Road, Erith (closed)	C of E Diocese (Rochester)	NCH Post Adoption Service, 12 Romney Place, Maidstone, Kent ME15 6LE
Brent	Part of Middlesex until 1965		
	Babies Hostel, Old Vicarage, Kingsbury Road, NW9 (up to 1938)	Church Adoption Society	
	Bellevue, 167 Willesden Lane, NW6	Brent SSD; Middlesex CC; Crusade of Rescue	Not traced; but worth checking as above
	Connaught House, Harlesden, NW10 (see Temple Guiting, Gloucester)	National Adoption Society	
	40 Exeter Road, NW2	Not known but thought to be an RC (M&B) home for German girls	Not traced; but worth checking with Catholic Children's Society (Westminster)
	St Mary's, 34 Craven Park, NW10	C of E Diocese (London)	Some with London Metropolitan Archives.
Bromley	Part of Kent until 1965		
	The Archivist, Bromley Central Library, no longer holds the Adoption Records of Bromley & Penge Magistrates' Courts. They have been reclaimed by Bromley Magistrates Court.		
	Denbridge House, 2 Wells Road, Bickley	C of E Diocese (Rochester)	Kent SSD has the records of the C of E Diocese (Rochester).
	Holy Child Nursery, Chislehurst (Children's Home only)	Southwark Catholic Children's Society	
	Lake View, 48–50 Thicket Road, SE20	Mission of Hope	
	Lilian Barker Home, 119 Croydon Road, SE20 (Children's Home)	Mission of Hope	
	Oakdene, 41 Anerley Park, SE20 (Hostel)	Mission of Hope	
	Penge Hotel, St Anne's, 45 Croydon Road, SE20	C of E Diocese (Rochester)	As above
	Ravensbourne(M&B), 9 Blyth Road & 20 Ravensbourne Road, Bromley	Rochester Diocesan Council for SW (Bromley and Orpington Branch)	As above
	Roy Heasman, 13 Crescent Road, Beckenham (from about 1977)	Church Army	Not traced; but worth checking as in London preface
	St Anne's, Orpington (Children's Home only)	Southwark Catholic Children's Society	

Homes and Shelters

Area	Name and Address	Run or used by	Records
	St Hilda's (Nursery), 13 Crescent Road, Beckenham (pre-1977)	Children's Society	
	St Joseph's, Orpington	Southwark Catholic Children's Society	
	Tower House, 43 Anerley Park, SE20 (Sick Infants Home)	Mission of Hope	
Camden	Barnardo's has Hampstead Deanery Register (Oct 1930–Oct 1949) but very little information. It also has Hendon & Hampstead case reports to Executive Committee (30 August 1933–6 December 1946).		
	Alexandra House, Maitland Park Road, St Pancras		London Metropolitan Archives have registers 1940–52 (Ref. LCC/WE/H/A/1) as well as Master's, Matron's and Chaplain's report books, and medical records.
	Coram Nursery, 41 Brunswick Square, WC1 (closed 1973)	Thomas Coram Foundation for Children (now Coram Family)	
	Cross Roads Club, 88–90 Alexandra Road, NW8	Thomas Coram Foundation for Children (administration only) (now Coram Family)	Not traced; BAAF has history. Worth trying as in London preface.
	Eagles Nest, 99 Haverstock Hill, NW3	Affiliated to National Council for One Parent Families	Not traced; worth checking as above.
	7 Fitzjohn's Avenue, NW3	C of E Diocese (London)	Not traced; worth checking as above.
	33 Fitzjohn's Avenue, NW3	Affiliated to National Council for One Parent Families	Not traced; worth checking as above.
	Hampstead Mother & Baby Home, 17 Daleham Gardens, NW3 (1918–1969) (previously known as Covenden, Hadley Wood)	C of E Diocese (London) Independent Trust	The Senior Archivist, Camden Local Studies & Archives Centre, 32–38 Theobalds Road, London WC1X 8PA; Minutes & papers 1903–70. Individual mothers, babies and adoptions 1 January 1953–6 June 1969.
	Hampstead Women's Shelter, 25 Agincourt Road, NW3	Rainer Foundation	Galleries of Justice, Shire Hall, High Pavement, Lace Market, Nottingham NG1 1HN; Fax: 0115 993 9828
	Henry Carter House, Camden Square (1953–4)	West London Mission	Adoption usually through NCH
	House of Refuge, 3 Camden Street NW1 (1852–)	C of E Diocese (London)	Not traced; worth checking as in London Preface
	London Haven, 2 Birkenhead Street, WC1 (still open)	London Female Preventative and Reformatory Institution	Register 1947–66 Rainer Foundation at Galleries of Justice as above
	Main Memorial (M&B), 141 West End Lane, NW6 and Cartwright Gardens, WC1 (previously known as Lanark Villas, Westminster)	Westminster WelCare Association; C of E Diocese (London)	London Metropolitan Archives have annual reports only 1938–1952. It is known that a number of private adoptions were arranged through Superintendent Miss Nicholson.

Area	Name and Address	Run or used by	Records
	Martin House (Hostel), 15 Oval Road, NW1	Martin Housing Limited; Crusade of Rescue	Not traced. Adoptions would usually have been through the Catholic Children's Society (Westminster).
	Pearson House, 11 Oval Road, NW1	Rainer Foundation	Minutes Aug 1946–Feb 1967. Registers 1957–64 at Rainer Foundation (as above). Also London Metropolitan Archives.
	62 Regents Park Road, NW1	Royal Free Hospital	No home records but some hospital records available. The Archivist, Royal Free Hospital, The Hoo, Lyndhurst Gardens, London NW3.
	43 Rosslyn Hill, NW3	C of E Diocese (London)	Not traced; worth checking as Preface
	Sacred Heart Convent (M&B), Highgate West Hill, N6	St Francis Children's Society	Records with referring agencies but worth checking with the Society for named individuals
	St Agatha's, 39 Lancaster Road, NW3	C of E Diocese (London)	Not traced; worth checking as Preface.
	St Agnes, Lyndhurst Terrace, NW3	Order of Divine Compassion	Not traced, but worth trying Catholic Children's Society (Westminster) for named individuals
	St Audrey's Rescue and Maternity Home, 10 Lancaster Place, NW3	Not known	Not traced, but worth checking with Catholic Children's Society (Westminster)
	St Faith's, 218 Camden Road, NW1 (Closed 1969) (previously known as St Margaret's and St Faith's, Myddleton Square, EC1 – see Tower Hamlets)	St Pancras WelCare; Camden WelCare; Rainer Foundation	Rainer Foundation at Galleries of Justice as above, has minutes only Dec 1960–Jan 1963. London Metropolitan Archives has Committee minutes 1950–67 (ref. A/LWC/399)
	St Margaret's (see St Faith's), 193 Albany Street, NW1		Rainer Foundation, minutes only. December 1960–January 1967.
	St Pelagia's, 25 and 27 Bickerton Road, N19 and 34 Highgate West Hill, N6. Children were sometimes sent to St William's Nursery.	Sisters of the Sacred Heart of Jesus and Mary; Crusade of Rescue	Catholic Children's Society (Westminster)
	Wadham Gardens, NW3 (Hostel for M&B)	London County Council	Not traced; worth checking as Preface.
Croydon	Part of Surrey until 1965		

The Archivist, Central Library, Katharine Street, Croydon CR9 1ET has indexed minutes of the Children's Committee of Croydon Board of Guardians up to 1930 and after that of Croydon B.C. They do mention the names of individual children and mothers and which homes they were sent to, although general information is limited. Croydon WelCare, 1 Ramsey Court, Church Street, Croydon CR0 1RF has some adoption records from 1961, mainly mid 60s to mid 70s.

Area	Name and Address	Run or used by	Records
	Beracah, Birdhurst Gardens, South Croydon (later Birdhurst Lodge, see below)	Mission of Hope for Children's Aid and Adoption	

Area	Name and Address	Run or used by	Records
	Birdhurst Lodge (M&B and Boys House), 14 South Park Hill Road, South Croydon (previously known as Beracah, see previous entry)	Mission of Hope for Children's Aid and Adoption	
	Blythswood (Hostel), 43 St Peter's Road, South Croydon	Mission of Hope	
	Cleevedon (M&B), 16–18 Tennison Road, SE25	Barnardo's; Children's Aid Society	
	Deanfield, St Peter's Road, South Croydon (Children's Home)	Mission of Hope	
	Deepdene, Hurst Road, South Croydon (1908–)	Mission of Hope for Children's Aid and Adoption	
	Delecote (NH), Bensham Manor Road, Thornton Heath	Church Adoption Society	
	Essendene, Hurst Road, South Croydon (1908–) (Children's Home)	Mission of Hope for Children's Aid and Adoption	
	Glazier House, 26 Stretton Road, Croydon (Early pregnancies)	C of E Diocese (Canterbury)	Not traced, but see prefaces to Croydon and London. Kent SSD have the records of Canterbury Diocese.
	Hurst House, 2 Hurst Road, South Croydon (1906–) (Children's Home)	Mission of Hope for Children's Aid and Adoption	
	Norwood House, 61 Crown Dale, SE19	LCC; Crusade of Rescue	London Metropolitan Archives has Register of Inmates (30.11.40–13.9.49), Admission & Discharge Registers (4.6.49–2.5.56)
	The Retreat, 19 and 35 Ross Road, SE25	National Free Church Women's Council	Hampshire SSD has some records of National Free Church Women's Council. Worth trying them, Croydon SSD and Christian Family Concern. London Metropolitan Archives also has some records of the organisation.
	St Monica's, 27–8 The Waldrons, Croydon (closed 1952)	C of E Diocese (Canterbury)	Worth trying Kent SSD which holds the C of E Diocese (Canterbury) records as well as London contacts.
	The Shrubberies (M&B), Woodside Green, Croydon	Children's Aid Society	Barnardo's
	Victoria House, Central Hill, Upper Norwood, SE19 (This could also be Lambeth.)	Not known	Not traced, but see prefaces to Croydon and London.
Ealing	Part of Middlesex until 1965		
	Alexandra House, Queen's Walk, W5	National Children's Home	

Area	Name and Address	Run or used by	Records
	Amherst Lodge (M&B), Amherst Road, W13 (closed)	Crusade of Rescue; Ealing SS; Middlesex CC	Any pre-1965 with London Metropolitan Archives. 1965–70 Ealing SSD. Some individuals' records Barnardo's.
	Connaught House, Acton Lane, W3	National Adoption Society	
	Ealing Deanery Hostel, 35 Windsor Road, Ealing, W5 (1927–40s)	C of E Diocese (London)	Some with London Metropolitan Archives.
Enfield	Part of Middlesex until 1965		
	149 Church Street, Lower Edmonton, N9	C of E Diocese (London)	Some with London Metropolitan Archives.
	Covenden (M&B), Beech Hill, Hadley Wood (later in Hampstead – see Camden)	C of E Diocese (London)	The Senior Archivist, Camden Local Studies & Archives Centre, 32–38 Theobald's Road, London WC1X 8PA. Minutes and papers 1903–70, individual mothers, babies and adoptions (1 January 1953–June 1969)
	100 Hertford Road, N9	C of E Diocese (London)	Not traced, but worth checking as in London preface.
	Ridge End House (Hostel), The Ridgeway, Enfield	Enfield WelCare	As above.
	St Joseph's (M&B), Enfield	Crusade of Rescue	Not traced, but worth checking with Catholic Children's Society (Westminster) for named individuals
	Private NH, 173 Palmerston Crescent, N13 (1932–7)	Dr George Grant Macdonald	Not traced. Probably worth checking as above.
Greenwich	London Metropolitan Archives has some WelCare papers 1969–70. WelCare (248 Nightingale Vale, London SE18 4HN) also has some.		
	92 Beresford Street, SE18	C of E Diocese (Southwark)	Not traced, but see above and London preface.
	Diocesan Medical House, 75 St Mary Street, Woolwich, SE18 (1913–1919); Moved to 80 Stockwell Park Road, Lambeth, SW9	C of E Diocese (Southwark)	London Metropolitan Archives has some 1931–35. Also worth checking as in London preface.
	The Plumstead MH, 23 Vicarage Park, SE18 (replaced by Stretton House)	C of E Diocese (Southwark)	London Metropolitan Archives
	59 Rectory Place, SE18	C of E Diocese (Southwark)	Not traced, but see above and London preface.
	Shaftesbury House, 10 Gloucester Place and 15 Circus Street, Greenwich, SE10	C of E Diocese (Southwark)	Not traced, but see above.
	The Woolwich MH, 32 Rectory Road, SE18	C of E Diocese (Southwark)	Not traced, but see above.

Homes
and Shelters

Area	Name and Address	Run or used by	Records
Hackney	Brent House 27–29 Devonshire Road, EC2 (Closed 1926) (transferred to Hope Lodge, see below)	Salvation Army	
	Cotland, 11 Springfield, E5 and 9 Amhurst Park, N16 (later Crossways, see below)	Salvation Army	
	Cotswold, 55–57 Downs Road, E5 (closed 1940 when some girls evacuated to Leeds)	Salvation Army	
	Crossways (M&B), 13 Laura Place, E5 (closed) (previously known as Cotland, see above)	Salvation Army	
	160 Dalston Lane, E8	Children's Aid Society	
	Hillsborough House, 181–183 Amhurst Road, E8	Salvation Army	
	Hope Lodge, 4 The Common, E5 (evacuated to Sheffield) (closed 1949)	Salvation Army	
	Ivy House (M&B), 271 Mare Street, E8 (closed 1913)	Salvation Army	
	Lorne House I (1909–1940), 16 Rectory Road, N16 (evacuated to Leeds)	Salvation Army	
	Lorne House II, 4 Clapton Common and 126–128 Lower Clapton Road, E5	Salvation Army	
	6 Pembury Road, E5	C of E Diocese (London)	Not traced, but worth checking as in London preface.
	East London M&B, 159 Richmond Road, E8	Possibly C of E Diocese (London)	Direct hit during World War II, but worth checking as in London preface.
	St Margaret's NH, 262 Victoria Park Road, E9	Privately owned NH	Not traced, but worth contacting National Children's Home, Hackney SSD and Barnardo's.
	St. Mary's M&B, 153 Stamford Hill, N16 (evacuated to Hemel Hempstead) (closed 1972)	C of E Diocese (Wantage Sisters)	Archives Sister, Community of St Mary the Virgin, St Mary's Convent, Challow, Wantage, Oxfordshire OX12 9DJ.
	Sapsworth House, 122–124 Lower Clapton Road, E5 (closed 1954)	Salvation Army	
Hammersmith	Fulham Shelter, 23 Barclay Road SW6	C of E Diocese (London)	Some with Barnardo's and London Metropolitan Archives.
	Charcroft House, Roseford Gardens, W12	Jewish Association for the Protection of Women and Girls	Some individual records at HQ Norwood Jewish Adoption Society and London Metropolitan Archives. Some Jewish adoptions arranged through NCAA.

Area	Name and Address	Run or used by	Records
	Nazareth House, Hammersmith Road, W6	Crusade of Rescue	Agency and Nazareth House Archives, Nazareth House, Hammersmith Road, London W6 8DE
	St Agnes, 36 Glenthorne Road, W6	C of E Diocese (London)	Many with Barnado's and some with London Metropolitan Archives (Ref. A/LWC/690–694)
	St James, 484 Fulham Palace Road, SW6 (moved to Ottershaw, Surrey)	C of E Diocese (London)	Not traced, but worth checking as in London preface.
	St Margarets, 466 Uxbridge Road, W12	C of E Diocese (London)	Not traced, but worth checking as in London preface.
Haringey	Part of Middlesex until 1965		
	Beacon Lodge (M&B), 109 Upper Tollington Park, N4 (1909–1928) (became Newbeacon – see below)	The Beacon Lodge Trust; C of E Diocese (London)	See below
	Beacon Lodge, 35 Eastern Road, N2 (1929–) (became M&B Hostel March 1978)	The Beacon Lodge Trust; C of E Diocese (London)	Still open. Good records. One book missing.
	House of Mercy, North Hill, N6	C of E Diocese (London)	Not traced, but worth checking as in London preface.
	Newbeacon, 79 Crouch Hill, N8 (1928–29) (became Beacon Lodge – see above)	The Beacon Lodge Trust; C of E Diocese (London)	
	Red Gables (M&B), Crouch Hill, N8	Haringey SS; Crusade of Rescue; Middlesex CC	Not traced. Worth checking as in London preface and Catholic Children's Society (Westminster) for named individuals.
	St Pelagia's, The Chestnuts, 684 High Road, Tottenham, N15	Sister Servants of the Sacred Heart of Jesus	Not traced, but worth checking with Catholic Children's society (Westminster) for named individuals.
Harrow	Part of Middlesex until 1965. Barnardo's has Diocesan Register 4 January 1968–1977.		
	Hillside (M&B), 5 Roxborough Park, Harrow; later 32 Harrow View, Harrow (closed)	Harrow/Ealing WelCare	Barnardo's 1 July 1953–2 June 1970. Some with London Metropolitan Archives.
	St Peter's (M&B), 2 Devonshire Road, Hatch End, Pinner (closed)	C of E Diocese (Tower Hamlets)	Some with London Metropolitan Archives.
Havering	Part of Essex until 1965		
	51 Junction Road, Romford	C of E Diocese (Romford)	County Archivist, Essex Record Office, Wharf Road, Chelmsford, CM2 6YT
Hounslow	Part of Middlesex until 1965		
	Devon Nook, Duke's Avenue, W4	Archdiocese of Westminster (RC)	Not traced, but worth checking with Catholic Children's Societies (Westminster; Arundel & Brighton, Portsmouth & Southwark)

Area	Name and Address	Run or used by	Records
	Madison Lodge (M&B Hostel) Osterley	Children's Aid Society	Barnardo's
	Nazareth House, Richmond Road, Isleworth	Crusade of Rescue	Agency and Nazareth House Archives, Nazareth House, Hammersmith Road, London W6 8DE
	St Agnes House, 53 Barrowgate Road, W4	C of E Diocese (London)	Barnardo's; London Metropolitan Archives
	St Anthony's Nursery, Feltham	Crusade of Rescue	Catholic Children's Society (Westminster)
	St Theresa's Nursery, Hatton Cross, Feltham	Crusade of Rescue	Catholic Children's Society (Westminster)
Islington	Cromwell House, N6	Association of Nursery Training Colleges; Mothercraft Training Society	Some with London Metropolitan Archives.
	38 Crouch Hill, N8	Jewish Association for the Protection of Women and Girls	Some records of individuals at Norwood Jewish Adoption Society HQ or at London Metropolitan Archives.
	30–32 Highbury Grove, N5	Jewish Association for the Protection of Women and Girls	Some Jewish adoptions arranged through National Children Adoption Association. See above.
	20–22 Highbury Quadrant, N5	Royal Free Hospital	No home records, but some hospital records available. The Archivist, Royal Free Hospital, The Hoo, Lyndhurst Gardens, NW3. London Metropolitan Archives has some information but mainly through RFH.
	17 Highbury Terrace, N5	Salvation Army	
	Hillside, 129 St John's Way, N19	London CC; Crusade of Rescue	London Metropolitan Archives. Admission and discharge registers 1930–53; daily numbers 1953–56; religious creed 1932–34; 1936–44.
	Hopedene, 15 Aubert Park, N5 (1963–85)	West London Mission	Adoptions usually through NCH. Also worth trying London Metropolitan Archives.
	Kingsway House, 28 Highbury Grove, N5 (1957–58)	West London Mission	London Metropolitan Archives, 2 volumes Committee Minutes Ref N/M/2/38/39. (1949–58) Adoptions usually through NCH.
	Legard Family Centre, Legard Road, N5	National Children's Home	
	Maternity Centre and School for Mothers, 6 and 7 Manor Gardens, N7	Affiliated to National Council for One Parent Families	Not separately traced but worth trying as in London preface particularly London Metropolitan Archives.

Area	Name and Address	Run or used by	Records
	Parkhurst, 35 Parkhurst Road, N7 (1922–39)	West London Mission	London Metropolitan Archives Ref N/M/2/105 (1922–31). Adoptions usually through NCH.
	24 Pemberton Gardens, N19	C of E Diocese (London)	Some with London Metropolitan Archives.
	St Nicholas (M&B), 31 Highbury Grove, N5 (transferred to Theydon Bois, Essex)	Crusade of Rescue	Catholic Children's Society (Westminster)
	St Pelagia's, 25–27 Bickerton Road, N19	Sister Servants of the Sacred Heart of Jesus; Crusade of Rescue	Not traced. Worth checking with Catholic Children's Society (Westminster) for named individuals.
	YLU Nursery, Legard Road, N5 (closed) Became Legard Family Centre – see above	National Children's Home	
	YWCA Hostel, 9 Aberdeen Park, N5	YWCA	Not traced. Worth checking as in London preface.
Kensington & Chelsea	Creaugh Nursery Training School, 38 Holland Villas Road, W14	National Adoption Society	
	Day Servants Hostel, 31 Danvers Street, SW3	By Committee	Not traced. Worth checking as in London preface.
	Fanny Hobson Hostel, 497 King's Road, SW10	Legion of Mary	Not traced. Worth checking with Catholic Children's Society Westminster and Arundel & Brighton, Portsmouth & Southwark.
	The Kensington Home, 2 Upper Phillimore Place, W8	By Committee	Not traced. Worth checking as in London preface.
	Kingsmead, 2 Dovehouse Street, SW3	LCC; Crusade of Rescue	London Metropolitan Archives. Admission and discharge registers.
	Loretta House (M&B), Pembridge Villas, W11	Crusade of Rescue	Not traced, but worth checking with Catholic Children's Society (Westminster) for named individuals.
	Nursery, 38 Holland Villas Road, W14 (till 1943)	Phyllis Holman Richards Adoption Society	
	19 Sloane Street, SW1	National Children Adoption Association	
	43 Smith Street, SW3	C of E Diocese (London)	Not traced. Worth checking as in London preface.
	Tower Cressey, Aubrey Road, W8 (closed)	National Children Adoption Association	
	14 Holland Park, W14 (1945–47); Moved to 49 North Side, SW18	WRVS	Not traced. Many adoptions arranged through National Children Adoption Association; Christian Family Concern; or Children's Society

Area	Name and Address	Run or used by	Records
Kingston-upon-Thames	Part of Surrey until 1965		
	The records of Kingston WelCare are held by the Kingston Museum and Heritage Service but accessible only through the Project Leader, Kingston WelCare, 53–55 Canbury Park Road, Kingston-upon-Thames KT2 6LQ.		
	45 Fairfield South, Kingston	C of E Diocese (Southwark)	Not traced. Worth checking as above and with SSD.
	26 Gibbon Road (M&B), Kingston	C of E Diocese (Southwark)	Not traced. Worth checking as above and with SSD.
	Kingston and District WelCare (Bedsits)	Kingston WelCare	Not traced. Worth checking as above and with SSD.
	18 Richmond Park Road (M&B), Kingston	C of E Diocese (Southwark); Kingston WelCare	Some with London Metropolitan Archives and worth checking as above.
Lambeth	London Metropolitan Archives has some details of the work of Lambeth Moral Welfare and M&B Homes. Also index cards 1940–66. Lambeth WelCare, St John's Community Centre, Frederick Crescent, SW9 6SN has a number of adoption records.		
	Anchorage Annexe, 131 Upper Tulse Hill, SW2	Children's Aid Society	Barnardo's & London Metropolitan Archives
	Anchorage Mission, 76–80 Jeffreys Road, SW4	Children's Aid Society; Southwark Diocesan Council for WelCare	Barnardo's & London Metropolitan Archives
	Annesley House (Hostel), 2a Christchurch Road, SW2	Women's Fellowship of the Methodist Church (now Network)	Records with NCH, 85 Highbury Park, London N5 1UD
	Bishop Billings Memorial Mission House (MH), 71 Upper Tulse Hill, SW2	Children's Aid Society; C of E Diocese (Southwark); Westminster Girls' Welfare	Barnardo's
	Buxted Lodge, 83 King's Avenue, SW4	Association of Infant Welfare and Maternity Centres and National Society of Day Nurseries	Not traced. Worth checking as in London preface.
	Carisbrooke (M&B), 149 Upper Tulse Hill, SW2	LCC from 1947, Lambeth BC from 1965	London Metropolitan Archives. Admission and discharge registers 1938–58
	Dunbar Lodge (MH for deaf and dumb), 20 King's Avenue, SW4	Southwark Diocesan Council for WelCare	Not traced. See Lambeth preface.
	Fellowship of St Michael and All Angels (M&B), 61 Christchurch Road, and 52 Palace Road, SW2 (closed 1968). Now St Michael's Fellowship, 42 Leigham Vale, SW16	Independent Trust	Rather scanty early records. The Director, St Michael's Fellowship, 1F Gleneagle Road, Streatham, SW16 6AY. Babies often placed by National Children Adoption Association, Children's Society or SSD.
	The Haven, 63 Kennington Park Road, SE11	Children's Aid Society	Barnardo's
	Hope House, 194 Clapham Road, SW9	Southwark Diocesan Council for WelCare	As above.

Area	Name and Address	Run or used by	Records
	Lambeth (M&B) Home, 127 Kennington Road, SE11 (1906–7; 1910–14). Moved to Wandsworth.	Southwark Diocesan Council for WelCare	London Metropolitan Archives has some WelCare papers 1915.
	The Limes (M&B), 5 Palace Road, SW2	Church Army; C of E Diocese (Southwark)	Not traced. See Lambeth preface.
	Magdalene Hospital, Drewstead Road, SW16	C of E Diocese (Southwark)	Not traced. See Lambeth preface.
	Medical House, 80 Stockwell Park Road, SW9 (closed 1935)	Southwark Diocesan Council for WelCare	London Metropolitan Archives has some records 1931–35.
	Cicely Northcote Trust, Northcote House, 148 Lambeth Road and 37a Royal Street, SE1	Independent Trust run for the benefit of patients of St Thomas' Hospital (Changed 1950s)	London Metropolitan Archives (St Thomas' Hospital)
	Rokeby (MH) 54 and 132 Leigham Court Road, SW16 (previously known as Morningside, Torquay)	Mission of Hope for Children's Aid and Adoption; Children's Aid Society	
	10 Rutford Road, SW16 (M&B)	Women's Fellowship of the Methodist Church (now Network)	Records with NCH, 85 Highbury Park, London N5 1UD
	St Anne's (M&B), 144 Leigham Court Road, SW16; 107 Tulse Hill, SW2 (became Assissi House, Grayshott, Surrey in 1940)	Dames of St Joan; Southwark Catholic Children's Society; Crusade of Rescue	Catholic Children's Society (Arundel & Brighton, Portsmouth & Southwark)
	St Christopher's (M&B), 179 Tulse Hill, SW2	Southwark Diocesan Council for WelCare; Church Army	Not traced. See Lambeth preface.
	St Christopher's (Pregnant Schoolgirls), 24 Palace Road, SW2	Church Army	As above.
	St Joan's Hostel, 9 Trinity Rise, Tulse Hill, SW2		Flatlet house, no records.
	St John Baptist (MH), 159 Tulse Hill, SW2	C of E Diocese (Southwark)	Not traced. See Lambeth preface.
	St Joseph's, 180 and 188 Clapham Road, SW9 (1939). 107 Tulse Hill, SW2 (1940, evacuated to Grayshott, Surrey)	Roman Catholic (Diocese of Southwark)	Catholic Children's Society (Arundel & Brighton, Portsmouth & Southwark)
	St Mary's House, 32 Macauley Road, SW4. Previously Battersea M&B, 9 Vicarage Road (closed 1986)	Southwark and Lambeth Diocesan Councils for WelCare	London Metropolitan Archives has some WelCare records including baptisms, 1905 onwards.
	St Michael's Fellowship, 42 Leigham Vale, SW16	Independent Trust	See Fellowship of St Michael and All Angels
	St Veronica, 22 Liston Road, SW4	C of E Diocese (Southwark)	Not traced. See Lambeth preface.
	Victoria House, Central Hill, Upper Norwood, SE19 (This could also be Croydon)	Not known. Affiliated to National Council for One Parent Families.	As above.

Area	Name and Address	Run or used by	Records
Lewisham	Lewisham WelCare records are at Lewisham Registry Database at Lewisham SSD. So also are any available records of Homes of all kinds which have been within the borough boundary. Any records pre-1965 are likely to be with London Metropolitan Archives. A few records might be with Central WelCare, Trinity House, 4 Chapel Court, Borough High Street, SE1 1HW. Many adoptions in the area were arranged through the Mission of Hope.		
	The Albany Institute, Creek Road, SE8 (HQ of the Deptford Fund) Several addresses	Charitable foundations	London Metropolitan Archives has purely administrative records.
	Ballantyne (M&B), Lushington Road, SE6 (including disabled children and those with learning difficulties)	Lewisham SSD; Crusade of Rescue	
	Castlebar, Sydenham Hill, SE26	National Children Adoption Association	
	1 Ladywell Road, SE13	Southwark Diocesan Council for WelCare	London Metropolitan Archives and above mentioned database
	308 New Cross Road, SE14	Lewisham WelCare	As above
	Stretton House (M&B), 273 Baring Road, Grove Park, SE12 (evacuated to Limpsfield 1939–46) (1928–1976)	Southwark Diocesan Council for WelCare	As above
	Sydenham Association for the Care of Friendless Girls, 31 Venner Road, SE26 (1910–14)	Southwark Diocesan Council for WelCare	London Metropolitan Archives, but probably purely administrative.
Merton	Partly in Surrey until 1965. Merton WelCare, 37 Western Road, Mitcham CR4 3ED has some records which could include details of mothers who were in homes in the area.		
	56 Gap Road, SW19	Southwark Diocesan Council for WelCare	Not traced. See London & Merton prefaces.
	47 Haydons Road, SW19	Southwark Diocesan Council for WelCare	As above.
	Haygarth-Witts Memorial Home (M&B), 54 The Ridgeway, SW19 (closed 1978)	Southwark Diocesan Council for WelCare	Some records with Director of Personal Services, Merton SSD; and some with London Metropolitan Archives
	Messenger House Trust, 17 Malcolm Road, SW19 and several other houses	Messenger House Trust	The Archivist, Planned Environment Therapy Trust Archive & Study Centre, Church Lane, Toddington, Cheltenham, Glos GL54 5DQ; Fax: 01242 620125
	2 Somerset Road SW19	Phyllis Holman Richards Adoption Society	
Newham	May have been partly in Essex until 1965.		
	St Agatha's, Disraeli Road (1915), 98 Romford Road, Forest Gate, E15 and 73 Carnarvon Road, Stratford, E15	Chelmsford Diocesan Committee for Family Care	County Archivist, Essex Record Office, Wharf Road, Chelmsford CM2 6YT

Area	Name and Address	Run or used by	Records
Redbridge	Part of Essex until 1965.		
	Records of Ilford East & West Ham WelCare are with Essex County Archivist, Essex Record Office, Wharf Road, Chelmsford CM2 6YT.		
	The Garden City (Nursery), Woodford Bridge	Barnado's	
	Hope Cottage, 80 Ingleby Road, Ilford	C of E Diocese (Chelmsford)	Essex County Archivist (see above)
	Southwood House, Bushwood Road, Barkingside	Barnardo's	
Richmond	Part of Surrey until 1965		
	Some adoption files from Richmond WelCare with Barnardo's. WelCare, 26 The Green, Twickenham TW2 5AB has some old ledgers.		
	Marryat House (Hostel), 13, 47 and 73 Mount Ararat Road, Richmond	Southwark Diocesan Council for WelCare; Richmond District Girl's Aid Association	Some with London Metropolitan Archives
	Moore House, Paynesfield Avenue, East Sheen, SW14	Southwark Diocesan Council for WelCare; Female Aid Society	Not separately traced, but worth checking as in London preface.
Southwark	London Metropolitan Archives has some details of work done with individuals by Southwark, Bermondsey & Newington Moral Welfare Association from 1918.		
	Castlebar, Sydenham Hill, SE26	National Children Adoption Association	
	24 De Crespigny Park, SE5 (closed 1925)	Camberwell and Dulwich Committee for Preventative and Rescue Work	London Metropolitan Archives has purely administrative records.
	107 Grange Road, SE1	C of E Diocese (Southwark)	Not separately traced, but see London preface.
	Hope House, 93 Grove Lane, SE5	Mission of Hope	
	House of Help, 201 Camberwell Grove, SE5	BWT Association (?British Women's Temperance)	Not traced. Worth checking as in London preface.
	The Moorings (MH), 2 Champion Park, Camberwell, SE5	Mission of Hope for Children's Aid and Adoption	
	Newington Lodge, 182 Westmoreland Road, SE17	LCC	London Metropolitan Archives
	St Pelagia's, 654 Rotherhithe Street, SE16	Sisters of the Sacred Heart of Jesus; Crusade of Rescue	Not traced. Worth checking with Catholic Children's Societies (Westminster) and (Arundel & Brighton, Portsmouth & Southwark)
Sutton	Part of Surrey until 1965.		
	Sutton WelCare owned the Haven and had registers from April 1955 and files from January 1966. They can be accessed by written request to the Chairman, Sutton WelCare, Sutton Family Centre, Robin Hood Lane, Sutton SM1 2SD		
	The Haven (M&B), 2 Camden Road, Sutton	Sutton MW Association, Southwark Diocesan Council for WelCare	As above and possibly some at London Metropolitan Archives.

Area	Name and Address	Run or used by	Records
Tower Hamlets	Bethany Hostel, 5 Bromley Street, E1; 583 Commercial Road, E1 (closed 1998).	East End Mission	Any available record of an individual is likely to be with Social Services
	Bow Hostel (M&B), 83 Bow Road, E3	C of E Diocese (London)	See London preface but many missing in that area.
	43 Hardinge Street, E1	C of E Diocese (London)	As above
	Pimlico House of Refuge, Commercial Road, SE1 (1852–)	C of E Diocese (London)	As above
	St Agnes House, 16–18 Follett Street, E14	C of E Diocese (London)	As above
	St Faith's, Myddleton Square, EC1 (moved to St Faith's, Camden)	Finsbury and Holborn WelCare, then Camden WelCare	London Metropolitan Archives has committee minutes 1950–67 (Ref. A/LWC/399). Rainer Foundation has minutes only December 1960–January 67. See London preface.
	4 The Terrace, Old Ford Road, E2	C of E Diocese (London)	See London preface but many missing in that area.
Waltham Forest	Part of Essex until 1965.		
	Buswood House, Browning Road, Leytonstone E11 (also known as F.B. Meyer Children's Home). Evacuated to Suffolk 1939–45.	Mission of Hope for Children's Aid and Adoption	
	Ellen Carville, 4 First Avenue; 9 Stainforth Road; 38 The Drive and 43 West Avenue Road, E17 (closed)	C of E Diocese (Chelmsford)	County Archivist, Essex Record Office, Wharf Road, Chelmsford CM2 6YT
	Hutchinson House – alternative name to Buswood.	See Buswood House	
	Loreto House, 23 Forest View, E4 (transferred from Theydon Bois)	Crusade or Rescue	Any records likely to be with Catholic Children's Society (Westminster)
	Shernhall Street, Walthamstow, E17 (1893–) (closed)	Mission of Hope for Children's Aid and Adoption	
	Vin's House, Walthamstow	Mission of Hope for Children's Aid and Adoption	
Wandsworth	London Metropolitan Archives has files 1953–76 from Wandsworth Council for WelCare; Battersea case books 1960–74; Some adoption files 1941–78. Wandsworth WelCare, 79 Trinity Road, Tooting, London SW17 7SQ		
	147 Battersea Rise, SW11	Southwark Diocesan Council for WelCare	See prefaces to Wandsworth and London.
	Beechwood (M&B), Putney Heath Lane, SW15 (1954-74)	National Children Adoption Association	

Area	Name and Address	Run or used by	Records
	Brent House (M&B), 6 North Drive, Streatham, SW16 (1961–68)	WRVS, Crusade of Rescue	Not traced. Most adoptions arranged through National Children Adoption Association; Christian Family Concern or Children's Society
	Brocklebank, 77 Swaffield Road, SW18	LCC	London Metropolitan Archives. Registers 1938–48.
	82 Chelverton Road, SW15 (M&B Hostel)	Southwark Diocesan Council for WelCare	See prefaces to Wandsworth and London.
	The Lambeth Home (moved from Lambeth 1914), 11 St Nicholas' Road, Upper Tooting (1914–31)	Southwark Diocesan Council for WelCare	See prefaces to Wandsworth and London.
	Mothercraft Hostel, 49 North Side, SW4 (Moved from W14)	WRVS	Not traced, but see above for agencies most frequently used.
	Putney Home for M&B, 14 and 15 Spencer Road, SW18 (till 1950); 15 Genoa Avenue, SW15 (closed 1968)	Southwark Diocesan Council for WelCare	Some WelCare case records 1963–68 with London Metropolitan Archives.
	St Anne's, 64 St Anne's Hill, SW18	Church Army; Southwark Diocese	See prefaces as above.
	St Marcella's, Tooting	Fellowship of St Michael and All Angels	Some records with The Director, St Michael's Fellowship, 1F Gleneagle Road, Streatham, SW16 6AX. Babies often placed through NCAA, Children's Society or SSD.
	St Margaret's Guest House, Cambridge Road, SW11	Church Adoption Society	
	St Mary's, 4 Chivalry Road, SW11	Southwark Diocesan Council for WelCare	Some records with London Metropolitan Archives.
	St Winifred House, 20 Thornton Road, SW12	Church Adoption Society	
Westminster	Barnardo's has Marylebone WelCare Register 1 January 1965–9 February 1968 and Case Record Book August 1965–December 1966. Westminster Social Welfare Committee Records 1936–71 with Catholic Children's Society (Westminster).		
	Blue Lamp, 39 Great Pulteney Street, W1	C of E Diocese (London)	Not traced but see London preface.
	Cross Roads Club (M&B), 21 Craven Hill Gardens, W2 and 11 Lyonsdown Road, North Finchley (Previously known as Cross Roads Club, Lemsford, Herts)	Thomas Coram Foundation for Children (administration only) (now Coram Family)	Not traced. Worth checking as in London preface. BAAF has history.
	Home for Female Orphans, 10 Grove Road, NW8	Church Adoption Society	
	Home of the Guardian Angel, Marlborough Place, NW8 (1939–1953)	Late Company of Mary Nuns; Sisters of Little Company of Mary; Crusade or Rescue	Some with Catholic Children's Society (Westminster); some babies were placed in homes run by Nazareth Sisters or Sisters of the Sacred Heart of Jesus.

Homes and Shelters

Area	Name and Address	Run or used by	Records
	House of Compassion, 63 Sutherland Street, SW1 (closed 1932)	C of E Diocese (London); Belgravia and Pimlico Association	Not traced, but see London preface.
	House of Refuge, 44 Vincent Square, SW1 (1856–)	C of E Diocese (London)	Not traced, but see London preface.
	4 Lanark Villas, W9 (MH) (1934 combined with Main Memorial, Camden)	C of E Diocese (London)	Not traced, but see London preface.
	Luxborough Lodge, 1 Luxborough Street, W1	LCC	London Metropolitan Archives has several registers.
	157–159 Marylebone Road, NW1	St Marylebone Female Protection Society	Not traced, but see London preface.
	Nutford Lodge, 27 Nutford Place, W1 (Married women and children)	Church Army	Not traced, but see London preface.
	St Agatha's (M&B), 48 St John's Wood Road, NW8	Mayfair Diocesan Union	London Metropolitan Archives has committee minutes 1914–46 (Ref. A/LWC/40–43). Annual Reports 1922–37 (Ref. A/LWC/ 295–308)
	St Anne's, 67 Denbigh Street, SW1	C of E Diocese (Southwark)	Not traced, but see London preface.
	St Barnabas, Greek Street, W1 (A privately run shelter which sometimes took pregnant women)		Not traced, but see London preface.
	St Christopher's, 1 Devonshire Terrace, W2	Church Army	Not traced, but see London preface.
	St Cyprian's, Bethesda, 38 Charlbert Street, NW8	Not known. Affiliated to National Council for One Parent Families	Not traced, but see London preface.
	St James House of Refuge, 15 St Marylebone Street (1860–) and Glasshouse Street, St James's, W1	Not known	Not traced, but see London preface.
	St John Baptist House, 162 Ebury Street, SW1	Belgrave Ladies Association	Not traced, but see London preface.
	St Mary Magdalen (MH), 25 Ranelagh Road, Paddington (1920–25). Moved in 1918 to Stamford Hill	C of E Diocese (London); Sisters of St Mary's, Wantage	Archive Sister, Community of St Mary the Virgin, St Mary's Convent, Wantage, Oxon OX12 9DJ
	The Stonehouse, Pimlico (1852–)	Possibly C of E Diocese (London)	Not traced, but see London preface.
	Victoria House, 76 Warwick Way, SW1 (closed)	Westminster (St Margaret's) WelCare	Barnardo's has a case book 23 March 1963–9 December 1967.
	11 Wilton Place, SW1 (Nursery)	Phyllis Holman Richards Adoption Society	

Area	Name and Address	Run or used by	Records
LUTON	Part of Bedfordshire until 1 April 1997		
Luton	St Faith's, 7 and 13 Napier Road, Luton (shelter)	St Albans Diocesan Council for Social Responsibility	
	Widecombe (M&B), 36 Grasmere Road, Streatley, Luton (ceased as M&B 1980)	St Albans Diocesan Council for Social Responsibility	
MANCHESTER	Because of boundary changes, it may sometimes be worth contacting Cheshire Record Office about individual records – County Archivist, Duke Street, Chester, Cheshire CH1 1RL. The records of the C of E Diocese (Manchester) are held by Manchester SSD.		
Altrincham	Shelter, 12 Willow Tree Road, Altrincham (1927–)	C of E Diocese (Chester)	Not traced. Worth contacting Cheshire Record Office, Manchester or Cheshire SSD.
Ancoats	Crossley Hospital, Mitchell Street, Ancoats (closed 1971)	Salvation Army	
Bury	Holly Mount, Tottington, Bury	Catholic Children's Rescue Society (Diocese of Salford)	
	St Mary's, Duke Street and 108 Manchester Road, Bury	C of E Diocese (Manchester)	Not traced. Worth contacting Manchester SSD who have some Manchester Diocesan records.
Eccles	Ennismore (M&B), 36 Half Edge Lane and 85 Regent Street, Eccles (closed)	C of E Diocese (Manchester)	As above
Fallowfield	Macalpine MH, 2 Willow Bank, Fallowfield	By committee	As above
Heywood	St Anne's (M&B), Simpson Hill, Heywood (closed)	C of E Diocese (Manchester); Manchester and District Child Adoption Society	Records of home destroyed but worth contacting adoption society.
Manchester	Diocesan (M&B), Upper Brook Street, Manchester 13	Manchester and District Child Adoption Society	
	Doriscourt Nursing Home, Whalley Range, Manchester	Catholic Children's Rescue Society (Diocese of Salford) Inc	
	Lorna Lodge, 133 Barlow Moor Road, Didsbury, Manchester	Manchester and Salford Methodist Mission now run by the Methodist Housing Association.	Worth trying Manchester or Tameside SSD. Some records probably destroyed. Some available by written request to The Manager, Lorna Lodge. Some adoptions through Ashton under Lyne Adoption Society or possibly National Children's Home.
	Marrilac House, 24 Laindon Road, Longsight, Manchester	Catholic Children's Rescue Society (Diocese of Salford)	Still open and records at the House
	Oakhill House, Cheetham Hill, Manchester	Salvation Army	Children often adopted through Lancashire Child Adoption Council.
	St Agnes, 40–42 and 54 Upper Brook Street, Chorlton-on-Medlock (closed 1925)	C of E Diocese (Manchester); Manchester and Salford Mission	Not traced, but may be with Manchester or Tameside SSD. Also worth trying NCH.

Area	Name and Address	Run or used by	Records
	St Agnes Home (M&B), 15 Mauldeth Road, Withington, Manchester 20 (previously known as Diocesan M&B Home)	C of E Diocese (Manchester)	Worth contacting Manchester SSD which has some Manchester Diocesan records
	St Katharine's, 222 Plymouth Grove, Chorlton-on-Medlock	C of E Diocese (Manchester)	As above entry
	St Mary's, Rusholme, Manchester	C of E Diocese (Manchester)	The Archivist, Archives & Local Studies, Central Library, St Peter's Square, Manchester M2 5PD has a baptism register 1899–1945 ref. M566/1/2
Marple	Brentwood Recuperative Centre, Church Lane, Marple	Community Council of Lancashire	The Secretary to the Trustees, Community Council of Lancashire, 15 Victoria Road, Fulwood, Preston PR2 8PS
Salford	Adswood, 460 Bury New Road, Salford 7	Salvation Army; Manchester and District Child Adoption Society	
	Moor Bank, Kersal, Salford	C of E Diocese (Manchester)	Worth contacting Manchester SSD which has some Manchester Diocesan records
	St Teresa's (M&B), 61 Broom Lane, Salford 7	Catholic Children's Rescue Society (Diocese of Salford) Inc; Sisters of Charity of St Vincent de Paul	Agency or Sisters of Charity of ST Vincent de Paul, The Provincial House, The Priory, The Ridgeway, London NW7
Stockport	80 Chatham Street, Stockport	C of E Diocese (Chester)	Not traced, but worth contacting the County Archivist Chester, Manchester & Chester SSD and local agencies
Wigan	St Margaret's House (M&B), Goose Green, Wigan (closed)	C of E Diocese (Liverpool)	Wigan Family Welfare, 537 Warrington Road, Spring View, Lower Ince, Wigan WN3 4TB, 1966–80

MEDWAY

Part of Kent until 1 April 1998

Poor Law records sometimes available through Kent SSD. Education Department adoption records destroyed in 1948.

Area	Name and Address	Run or used by	Records
Chatham	12 New Road, Chatham	C of E Diocese (Rochester)	Some records with Kent SSD
Gillingham	St Lawrence (M&B), 78 Rock Avenue, Gillingham	C of E Diocese (Canterbury and Rochester)	Kent SSD
Rochester	St Lawrence, 102 Borstal Road, Rochester	C of E Diocese (Rochester)	Kent SSD
	25 Star Hill, Rochester	C of E Diocese (Rochester)	Not separately traced but Kent SSD may have records of individuals

MERSEYSIDE

A number of records from Sefton Choices, sponsored by the C of E Diocese of Liverpool, are held by The Archivist, Liverpool Central Library, William Brown Street, Liverpool L3 8EW.

Area	Name and Address	Run or used by	Records
Birkenhead	Nazareth House, Manor Hill, Birkenhead	Shrewsbury Diocesan Children's Rescue Society	Agency and Nazareth House Archives. Nazareth House, Hammersmith Road, London W6 8DE

Area	Name and Address	Run or used by	Records
	St Faith's (M&B), 24 Palm Grove, Birkenhead	C of E Diocese (Chester)	Not traced, but worth trying Wirral SSD & County Archivist, Cheshire Record Office, Duke Street, Chester, Cheshire CH1 1RL
Crosby	Nazareth House, Liverpool Road, Crosby	Liverpool Catholic Social Services	Agency and Nazareth House Archives, as above
Freshfield	Clumber Lodge, Victoria Road, Freshfield	Liverpool Catholic Social Services	
Heswall	Gayton Grange (M&B), Heswall, Wirral	C of E Diocese (Chester)	Worth trying County Archivist, Chester Record Office as above
Hoylake	Prospect House (M&B), 7 Trinity Road, Hoylake, Wirral	Cheshire Social Services; Manchester and District Child Adoption Society	
Liverpool	Catholic Female Orphanage, Druids Cross Road, Liverpool 18 (closed 1955)	Liverpool Catholic Social Services	
	Chesterfield House, Edge Lane, Liverpool	Salvation Army	
	Cradlehurst Edge Lane (previously known as Chesterfield House. 1939 transferred to Elmswood.)	Salvation Army	
	282 Edge Lane, Fairfield, Liverpool (MH)	Salvation Army	
	Elmswood, N. Mossley Hill Road, Liverpool 18	Salvation Army	
	38 Grey Road, Liverpool 9 (Flatlets 1967–77)	Liverpool Catholic Social Services	
	House of Help, 162 Grove Street, Liverpool	By Committee	Not traced, but worth trying local agencies, Liverpool SSD and Liverpool Archivist as above
	House of Providence, Kelton, Woodlands Road, Liverpool 17 (closed 1968)	Liverpool Catholic Social Services	
	Laurel House (transferred to St Hilda's, see below)		
	Leyfield School, West Derby, Liverpool 12 (closed 1956)	Liverpool Catholic Social Services	
	Magdalen Home, 8 Mount Vernon Green, Edgehill, Liverpool	C of E Diocese (Liverpool)	Worth trying local agencies, Liverpool SSD and Liverpool Archivist as above
	Mater Dei Hostel, Berkeley House, Blundellsands, Liverpool 23 (closed 1967)	Liverpool Catholic Social Services	
	Our Lady's Home, 12 Holly Road, Fairfield, Liverpool 7 (closed 1975)	Liverpool Catholic Social Services	

Area	Name and Address	Run or used by	Records
	Rosemont, 311 Edge Lane, Liverpool	Poor Servants of Mother of God	Not traced; Adoptions probably through Liverpool Catholic SS
	St Edward's School, Thingwall Hall, Liverpool 14 (until 1957)	Liverpool Catholic Social Services	
	St Faith's (MH), 12 Gambier Terrace, Liverpool	C of E Diocese (Liverpool)	As for Magdalen Home above
	St Hilda's (previously Laurel House), 1 Linnet Lane, 14 Ullet Road and 4 Everton Terrace, Liverpool (closed)	C of E Diocese (Liverpool)	As above
	St Monica's (M&B), 13 Croxteth Road, Liverpool (closed)	C of E Diocese (Liverpool)	As above
Southport	Marshfield, 37 Park Crescent 1940–43	Salvation Army	
	St Katharine's, 5 Lathom Road, Southport	Affiliated to National Council for One Parent Families	As for Magdalen Home above
Wallasey	St Barnabas Home for Orphans, 19 Montpelier Crescent, New Brighton, Wallasey	Mrs C. Whishaw	Not traced, but Mrs Whishaw is said to have arranged many adoptions
	Steel House, 29 St Martin's Lane, Wallasey	C of E Diocese (Chester)	See preface to Cheshire as this was in Chester Diocese
Waterloo	St Mary's, 10 Garden Road, Seaforth and 25 Grosby Road, South Waterloo	C of E Diocese (Liverpool)	As for Magdalen Home above
	St Gabriel's, Knolle Park, Woolton	Liverpool Catholic Social Services	

MIDDLESBROUGH

Part of Cleveland until 1 April 1996

Although not a registered adoption agency, Cleveland Family Welfare Council negotiated placements with other agencies. It closed in 1979. Durham Diocesan Family Welfare Council holds some index cards and case books.

Area	Name and Address	Run or used by	Records
Middlesbrough	Holy Cross Home (M&B), 74 St Paul's Road, and 92 Lothian Road, Middlesbrough (closed)	C of E Diocese (York); Adoptions normally through York Adoption Society, Durham Diocesan Family Welfare Council or Northern Counties Adoption Society	No separate records traced. Worth contacting agencies and SSDs. Some early adoptions arranged by the Superintendent Health Visitor (now deceased) in the Middlesbrough Health Department.
	St Theresa's, 176 Borough Road and 261 Marton Road, Middlesbrough	Middlesbrough Diocesan Rescue Society	

MIDLANDS
Birmingham

Birmingham City Archives, Central Library, Chamberlain Square, Birmingham B3 3HQ holds records of the Birmingham Association for the Unmarried Mother and Her Child from 1953. Because these are not indexed it is extremely difficult to trace an individual. The archives also contain some records of the Birmingham Diocesan Association for Moral Welfare, records of some Birmingham Union, later Birmingham City Council, Children's Homes as well as those of the Princess Alice Orphanage run by the National Children's Home which holds the case files, the Josiah Mason Orphanage and the Middlemore Homes which emigrated most of their children to Canada or Australia.

Area	Name and Address	Run or used by	Records
	Beechcroft, 15 Belle Walk, Moseley, Birmingham 13	Public Health Department, Birmingham	Pre-1950 records not traced. Some adoption records with Birmingham SSD. Others with agencies which used the Home.

Area	Name and Address	Run or used by	Records
	Bonner House, 172 Sellywood Road, Bourneville, Birmingham 30	National Children's Home	
	35 Braithwaite Road, Sparkbrook, Birmingham 11	C of E Diocese (Birmingham)	Not traced. Worth trying Birmingham SSD for named individuals and City Archives.
	Crowley House M&B Hostel	Middlemore Homes	The Secretary of the Trustees, 55 Stevens Avenue, Bartley Green, Birmingham B32 3SD
	The Grange, Rescue Maternity Home, 42 Park Hill, Moseley 13 (1960–65)	The Grange Trust	Not traced. Worth contacting Birmingham SSD and local agencies.
	The Hawthorns, Ladywood Road, Edgbaston	Salvation Army	
	The Hostel, 276 Monument Road, Edgbaston, Birmingham 16	Affiliated to National Council for One Parent Families	Not traced. The Archivist as above has a small amount of material from the Birmingham branch.
	Lahai-Roi (MH), 42 Park Hill, Moseley, Birmingham 13	Lahai-Roi Adoption Society	Not traced. Worth contacting Birmingham SSD and local agencies about named individuals.
	Lyncroft House, 88–101 Handsworth Wood Road, Birmingham 20	Salvation Army	
	St Paul's, 1 High Street, Coleshill, Birmingham	Father Hudson's Homes	
	Trentham House, 12 Devonshire Road, Handsworth Wood, Birmingham 17 (1966–) now at 47–49 Broad Road, Acock's Green, Birmingham B27 7UX	Birmingham Diocesan Council for Family and Social Welfare; run by St Basil's Centre Ltd	Not traced. Worth trying Birmingham SSD and County Archivist as above for named individuals.
	Woodville (MH), 176 Raddlebarn Road, Selly Oak, Birmingham 29	Father Hudson's Homes, Birmingham Catholic Maternity and Child Welfare Council	
Coventry	Coventry SSD holds copies of court reports in respect of adoption orders made in Coventry from 1927. The City Archivist, Mandela House, Bayley Lane, Coventry CV1 5RG holds records of children in the care of the SSD; Children's Homes; Registers of Adoptions, permanent, withdrawn and dismissed; Notifications of Births to the Medical Officer of Health and the Register of the Midwife for Foleshill.		
	St Faith's, St Nicholas Street (1920–24, 143 Warwick Road and 50 Holyhead Road, Coventry	C of E Diocese (Coventry); Birmingham Diocesan Board for Social Responsibility	City Archivist as above 1897–1928. From 1928 Coventry SSD.
Kingswinford	Broadfield House, Steam Road, Kingswinford	Staffordshire CC	Individual records may be with Staffordshire SSD
Smethwick	Astbury House (M&B), 27 Littlemoor Hill, Smethwick, Warley (sold 1987), mainly a children's home	C of E Diocese (Birmingham); Warley Rural District Association of Birmingham; Sandwell SSD	Worth contacting Sandwell SSD and Birmingham Archivist as above.

Area	Name and Address	Run or used by	Records
	35 Broomfield, Smethwick	Church Moral Aid Society until June 1952	Not traced. As previous entry.
Solihull	Corner Oak, 1 Homer Road, Solihull	Father Hudson's Homes	
	Francis Way, 124 Four Ashes Road, Bentley Heath, Knowie, Solihull	Father Hudson's Homes, Birmingham Catholic Maternity and Child Welfare Council	Father Hudson's Society
Sutton Coldfield	Florence Nursery, Princess Alice Drive, Chester Road North, Sutton Coldfield (closed)	National Children's Home	
Walsall	St Agnes, 7 St Paul's Terrace, Walsall (closed 1923)		Not traced. Worth trying SSD and City Archivists as above.
Wolverhampton	Mrs Hay Memorial Home, 36 Merridale Road and 38 Park Road East, Wolverhampton	C of E Diocese (Lichfield)	Individual records may be with Staffordshire SSD
	Mrs Legge Memorial Home, 87 and 89 New North Road and 134 Tettenhall Road, Wolverhampton	C of E Diocese (Lichfield)	As previous entry
	St Winifred's, Whitmore Reans, Wolverhampton	C of E Diocese (Lichfield)	As previous entry
	Wolverhampton Clinic, Cleveland House, Vicarage Road, Wolverhampton	C of E Diocese (Lichfield)	As previous entry
MILTON KEYNES	Part of Buckinghamshire until 1 April 1997		
Fenny Stratford	Richmond House, Bletchley Road, Fenny Stratford	C of E Diocese (Oxford)	Not traced. Worth trying Bucks and Oxon SSD and PACT
NORFOLK	The Board for Social Responsibility, Diocesan House, 109 Dereham Road, Easton, Norwich NR9 5ES has the records of the C of E Diocese, Norfolk		
Great Yarmouth	St Paul's Lodge (M&B), Salisbury Road, Great Yarmouth (closed as M&B)	C of E Diocese (Norwich)	Social Responsibility Officer as above 1959–1974
Hunstanton	St Katharine's, Alexandra Road, Hunstanton	C of E Diocese (King's Lynn)	Not separately traced. See above.
King's Lynn	Lyndene, 53 Wisbech Road, King's Lynn	C of E Diocese (Norwich)	As above
Norwich	St Augustine's Lodge, 21 Lady Lane and 53 Bethel Street, Norwich	C of E Diocese (Norwich)	As above
	53 Surrey Street, Norwich	C of E Diocese (Norwich)	As above
Sheringham	RC Nursery, Sheringham (1948–74)	St Francis' Children's Society	

Area	Name and Address	Run or used by	Records
NORTHANTS	Any available Diocesan records are likely to be held by Family Care, 222 Dogsthorpe Road, Peterborough PE1 3PB. They hold some adoption records for Cambridge and Northamptonshire. Agencies used were usually the Children's Society, Leicestershire Diocesan Board for Social Responsibility, or East Anglia Adoption and Family Care Association.		
Northampton	Elmleigh (M&B), 114 Harleston Road, Northampton	National Adoption Society	
	St Saviour's, 103 Harleston Road and 21a Manor Road, Kingsthorpe, Northampton	Leicester Diocesan Board for Social Responsibility; C of E Diocese (Peterborough)	Probably with Family Care (as above)
	Spencer Leeson House, 11–12 Langham Place, Northampton	Peterborough Diocesan Family and Social Welfare Council	As above
	9 St George's Avenue, Northampton	Peterborough Diocesan Family and Social Welfare Council	As above
NORTHUMBERLAND			
Corbridge	Dilston Hall, really a maternity hospital used by mother & baby homes	Durham Family Welfare; Northern Counties Adoption Society	
Morpeth	Bowmer Bank, Morpeth	Northumbrland CC	Manager, Adoption & Fostering Team, Tweed House, Hepscott Park, Stannington Morpeth, Northumberland NE61 6NF
NOTTINGHAM CITY	Part of Nottinghamshire until 1 April 1998. The records of the C of E Diocese (Southwell) are held by the Principal Archivist, Nottinghamshire Archives County House, Castle Meadow Road, Nottingham NG2 1AG.		
Lenton	Nazareth House, Lenton Society	Nottingham Catholic Children's Society	Agency and Nazareth House Archives, Nazareth House, Hammersmith Road, London W6 8DE
Nottingham	Fern Mount, 16 Gorsey Road, Nottingham (1965–69)	Southwell Diocesan Council for Family Care	
	Mothers' Hostels, 95 Queen's Drive and 8 Mapperley Road, Nottingham	Probably old Nottingham City Health Department	Individual case files may be with Health Authority Archives
	St Joseph's (M&B), 130–132 Radcliffe Road, West Bridgford, Nottingham	Catholic Children's Society (RC Diocese of Nottingham) which covers Derbyshire, Lincolnshire, Leicestershire and Nottinghamshire. Also took Irish girls.	
	Southwell House Shelter, 49 Leen Side, Nottingham (1924–32)	Southwell Diocesan Council for Family Care	No records of home but might have adoption records
	32 Canmer Street, Nottingham (1932–37)	Southwell Diocesan Council for Family Care	As previous entry
NOTTINGHAMSHIRE			
Clipstone	Gwendoline Grove House (M&B), Mansfield Road, Clipstone, Nr Mansfield (1969–)	Southwell Diocesan Council for Family Care; Leicester Diocesan Board for Social Responsibility	

Area	Name and Address	Run or used by	Records
Colston Bassett	Colston Bassett Nursery, Garden Cottage, Colston Bassett	Nottingham Catholic Children's Society	
Mansfield	Grosvenor House, 1 Grove Street, Mansfield (1946–69)	Southwell Diocesan Council for Family Care; Leicester Diocesan Board for Social Responsibility	
Newark	St Catherine's House (M&B), 15 Wilson Street, Newark (1929–62)	Southwell Diocesan Council for Family Care	
Worksop	27 George Street, Worksop	C of E Diocese (Southwell)	Worth trying Principal Archivist as previous entry.

OXFORDSHIRE — It is known that pre-1967 Diocesan records were destroyed. Adoptions were usually arranged through the Children's Society or Father Hudson's Homes, Birmingham. Oxfordshire SSD has manual records dating back at least to the creation of children's departments in 1948, and sometimes beyond that e.g. Guardian *ad litem* reports.

Area	Name and Address	Run or used by	Records
Abingdon	Oakley House, Frilford Heath	Barnardo's	
Littlemore	St Mary's, Littlemore. Before 1929 known as Lawn Upton. Closed September 1949.	Founded privately around 1857. Run by the sisters of St John the Baptist, Clewer.	BAAF has history of home but records not traced
Oxford	Clark's House (M&B), 7 Clark's Row, St Aldgate's, Oxford (closed 1977)	Oxford DHSS	Not traced. Worth trying Oxford SSD and PACT as well as national agencies.
	Floyd's Row, St Aldgate's, Oxford	C of E Diocese (Oxford)	As above
	Manor House, Holywell, Oxford	C of E Diocese (Oxford)	Not traced and as above
	Skene House, Charles Row, Oxford	C of E Diocese (Oxford)	Possibly some with London Metropolitan Archives. Worth trying as above
	St Frideswide's Cottage, 59 St John's Road, Oxford	Oxford Ladies' Association for the Care of Friendless Girls	As previous entries

PLYMOUTH — Part of Devon until 1 April 1998

The Archivist, Plymouth & West Devon Record Office, Unit 3, Clare Place, Coxside, Plymouth, Devon, PL4 0JW, holds the Plymouth Public Assistance Committee Minutes & registers of people in institutions 1930–48 (Ref 54). They include some references to adoption, fostering and care. Adoptions which took place in the Juvenile Courts are held in a strong room at the Plymouth & Torquay Magistrates' Court.

The County Archivist, Devon Record Office, Castle Street, Exeter EX4 3PU, holds the records of the C of E Diocese (Exeter) but they may not contain much that relates to adoption.

Access to all the above should be through an adoption counsellor.

Area	Name and Address	Run or used by	Records
Plymouth	Abbotsfield, Seymour Road, Mannamead (evacuated to Bradninch 1940, returned to Plymouth 1961 and later became the Mayflower Home).	Salvation Army	
	Devon and Cornwall Female Orphanage	Aid for Girls Trust	Probably Plymouth and West Devon Record Office (as above)
	Mayflower Home, Courtfield Road, Plymouth (previously known as Dunmore House, see Bradninch)	Salvation Army	

Area	Name and Address	Run or used by	Records
	Nazareth House	Plymouth Diocesan Catholic Children's Society	Agency and Nazareth House Archives, Nazareth House, Hammersmith Road, London W6 8DE
	St Margaret's, 17 Portland Villas, Plymouth (1880–1935)	C of E Diocese (Exeter)	Not traced, but worth contacting SSD and Devon Record Office as above
	St Ursula's (MH), 1 Edith Avenue, Plymouth	C of E Diocese (Exeter)	As above
	Southview (M&B), 2 Woodside, Plymouth	Plymouth and District Association for Girls' Welfare	Registers 1961–69 (Ref 1716) with the Archivist as above.
Plympton	St Theresa's Orphanage (1875–1931)	Sisters of Charity of St Vincent de Paul	Provincial Archivist, Sisters of Charity of St Vincent de Paul, Provincial House, The Ridgeway, London NW7
POOLE	Part of Dorset until 1 April 1997		
	The Senior Archivist, Wiltshire & Swindon Record Office, Bythesea Road, Trowbridge, Wilts BA14 8BS holds the general records of the C of E Diocese (Salisbury) but there are few references to individuals. Many adoptions were probably arranged through St Gabriel's or the Avon and Wilts agencies.		
Canford Magna	Knighton Lodge (M&B)	Mission of Hope for Children's Aid and Adoption	Mission of Hope or Hampshire SSD
Parkstone	Oak Tree Lodge (M&B), Pottery Lane, Parkstone	C of E Diocese (Salisbury)	Not traced. Worth trying SSD and Senior Archivist as above
	St Faith's, Mount Road, Parkstone	C of E Diocese (Salisbury)	As above
	St Monica's, 17 and 19 St Peter's Road, Parkstone (closed)	C of E Diocese (Salisbury)	As above
PORTSMOUTH	Part of Hampshire until 1 April 1997		
Southsea	Woodlands, 22 Albany Road, Southsea (1919–37)	National Free Church Women's Council	Index cards only (1919–37) with Hants SSD. Access through Portsmouth SSD. London Metropolitan Archives might also have some for the organisation.
	16 St David's Road, Southsea	C of E Diocese (Portsmouth)	Hampshire SSD has records of some individuals but none of home itself. Access through Portsmouth SSD.
READING	Part of Berkshire until 1 April 1998		
	It is known that pre-1967 Oxford Diocesan Records were destroyed. Adoptions were usually arranged through the Children's Society, Father Hudson's Homes or PACT.		
Reading	St Monica's, 23 Russell Street, Christchurch Road, Reading	C of E Diocese (Oxford)	Not traced but worth trying above-mentioned contacts

Homes and Shelters

Area	Name and Address	Run or used by	Records
SHROPSHIRE	Staffordshire SSD holds the records of the C of E Diocese of Lichfield. Shropshire Records and Research Centre, Castle Gates, Shrewsbury SY1 2AQ has archives of Poor Law union workhouses, schools and Shrewsbury newspapers from 1772. www.shropshire-cc.gov.uk/research.nsf		
Newcastle	2 Enderley St, Lichfield (M&B)	C of E Diocese (Lichfield)	Not traced. Worth trying Shropshire & Staffordshire SSD for individuals.
Shrewsbury	Chaddeslode, Crescent Lane and Abbey Foregate, Shrewsbury	C of E Diocese (Lichfield)	As above
SLOUGH	Part of Berkshire until 1 April 1998. Known that pre-1967 Oxford Diocesan Records were destroyed. Adoptions were usually arranged through Children's Society, Father Hudson's Homes or PACT.		
Slough	3 Belgrave Place, Uxbridge Road; now at 11 Sussex Place, Slough	C of E Diocese (Oxford)	Limited information with PACT, 7 Southern Court, South Street, Reading RG1 4QS
SOMERSET	The County Archivist, Somerset Records Office, Obridge Road, Taunton, TA2 7PU holds registers for a large number of Children's Homes in Somerset and also of Public Assistance institutions in Axbridge, Bridgwater, Chard, Clutton, Dulverton, Frome, Keynsham, Langport, Shepton Mallet, Taunton, Wellington, Wells, Wincanton & Yeovil.		
Chard	Braeside (M&B), Crewkerne Road, Chard	Somerset SSD	Records lost. Probably worth trying SSD, Avon and N. Wilts and national agencies.
Dulverton	Exmoor House, Dulverton	Somerset CC. An old workhouse with a wing for unmarried mothers.	A number of admission and discharge registers for periods between 1856 & 1932. Registers of births 1866–1927. County Archivist as above.
South Petherton	The Old House, S. Petherton	Affiliated to National Council for One Parent Families	Records lost. Probably worth trying SSD, Avon and N. Wilts and national agencies.
SOUTHAMPTON	Part of Hampshire until 1 April 1997		
Southampton	Hope Lodge, (M&B), Cross Street and 41 Belmont Road, Portswood, Southampton	Southampton Refuge Trustees; C of E Diocese (Winchester)	Hants SSD, access through Southampton SSD
	Ilfra, Bassett Crescent East, Southampton	Southampton Refuge Trustees	Records 1964–71 as above
	Nazareth House, 33 Hill Lane, Southampton	St Francis Children's Society; Portsmouth Catholic Social Service Council	Agencies and Nazareth House Archives, Hammersmith Road, London W6 8DE
SOUTHEND-ON-SEA	Part of Essex until 1 April 1998		
Southend-on-Sea	Nazareth House, Southend-on-Sea	Crusade of Rescue	Nazareth House Archives. Nazareth House, Hammersmith Road, London W6 8DE
Westcliffe-on-Sea	St Monica's, 26 and 44 Sutton Road and 154 York Road, Southend-on-Sea (1956 became Beechwood).	C of E Diocese (Chelmsford)	The County Archivist, Essex Record Office, Wharf Road, Chelmsford CM2 6YT
Beechwood	Beechwood, 2 Westborough Road, Westcliff-on-Sea, Chelmsford	Chelmsford Diocesan Committee for Family Care	The County Archivist, as above

Area	Name and Address	Run or used by	Records
STAFFORDSHIRE	Staffordshire SSD holds the records of Lichfield Diocesan Association for Family Care and the C of E Diocese (Lichfield).		
Burton-upon-Trent	Home for Girls (M&B), 53 Union Street, Burton-upon-Trent	Burton-upon-Trent Association for the Protection of Girls (affiliated to C of E Diocese, Lichfield)	Assistant Director (Adoption Unit) Staffordshire SSD (after being lodged with Lichfield Diocesan Association)
Lichfield	Beacon Holme, Lichfield.	C of E Diocese (Lichfield)	Not separately traced. See above preface.
	Lyncroft House, Stafford Road, Lichfield	Salvation Army	
	2 Enderley St, Lichfield (M& B)	C of E Diocese (Lichfield)	Not separately traced. See above preface.
Newcastle-under-Lyme	Elizabeth House, 7 Sidmouth Avenue, Newcastle-under-Lyme	The Elizabeth Trust	Not traced. Worth trying Staffordshire SSD for named individuals.
Stafford	Glentworth Mothercraft Hostel, Rowley Bank, Stafford, 31 March 1947–30 June 1950	WRVS	WRVS have no records. Some adoptions dealt with by Lichfield Diocesan Association so individual records may be with Staffordshire SSD. Others might be with National Children Adoption Association or Mission of Hope or Children's Society
	House of Mercy, Sandon Road, Stafford (Became Reform School)	C of E Diocese (Lichfield)	Not traced. See above preface.
SUFFOLK	The Public Service Manager, Bury St Edmunds Records Office, 77 Raingate St, Bury St Edmunds Suffolk IP3 32AR holds the records of the St Edmundsbury & Ipswich Diocesan Board of Social Responsibility 1957–1973. They do not hold records of individual Homes, but may well have records of individuals who resided in them.		
Bungay	Ditchingham House of Mercy, Bungay	C of E Diocese (Norwich)	See above preface. Also the C of E Diocese (Norwich) records are held by the Board for Social Responsibility, Diocesan House, 109 Dereham Road, Easton, Norwich NR9 5ES.
Bury St Edmunds	St Elizabeth's, 11 Lower Baxter Street, Bury St Edmunds	C of E Diocese (St Edmundsbury and Ipswich)	Try Bury St Edmund's Record Office. As above.
Ipswich	Highlands, 52 Belstead Road, Ipswich	C of E Diocese (St Edmundsbury and Ipswich)	As above
Long Melford	Montgomery House (Nursery), Long Melford	Barnardo's	
Lowestoft	Parkview, 3 Yarmouth Road, Lowestoft	C of E Diocese (St Edmundsbury and Ipswich)	Try Bury St Edmunds Record Office. As above
	St Bridget's, North Parade, Lowestoft	C of E Diocese (Norwich)	As above and Board for Social Responsibility, Norwich
Needham Market	Beatrice Elizabeth House, Barking Road, Needham Market. Hutchinson House Children's Home, evacuated there 1939–45 war.	Homeless Children's Aid and Adoption	Not traced. Worth checking for an individual with the Homeless Children's Aid and Adoption records.

Area	Name and Address	Run or used by	Records
SURREY	The records of the Diocese of Guildford's Dept of Social Responsibility throughout Surrey are with the County Archivist, Surrey History Centre, 130 Goldsworth Rd, Woking, Surrey GU21 1ND. The records are mainly administrative and historical but do contain details of some individuals – and maternity case records 1962–1972. Access should normally be through an adoption counsellor. Always worth trying Surrey SSD.		
Caterham	George Simon Home (M&B), 57 Tupwood Lane, Caterham	Rainer Foundation	Rainer Foundation, The Galleries of Justice, Shire Hall, High Pavement, Lace Market, Nottingham NG1 1HN
Dorking	Edgcombe, Horsham Road Renamed St Aubyn's (1944–66)	C of E Diocese (Guildford)	Surrey History Centre as above
	St Aubyn's, Horsham Road, Dorking (1929–66)	C of E Diocese (Guildford)	As above
	St Faith's, Horsham Road, Dorking (1911–22)	C of E Diocese (Guildford)	As above
	19 Rothes Road, Dorking (1910–11)	C of E Diocese (Guildford)	As above
Epsom	Waltham House Hostel and Foster Home, Worple Road, Epsom	C of E Diocese (Epsom)	Worth trying both Surrey SSD and Surrey History Centre as above
Grayshott	Assisi (M&B), Grayshott (previously known as St Joseph's)	Portsmouth Catholic Social Service Council; Crusade of Rescue; St Francis Children's Society	Records 9 January 1952–7 October 1975 with Catholic Children's Society (Arundel & Brighton, Portsmouth & Southwark). Earlier records believed to have been destroyed.
	St Josephs, Hammer Lane, Grayshott (later Assisi (M&B) – see previous entry)		
	St Nicholas, Hammer Lane, Grayshott (previously known as St Nicholas, Islington)	Crusade of Rescue	Not traced but the records of individuals might be with Catholic Children's Society (Westminster) or CCS (Arundel & Brighton, Portsmouth & Southwark)
Guildford	Avondale, Sydney Road, Guildford 1961–69	C of E Diocese (Guildford)	Surrey History Centre and SSD as above
	Hope Lodge, The Guildford Rescue Home, 6 Wellington Place, Guildford 1936	C of E Diocese (Guildford)	Surrey History Centre and SSD as above
	New Hope Lodge, Nightingale Road, Guildford 1938–1952; re-opened as M&B House 1958	C of E Diocese (Guildford)	Surrey History Centre and SSD as above
Haslemere	Home of the Good Shepherd, (M&B) Shepherd's Hill Haslemere 1924–57	C of E Diocese (Guildford)	Surrey History Centre and SSD as above
Leatherhead	St Monica's, Kingston Road, Leatherhead (closed 31 July 1938)	C of E Diocese (Guildford)	Surrey History Centre and SSD as above.

Area	Name and Address	Run or used by	Records
Limpsfield	Stretton House (M&B) evacuated from London 1939, moved to Fairacre and then to Monkschester 1940. Closed 1944, reopened Lewisham 1946	C of E Diocese (Southwark)	Limited records London Metropolitan Archives
Ottershaw	St James, Ottershaw (previously known as St James, Hammersmith)	C of E Diocese (London)	Not traced but worth checking with Barnardo's for named individuals.
Oxted	Pasteus, Pasteus Road, Oxted (closed)	National Children's Home	
Redhill	6 Brownlow Road, Redhill	Reigate Deanery WelCare Association	Surrey History Centre and SSD as above
	Denmark NH, Linkfield House, Redhill (1948–)	Privately run by Mrs G H James, Matron	Not traced, worth trying Surrey SSD
Walton Heath	Castle House, Walton Heath	Mission of Hope for Children's Aid and Adoption	Any available records with the Archivist, Croydon Local Studies Library, Beatrice Ave, Norbury, London SW16 4UW or Croydon SSD
Walton-on-Thames	Emly House, Rydens Avenue, Walton-on-Thames. Demolished June 1968. Replaced by West Lodge.	C of E Diocese (Guildford)	Surrey History Centre and SSD as above
	West Lodge (M&B), 185 Sidney Road, Walton-on-Thames (1969–79)	C of E Diocese (Guildford)	Surrey History Centre and SSD
Woking	Ashwood, Ashwood Road, Woking (closed)	National Children's Home	
	Dorincourt (M&B), Woodham Rise, Woking	Surrey SSD	Surrey SSD may have records of individuals
	Fairview, Ferndale Road, 1927/8–1929	Woking Deanery C of E Diocese (Guildford)	Surrey History Centre and SSD
	Pembroke, Woking	Woking Deanery C of E Diocese (Guildford)	Surrey History Centre and SSD
	St Margaret's (M&B), 22–23 Ferndale Road, Woking (1903–69)	Woking Deanery C of E Diocese (Guildford)	Surrey History Centre and SSD
TORBAY	Part of Devon until 1 April 1998. The Court House, Union Street, Torquay TQ1 4BP holds the records of adoptions within the Petty Sessional areas of S. Hams, Teignbridge and Torbay. Access only through an adoption counsellor.		
Torquay	3 Bampfylde Road, Torre and 12 Bexley Terrace, Torre, Torquay (closed 1949–51)	C of E Diocese (Exeter)	Not traced. Worth contacting SSD, Council for Christian Care and County Archivist, Devon Record Office, Castle Street, Exeter, EX4 3PU.
	Morningside, Barrington Road, Torquay	Children's Aid Society	Barnardo's and London Metropolitan Archives
	St Vincent's Orphanage, Torquay	Sisters of Charity of St Vincent de Paul	Provincial Archivist, Sisters of Charity of St Vincent de Paul, Provincial House, The Ridgeway, London NW7. Register 1889–1982.

Area	Name and Address	Run or used by	Records
TYNE & WEAR	Northumberland Record Office, Melton Park, North Gosforth, Newcastle upon Tyne NE3 5QX holds mainly administrative records of Newcastle Diocesan Council for Moral & Social Welfare. They cover the areas of Newcastle, Alnwick, Hexham, Morpeth, Tynemouth and Wallsend.		
Birtley	Eighton Lodge (M&B), Low Eighton, Low Fell, Birtley (previously known as St Faith's, see next entry)	C of E Diocese (Durham)	Durham Family Welfare
Gateshead	St Faith's, 4 King James Street and 8 Grasmere Street, Gateshead; replaced by Eighton Lodge 1968 (see previous entry)	C of E Diocese (Durham)	Durham Family Welfare
Gosforth	House of Mercy, Salters Rd, Gosforth 1891–1942 when it became an Approved School	C of E Diocese (Newcastle)	Northumberland Record Office as above. Also has history of the Home.
Newcastle upon Tyne	Catherine House, Osborne Road, Jesmond, Newcastle (transferred to Hope Dean, see later entry)	Salvation Army	
	Clifton House, Clifton Road, Newcastle	C of E Diocese (Newcastle)	Annual Reports 1941–43, Northumberland Record Office as above
	Elswick Lodge (M&B), Park Road, Newcastle (closed)	C of E Diocese (Newcastle); Northern Counties Adoption Society; Durham Diocesan Family Welfare Council	Committee meetings and Annual Reports, Northumberland Record Office
	Hope Dean, Jesmond Park Estate, Newcastle (previously known as Catherine House, see previous entry)	Salvation Army	
	Hopedene, Elswick Rd, Newcastle (closed 1974)	Salvation Army	
South Shields	St Agnes Hostel, 5 Lovaine Row, Newcastle	Hexham and Newcastle Diocesan Rescue Society	
Sunderland	Wayside, Benton Bank, Newcastle	Hexham and Newcastle Diocesan Rescue Society	
	Wilberforce, 41 Jesmond Road Newcastle	C of E Diocese (Newcastle)	Half-yearly Report 1904 Northumberland Record Office
	St Vercas', 9 Challoner Terrace West, South Shields	C of E Diocese (Durham)	Bombed – records probably destroyed
	The Limes, Parker Memorial Home (M&B), 25 Kayll Road, Sunderland	Sunderland County Borough Council; Durham Diocesan Family Welfare Council	
	St Agatha's, 17 Merton Street, Sunderland	C of E Diocese (Durham)	Bombed – records possibly destroyed
WARRINGTON	Part of Cheshire until 1 April 1998		
Warrington	Good Samaritan Home, 33 Wilson Patten Street, Warrington	C of E Diocese (Chester and Liverpool); Church Army	No record of Home but worth approach to Cheshire County Archivist, Chester Record Office, Duke Street, Chester, Cheshire CH1 1RL through Cheshire SSD

Area	Name and Address	Run or used by	Records
	Waverley House (M&B) Victoria Rd, Grappenhall, Warrington and 263 Waverley Place Warrington (closed 1982)	C of E Diocese; Liverpool Board of Mission and Social Responsibility; Social Services	As above
WARWICKSHIRE			
Leamington	Fairhaven, 6 Church Hill; 76 Leam Terrace, Leamington Spa (1956–67)	Leamington and Warwick Girls' Shelter Association. Connection with Gay Block Maternity Wing, Warneford Hospital	Not traced; worth trying Coventry SSD for records of individuals.
Rugby	Hamilton House (M&B), 12 Bilton Rd, Rugby (closed)	C of E Diocese (Coventry)	Not traced; worth trying Coventry SSD for named individuals
Stratford upon Avon	The Limes, Alcester Road, Stratford upon Avon	Warwickshire CC	Warwickshire SSD
WEST BERKSHIRE	Part of Berkshire until 1 April 1998		
Newbury	York House (M&B), 50 Andover Road, Newbury	Berkshire Social Services	Not traced; worth contacting SSD for named individuals
WEST SUSSEX	The County Archivist, W. Sussex Record Office, County Hall, Chichester, W. Sussex, PO19 1RN has general records of the Chichester Diocesan M W Association for the 1940s and 1950s but they do not include case files. They also hold incomplete records of Juvenile Courts at Petty Sessions & school admissions registers. Chichester Diocesan Association for Family Social Work (now for Family Support Work) was responsible for most of the C of E Diocese (Chichester) Homes in E & W Sussex, Brighton & Hove. Casework files were destroyed after 10 years. The records of any adoptions arranged by the Society are with E Sussex SSD.		
Horsham	Forest House, Winterpit Lane, Manning's Heath, Horsham	National Children's Home	
	Memorial Centre for Babies, South Lodge, Lower Beeding, Horsham	Phyllis Holman Richards Adoption Society	Parents for Children. Records from 1958 only
Thakeham	Merrywood Nursery, Thakeham (nursery only)	Southwark Catholic Children's Society	
Worthing	St Monica's, 15 Grafton Road, Worthing	C of E Diocese (Chichester)	As in preface above
	Worthing House, 61 South Street, Tarring, Worthing (Flat let House)	C of E Diocese (Chichester)	As in preface above
WILTSHIRE	Because the Senior Archivist, Wiltshire & Swindon Record Office, Bythesea Road, Trowbridge, Wiltshire BA14 8BS holds the general records of the C of E Diocese (Salisbury), it may be worth checking whether named individuals are in the records even when there are no records of the individual Home. Many adoptions were probably arranged by The Avon and N. Wiltshire Agency.		
Devizes	The Girls' Hostel (M&B), 4 Trafalgar Place and Bath Road, Devizes (closed)	C of E Diocese (Salisbury)	It is possible that some records which were with Winchester Council for SR are now with Hampshire SSD
Marlborough	Magdalen Convalescent Home, 30 Weymouth Street, Marlborough		Not traced

Area	Name and Address	Run or used by	Records
Salisbury	Beckinsale House (M&B), 121 Rampart Road, Salisbury	C of E Diocese (Salisbury)	Some records with Senior Archivist as above
	42 Harcourt Terrace, Salisbury	C of E Diocese (Salisbury)	Not traced
	Hope House, 56 Mill Road, Salisbury	C of E Diocese (Salisbury)	Not traced
	House of Industry – later became Beckinsale House	C of E Diocese (Salisbury)	Senior Archivist as above
	Moorland House, St Martins Church Street, Salisbury	May have been an office, not a Home. C of E Diocese (Salisbury)	Not traced; see preface above
	16 Rolleston Street, Salisbury	C of E Diocese (Salisbury)	Not traced
Warminster	St Denys, 4 Lyme Avenue, Warminster (closed 1932)	C of E Diocese (Salisbury)	Not traced
WINDSOR and MAIDENHEAD	Part of Berkshire until 1 April 1998. It is known that pre-1967 Oxford Diocesan Records were destroyed. Adoptions were usually arranged through the Children's Society, Father Hudson's Society or PACT.		
Maidenhead	St Agnes Lodge, 52 Clare Road, Maidenhead (closed 1938)	C of E Diocese (Oxford)	Not traced
Windsor	Berkshire County Home, Windsor	Portsmouth Catholic Social Service Council	
	Burnell House (M&B), 27 Bolton Avenue, Windsor	Berkshire Social Services	Oxford Diocese until mid 60s, then Berks CC. A few files with PACT and Berks Record Office but these might be G & L reports only.
	St John Baptist Orphanage		With Convent of St John Baptist, Hatch Lane, Windsor
	St Michael's, 56 Frances Road, Windsor	C of E Diocese (Oxford)	PACT, 7 Southern Court, South Street, Reading RG1 4QS has incomplete set of index cards
WORCESTER	Part of Hereford and Worcester until 1 April 1998		
Kidderminster	Greenhill Hostel, Chester Road, Kidderminster (closed)	C of E Diocese (Worcester)	Not traced; Worth trying SSD and Worcester Diocesan Association for Family and Social Service
Malvern	Barsham House, 33 Graham Road, Malvern (closed)	C of E Diocese (Worcester)	Not traced; as above
Malvern Link	Home of the Good Shepherd, Romelagh Road, Malvern Link	Religious House, Community of the Holy Name; C of E Diocese (Worcester)	Not traced; as above
	St Catherine's, St Edward's House, Merick Road, Malvern Link	Convent of the Holy Name; C of E Diocese (Worcester)	Not traced; as above
Worcester	Field House, Wylds Lane, Worcester	C of E Diocese (Worcester)	Not traced; as above
	58 Woolhope Road, Worcester (closed 1923)	C of E Diocese (Worcester)	Not traced; as above

Area	Name and Address	Run or used by	Records
THE WREKIN	Part of Shropshire until 1 April 1998		
Wellington	Myford House, Horsehay, Nr Wellington	C of E Diocese (Lichfield)	Not separately traced but Staffordshire SSD has the records of C of E Diocese (Lichfield)
YORKSHIRE	Most adoptions in York Diocese arranged through Church of England Children's Society, York Adoption Society or Barnardo's.		
Barnsley	7 Longman Road, Barnsley	Barnsley Deanery MW	Not separately traced but worth contacting SSD and above agencies.
Bradford	Bradford District Archives, 15 Canal Road, Bradford BD1 4AT has: Records of Bradford B C Education Department which include an incomplete series of adoption orders 1929–64 (Ref:BBD 3/2/118–123): Records of Bradford B C Welfare Department including various Children's Registers, 1899–1966 (Ref: BBD 4/13) and Bradford Union Register of Adoptions 1899–1949: Bradford B C Town Clerk records which include Bradford Union Register of adopted children (under control of the Guardians) 1899–1952 (Ref: 40D 80/25) and admission registers for children's homes 1906–53 (Ref: 40 D80/37). Bradford Poor Law records which include Children's Homes returns 1903–31 (Ref: BU)		
	Holybrook House, Romanby Shaw, Greengates (closed)	C of E Diocese	Not separately traced but worth contacting SSD and above agencies
	Oakwell House (M&B), 8 Oak Avenue, Bradford 8	City of Bradford Health Committee	As above
	St Monica's, 10 and 11 Belle Vue, Manningham, Bradford 8	Bradford Church Committee for Rescue Work	County Archivist, Bradford District Archives (as above). Baptisms of children born in the home are recorded in the registers of St Mary Magdalene, Manningham, Bradford (Ref: 21 D80)
Bramley	Carmel House, Houghley Lane, Bramley	Leeds Diocesan Rescue and Child Welfare Society	
	Cowgill House, Houghley Lane, Bramley	Leeds Diocesan Rescue and Child Welfare Society	
	Mount Cross, Broad Lane, Bramley (closed 1972)	Salvation Army	Some destroyed by fire
Halifax	St Margaret's House (M&B), 8 Balmoral Place, Halifax (closed)	C of E Diocese (Wakefield)	Records destroyed
Harrogate	Roberts House Nursery, Harrogate	Barnardo's	
	St Agnes (Babies Home), 33 Regent Parade, Harrogate (closed)	C of E Diocese (Ripon)	Not separately traced but West Yorkshire Archive Service, Leeds has the records of the Diocese of Ripon
	St Monica's (M&B), 35 Regent Parade, Harrogate (closed)	C of E Diocese (Ripon); Durham Diocesan Family Welfare Council.	Leeds Family Welfare (Ripon Diocesan Board of Social Responsibility), Holy Trinity Church, Boar Lane, Leeds LS1 6HW 1967–72

Homes and Shelters

Area	Name and Address	Run or used by	Records
Huddersfield	16 Queen's Square, Huddersfield (M&B) until 1965.	Huddersfield Methodist Mission C of E Diocese. (Huddersfield)	Records of these homes with the Archivist, Kirklees District Archives, Central Library, Princess Alexandra Walk, Huddersfield HD1 2SU. Permission to access records must be obtained from the Superintendent, Minister of Huddersfield, Methodist Mission, Lord Street, Huddersfield
	Bryanwood, Bryan Road, Edgerton, Huddersfield. Closed 1978. In 1970 amalgamated with St Katharine's (M&B), 10 Kingsmill Lane, Huddersfield. Closed on amalgamation	As above	
Leeds	The Principal District Archivist, West Yorkshire Archive Service, Chapeltown Road, Sheepscar, Leeds, LS7 3AP holds records of Leeds Board of Guardians and Public Assistance Committee 1844–1948, some received from the Health Authorities and the records of the Diocese of Ripon, most Anglican parishes in The Archdeaconry of Leeds and some in the Diocese of Bradford (not formed until 1920). Also held are records from non-conformist churches including those of the Yorkshire Congregational Union 1813–1968, several United Reform Churches, Mill Hill Unitarian Chapel and numerous Methodist Circuits.		
	Leeds Family Welfare (Ripon Diocesan Board of Social Responsibility), Holy Trinity Church, Boar Lane, Leeds, LS1 6HW holds the records of Leeds Moral Welfare (1964–1985) and of the Ripon Diocesan Board of Social Responsibility in the period 1966–72. They negotiated adoption placements usually through Durham Family Welfare and York Adoption Society.		
	Browning House, 126 Chapeltown Road, Leeds 7	York Adoption Society; C of E Diocese (Ripon)	Browning House has admission and discharge records. Some adoption records held by Leeds SSD, W. Yorkshire Archive Service Leeds has the records of the Diocese of Ripon
	Cotland (closed) (Previously known as Cotland London)	Not known. Previously thought to be Salvation Army	Suggest trying SSD; W. Yorks Archives, Leeds.
	Emmaus Housing Association, 6 Grove Lane, Leeds 6		Worth trying N. Yorks SSD
	Fallodon Nursing Home, 4 Allerton Park, Leeds 17		Leeds SSD. Matron arranged adoptions often with local GPs
	Hope Hospital, 126 Chapeltown Road, Leeds: now Browning House M&B	Leeds Public Health Department	Admission and Discharge Records
	St Faith's, 20 Brunswick Place, 18 Moorland Road and 63 Clarendon Road, Leeds 6 (closed)	C of E Diocese (Ripon)	Not traced but W. Yorks Archive Service Leeds has records of Diocese of Ripon. Also worth trying SSD and agency
	St Margaret's, 18 Clarendon Road, Leeds 2	RC	Not traced, but for individuals worth trying Catholic Social Welfare Society (Leeds)
	St Margaret's (M&B), 31 Moor Road, Headingley, Leeds 6, and possibly 18 Clarendon Road, Leeds 2	Leeds Diocesan Rescue and Child Welfare Society	

Area	Name and Address	Run or used by	Records
	Spring Grove, Alexander Road, Leeds (closed 1942)	Salvation Army	
	Wyther Hostel, Armley Ridge Road, Leeds 12 and 40 Wakefield Road	Leeds Corporation	Adoption records Leeds SSD
Pontefract	The Haven or St Giles (M&B), 1–3 Linden Terrace, Pontefract	C of E Diocese (Pontefract and Wakefield)	Records probably destroyed but files of some adopted individuals may be with Wakefield SSD
Ripon	The Red House, Ripon	Barnardo's	
	St Clare's, 6 Claremont	C of E Diocese (Ripon)	Not separately traced but W Yorks Archives Service, Leeds has records of the Diocese of Ripon. Also worth trying SSD and agency.
	6 Skell Bank	C of E Diocese (Ripon)	As above
Scarborough	St Margaret's Home, 21 Albemarle Crescent, Scarborough (closed) (previously known as St Mary's)	C of E Diocese (York). Durham Diocesan Family Welfare Council	Worth trying N. Yorkshire SSD and agencies
Sheffield	The Archivist, Sheffield Archives, 52 Shoreham Street, Sheffield, S1 4SP hold the Records of the C of E Diocese (Sheffield), the RC Diocese of Hallam and numerous records of Methodists, Quakers, etc, records of the Leeds (RC) Diocesan Rescue Protection and Child Welfare Society 1974–1977: Records of a number of Children's Homes and a Register of children adopted under the Poor Law Act 1899 by the Ecclesall Board of Guardians 1902–1924, and a file on Sheffield and District Child Adoption Association 1968–1977.		
	Hope Lodge, Sheffield (previously known as Hope Lodge, London)	Previously thought to be Salvation Army	Not traced. Worth trying SSD and Yorkshire agencies.
	Oakdale House, Paradise Square, Glossop Road, Broomspring Lane, and 68 Carter Knowle Road, Sheffield (shelter) (still open)	Individual charity	Sheffield Archives (as above) have records 1886–1952 (Ref LD1378–1415)
	St Agatha's (M&B), 22 Broomsgrove Road, Sheffield 10 (closed)	C of E Diocese (Sheffield)	Sheffield Archives (as above) have Admissions Register 1931–73 and Baptism Register 1952–62
	Sheffield House of Help, another name for Oakdale House		
	19–21 Hucklow Rd, Sheffield 5 (M&B)	Sheffield Public Health Department	Enquiries to Sheffield SSD
	22 Paradise Square, Sheffield 1	Leeds Diocesan Rescue and Child Welfare Society	
Steeton	Park House, Steeton, Keighley: evacuated from Hull, later returned to Sutton-upon-Hull, Humberside	C of E Diocese (York)	
Wakefield	The principal District Archivist, W. Yorks Archive Service, Newstead Road, Wakefield WF1 2DE holds the records of the C of E Diocese (Wakefield), numerous Methodist circuit and chapel records, those of the Yorks Baptist Association and other individual Baptist and reformed churches. Some RC registers have also been filmed.		

Homes and Shelters

Area	Name and Address	Run or used by	Records
York	Clifton Home, York	C of E Diocese (York); Durham Diocesan Family Welfare Council	Most adoptions done through Barnardo's, Children's Society and York Adoption Society
	Heworth Moor House (M&B), 56 Heworth Green, York (closed 1997)	C of E Diocese (York); Durham Diocesan Family Welfare Council	The Borthwick Institute of Historical Research, St Anthony's Hall, Peasholme Green, York YO1 7PW

WALES

Most adoptions from Denbighshire and Flintshire (previously Clwyd) were through Bangor Diocesan Council for Moral Welfare, particularly if Welsh, or the Lancashire and Cheshire Child Adoption Council. Placements were also made through the Children's Society, Barnardo's, National Children's Home, National Adoption Society, Leicester Diocesan Board for Social Responsibility, St David's Adoption Society, Lichfield Diocesan Association for Family Care, and if Roman Catholic, Leeds Diocesan Rescue and Child Welfare Society or Menevia Diocesan Rescue Society.

CARDIFF	Previously part of South Glamorgan. Became a unitary authority 1 April 1996.		
Cardiff	Cardiff M&B Home, 65 Cowbridge Road West, Cardiff	Llandaff Diocesan Committee for Social Responsibility	Carmarthenshire SSD has the records of St David's Diocesan Moral Welfare Committee. Most adoptions through Children's Society or SSD.
	Edward Nicholl House, Penylan, Cardiff (Children's Home)	Children's Society	Some adoptions through St David's Adoption Society as well as Children's Society
	Family Centre, Cardiff	C of E Children's Society (Wales)	
	Northlands, 202 North Street, Cardiff	Salvation Army	
	St Margaret's, Church Terrace, Roath, Cardiff	Church in Wales Diocese (Llandaff)	Carmarthenshire SSD has the records of St David's Diocesan Moral Welfare Committee. Most adoptions through Children's Society or SSD.
	Hope Lodge, 81 Newport Road (1910–1922), Cardiff	Salvation Army	

CARMARTHENSHIRE	Previously part of Dyfed. Became a unitary authority 1 April 1996.		
Carmarthen	Plas Newydd Mothercraft Hostel, Burry Port, Camarthen (1946–)	St David's Diocesan MW Committee and WRVS	Carmarthenshire SSD has records of agency. Some possibly with National Children Adoption Association or Mission of Hope or Children's Society.

FLINTSHIRE	Previously part of Clwyd. Became a unitary authority 1 April 1996.		
Flint	Petit House, Flint (previously known as St Clare's, see next entry)	Catholic Children's Society (Wales)	
Pantasaph	St Clare's, Llanelwy (1963–65) (later Petit House, see above entry)	Catholic Children's Society (Wales)	

Where to find adoption records 99

Area	Name and Address	Run or used by	Records
GWYNEDD			
Criccieth	Nazareth House, Criccieth (until 1966)	Catholic Children's Society (Wales)	Agency and Nazareth House Archives, Nazareth House, Hammersmith Road, London W6 8DE
MONMOUTHSHIRE	Previously part of Gwent. Became a unitary authority 1 April 1996.		
Abergavenny	Nantyderry House	Affiliated to National Council for One Parent Families	Not traced
Chepstow	St Anne's Home, Crossways Green, Chepstow	Catholic Children's Society (Wales)	The Archivist, Good Shepherd Sisters, Cranbrook Road, Staplehurst, Kent TN12 0ER
	St Joseph's Hostel, Crossways Green, Chepstow	Catholic Children's Society (Wales)	As above
NEWPORT	Previously part of Gwent. Became a unitary authority 1 April 1996.		
Caerleon	St Cadoc's Family Home, 11a Norman Street, Caerleon	C of E Children's Society	
Newport	Family Care Housing Association Ltd, 55 York Place, Newport	Family Care Housing Association	The Director of Housing Services, 11 Devon Place, Newport, South Wales NP20 4NP
	St Faith's, 15 Clytha Square, Newport	Monmouth Diocesan Association for Moral Welfare	Not traced but worth trying St David's Adoption Society
	The Shelter (M&B), York Place, Newport (closed)	Monmouth Diocesan Association for Moral Welfare	As above
SWANSEA	Previously part of West Glamorgan. Became a unitary authority 1 April 1996.		
	Cadle Mill Family Centre, Blaen-y-Maes; Cwmdonkin (M&B), 10a and 67 Heathfield, Swansea	Church in Wales; Swansea and Brecon Diocesan Council for Social Work	Adoptions probably arranged through St David's Adoptoin Society or Swansea Diocesan Council
	Nazareth House, Clyne Common, Bishopston (closed)	Catholic Children's Society (Wales)	Agency and Nazareth House Archives, Nazareth House, Hammersmith Road, London W6 8DE
	St David's, Eastmoor Park, Nr Swansea	Church in Wales Diocese (St David's)	Adoptions probably arranged through St David's Adoption Society or Swansea Diocesan Council
VALE OF GLAMORGAN	Previously part of South Glamorgan. Became a unitary authority 1 April 1996.		
Penarth	56 Stanwell Road, Penarth (closed); moved to Cowbridge Road in 1967 (see Cardiff entry)	Church in Wales Diocese (Llandaff)	
WREXHAM	Previously part of Clwyd. Became a unitary authority 1 April 19.		
Bersham	Bersham Hall (M&B), Bersham, Nr Wrexham	Health Department, Denbighshire CC;	Worth contacting Wrexham SSD; Lancashire and Cheshire Child Adoption Council (Liverpool SSD)

Area	Name and Address	Run or used by	Records
Wrexham	Llanelwy, 35 Holt Road, Wrexham (1945–78) (mainly a shelter and then a residential home run by Clwyd CC)	Church in Wales Diocese (St Asaph)	Worth contacting Wrexham or Gwynedd SSD
	Llansbury, 28 Grosvenor Road, Wrexham (1942–45) (replaced by Llanelwy, see above entry)		
	Pas Gwyn, Nazareth House, 2 Hillsbury Road, Wrexham (1967–74) (previously known as Nazareth House)	Catholic Children's Society (Wales); Shrewsbury Diocesan Children's Rescue Society; Liverpool Catholic Social Services	Agencies and Nazareth House Archives, Nazareth House, Hammersmith Road, London W6 8DE

SCOTLAND

ABERDEEN CITY	Previously a part of Grampian Region. Became a unitary authority 1 April 1996.		
Aberdeen	Castlehill, 38 Castle Street, Aberdeen	Aberdeen Association of Social Service	Agency records are with Aberdeenshire SWD
	Maternity House, 25 Westfield Terrace, Aberdeen; became Richmondhill (M&B), 18 Richmondhill Place and 22 Kingsgate, Aberdeen	Family Care; Voluntary Service Aberdeen	
DUNDEE CITY	Previously part of Tayside. Became a unitary authority 1 April 1996.		
Dundee	Florence Booth House (M&B), Harefield Road, Lochee (also known as Clement Park)	Salvation Army; Family Care; Dundee Association for Social Services	Salvation Army
	St Ronan's (M&B), Dalkeith Road, Dundee (1928–73)	East Lothian Social Welfare Department; Episcopal Church of Scotland; Family Care	Scottish Adoption Association, 2 Commercial St, Leith, Edinburgh EH6 6JA or Dundee City SS
	Seafield Lodge, 93 Magdalen Street	Salvation Army	
EAST AYRSHIRE	Previously part of Strathclyde. Became a unitary authority 1 April 1996.		
Kilmarnock	Tankerha, 79 London Road, Kilmarnock (1950–)	Church of Scotland Committee on Social Responsibility	
EAST LOTHIAN	Previously part of Lothian region. Became a unitary authority 1 April 1996.		
Musselburgh	Levenhall and Leven Lodge (M&B), 47c Ravensaugh Road, Musselburgh (closed)	Church of Scotland Committee on Social Responsibility	
	Robertson Orphanage (1949–) (see Hawthornbrae, Edinburgh)		
EDINBURGH CITY	Previously part of Lothian Region. Became a unitary authority 1 April 1996.		
Balerno	Ravelrig, Balerno, Lothian	Barnardo's (Edinburgh)	Family Care

Area	Name and Address	Run or used by	Records
Edinburgh	Avenel (Babies Home and School of Mothercraft), 30 Colinton Road, Edinburgh 10 (closed 1978)	Family Care; Scottish Adoption Association	Not traced. Adoptions may have been arranged by any of the agencies using it.
	Bonnington Bank, Ferry Road, Leith (transferred to Tor, Edinburgh, see below)		Not traced. Worth trying Scottish Adoption Association, 2 Commercial St, Leith, Edinburgh EH6 6JA.
	Castle Rock Housing Association, 26 York Place, Edinburgh	Shelter Housing Aid	
	Dunforth, 46 Park Road, Edinburgh (1948–)	Church of Scotland Committee on Social Responsibility	
	Edinburgh Home for Mothers and Infants, 17 Claremont Park, Edinburgh (closed 1981) (also known as Claremont Park)	Family Care	Family Care
	Edzell Lodge (Children's Home), 35 Inverleith Terrace, Edinburgh (until 1964). Now at 11 Newbattle Terrace, Edinburgh	Family Care	
	Forbes Road (Residential Nursery), 3 Forbes Road, Edinburgh 10 (1944–57)	Scottish Adoption Association Ltd; Family Care	
	Guild of Service (Children's Home), 37 Frederick Street, Edinburgh (until 1955)	Scottish Adoption Association Ltd; Family Care	Family Care
	Haig Ferguson Memorial Home (M&B), 4 Lauriston Park, Edinburgh (closed) (also known as Lauriston Park)	Family Care; Simpson Memorial Maternity Pavilion, Royal Infirmary, Edinburgh; Scottish Council of Single Parents	Scottish Adoption Association. As above.
	Hawthornbrae, 46 The Causeway, Duddington, Edinburgh (1949–) (formerly Robertson Orphanage, Musselburgh)	Church of Scotland Committee on Social Responsibility	
	Lord & Lady Polwarth Home (Nursery), 22 Colinton Road, Edinburgh	Church of Scotland Committee on Social Responsibility; Family Care	
	Malta House, 1 Malta Terrace (1957–77). Transfered to Wallace House		
	Margaret Cottage (Children's Home), Belmont Road, Juniper Green, until 1960, then 11 Newbattle Terrace, Edinburgh (Closed 1963)	Family Care	
	St Andrew's, Joppa, Edinburgh	Church of Scotland	

Area	Name and Address	Run or used by	Records
	The Shelter (Children's Home), 41 Polwarth Terrace, Edinburgh (closed)	Royal Scottish Society for the Prevention of Cruelty to Children; Family Care	Some records with Children First, Melville House, 41 Polwarth Terrace, Edinburgh EH11 1NU
	Tor (M&B), Corstorphine Road, Edinburgh 12 (previously known as Bonnington Bank, Leith) (closed 1970)	Family Care	Not separately traced. Adoptions may have been arranged by one of the agencies using it.
	Wallace House, 3 Boswall Road, Edinburgh (previously known as Malta House)	Church of Scotland Committee on Social Responsibility	
Leith	Bonnington Bank House, Ferry Road, Leith (later known as Tor, Corstorphine Road, Edinburgh 12)	Family Care	
GLASGOW CITY	Previously part of Strathclyde Region. Became a unitary council 1 April 1996.		
Glasgow	Atholl House (M&B), 63 Partickhill Road, Glasgow	Scottish Council of Single Parents; Family Care	Families for Children, 115 Wellington Street, Glasgow G2 2XT
	Clevedon House, Clevedon Road, Kelvinside (now known as Fraser of Allander, see later entry)		
	Florentine, 33 Queen Mary Avenue, Glasgow (1949–) (Formerly Whiteriach Orphanage)	Church of Scotland Committee of Social Responsibility	
	Fraser of Allander (M&B), 5 Clevedon Road, Kelvinside, Glasgow (previously known as Clevedon House)	Salvation Army; Family Care	
	4 Grafton Street (M&B)	Committee of Magdalene Institute	Not traced. Worth trying local agencies and SWD for individuals.
	Homeland, 25 St Andrew's Drive, Pollockshields (1939–64)	Salvation Army	
	The Knowe (M&B), 301 Albert Drive, Pollokshields, Glasgow (closed)	Salvation Army; Family Care	
	Lansdowne House (M&B), 44 Sutherland Avenue (and various other addresses), Glasgow (closed)	Church of Scotland Committee on Social Responsibility; Family Care	
	Red Hall, 1014 Great Western Road 1936. Became Homeland, 1938	Salvation Army	
	St Gerard's (M&B), Nithsdale Road, Glasgow (see Bishopton)	St Margaret of Scotland	Agency or The Archivist, Good Shepherd Sisters, Cranbrook Road, Staplehurst, Tunbridge, Kent TN12 6ER

Area	Name and Address	Run or used by	Records
	Walpole Housing Association, 6 Craigpark, Dennistown, Glasgow		
PERTHSHIRE & KINROSS	Previously part of Tayside. Became a unitary authority 1 April 1996.		
Perth	Melville House (Hostel), 124 Scott Street, Perth (until 1960)	Dundee Association for Social Services; National Vigilance Association of Scotland; Family Care	
	Perth Society, 50 Balhousie Street, Perth (closed)	Episcopal Church in Scotland; Family Care	
RENFREWSHIRE	Previously part of Strathclyde Region. Became a unitary authority 1 April 1996.		
Bishopton	St Gerards, Old Bishopton House, Bishopton (previously known as St Gerards, Glasgow or Bishopton)	St Margaret of Scotland; Good Shepherd Sisterhood	The Archivist, Good Shepherd Sisters, Cranbrook Road, Staplehurst, Tonbridge, Kent TN12 6ER
SCOTTISH BORDERS COUNCIL	Before 1 April 1996 was made up of Berwickshire, Ettrick and Lauderdale, Roxbrough and Tweedale		
Galashiels	Woodlands, Windyknowe Road, Gallashiels (1954–)	Church of Scotland Committee on Social Responsibility	Agency's records are with Scottish Adoption Association, 2 Commercial St, Leith, Edinburgh EH6 6JA
SOUTH LANARKSHIRE	Previously a part of Strathclyde Region. Became a unitary authority 1 April 1996.		
Rutherglen	Westlands, 2 Upper Bourtree Drive, High Burnside, Rutherglen (1968–)	Church of Scotland Committee on Social Responsibility	

NORTHERN IRELAND

Belfast	Belfast Midnight Mission, 25–31 Malone Place, Belfast	By Committee	
	Marianville, 511 Ormeau Road, Belfast BT7 3GS	Down & Connor Catholic Family Welfare Society	
	Mater Dei Hostel, 298 Antrim Road, Belfast	Catholic Family Care Society (NI)	
	Thorndale House, Duncairn Avenue, Belfast (closed 1979)	Salvation Army	
Newry	Marion Vale, Newry	Down & Connor Catholic Family Welfare Society	

EIRE

There were a great many children's homes all over Eire, mainly run by religious orders. Under the Freedom of Information Act (1999) people who were raised in residential care can apply for information to: Freedom of Information Section, Department of Education, Marlboro Street, Dublin 1. Barnardo's adoption advice service is very willing to help anyone making enquiries.

Cork	Sean Ross Abbey (M&B)	Sean Ross Abbey Adoption Society	Senior Social Worker, The Sacred Heart Adoption Society, Blackrock, Cork Fax: 00 353 21 359395

Area	Name and Address	Run or used by	Records
Dublin	Bethany Home (M&B), 112 Orwell Road, Rathgar, Dublin 6 (closed)	Church of Ireland Diocese	PACT, 15 Belgrave Road, Rathmines, Dublin 6 Fax: 00 353 1 4966565
	Denny House, 83 Eglington Road, Dublin 4	Any Protestant denomination	
	Magdalene House: became Denny House (see above)		
	St Patrick's Home (M&B), Navan Road, Dublin	Eastern Health Board	The Matron, Eglinton House, Eglinton Road, Donnybrook, Dublin 4
Co Dublin	Glensilva, 95 Monkstown Road, Monkstown, Co Dublin		The Secretary, Mrs Smylys Homes, 15 Rock Road, Blackrock, Co Dublin
	Racefield, Lower Mountown Road, Dun Laoighre, Co Dublin		The Secretary, Mrs Smylys Homes, 15 Rock Road, Blackrock, Co Dublin
	Mrs Smylys Homes, 15 Rock Road, Blackrock, Co Dublin Fax: 00 353 1 2832071		Secretary
Co Meath	Ard Mhuire, Good Shepherd Convent, Dunboyne, Co Meath (closed 1991)		Senior Social Worker, Child & Family Centre, NE Health Board, Dublin Road, Drogheda, Co Louth Fax: 00 351 4133067

5 • Personnel in agencies and homes

Name of Worker	Organisation or Home	Area	Role	Date

Experienced counsellors find that people who are searching sometimes remember the name of a worker when they have completely forgotten the name of the agency with which they were involved. We have therefore listed many of the workers in agencies, homes or church welfare, with such appropriate information as we have available. Names may sometimes be duplicated because information has come from a wide variety of sources and the time span involved has made absolute verification impossible. We are very grateful to all the present staff of many organisations who have gone to a great deal of trouble to provide these facts.

Name of Worker	Organisation or Home	Area	Role	Date
Adams, Margery, Sister (Church Army)	St Albans Adoption Society	N. Bedfordshire	Social Worker	1954–62
Adams, Sister	Heworth Moor House	York	Matron	
Agren, Anita	The Children's Society		Social Worker	1975–78
Akerman, Miss	Cambridge Shelter for Girls	Cambridgeshire	Superintendent	1925/6–1926/7
Alcock, Miss	Church of England	St Pancras	Welfare Worker	1963
Alderson, Laura, Miss	Cambridge Shelter for Girls	Cambridgeshire	Superintendent	1923/4–25
Allen, M, Mrs	The Children's Society	Midlands Region	Social Worker	1979–81
Aloysius, Sister	Catholic Children's Rescue Society	Diocese of Salford	Social Worker	
Amah, Mrs	Prospect House, Hoylake	Merseyside	Matron	
Ambrose, Sister	Catholic Care	Diocese of Leeds		
Amor, V, Miss	St Faith's, Loughton	Essex	Superintendent	Aug 1975 -
Ancilla, Sister (later known as Sister Breda Murphy)	Catholic Children and Family Care Society, Wales	Cardiff	Social Worker	
Andrew, Clara, Miss	National Children Adoption Association		Founder Previously worked with Miss Whishaw in Liverpool	From 1917
Anna, Sister	Catholic Children's Rescue Society	Diocese of Salford	Moral Welfare Worker	
Annette, Maud, Miss	Southwell Diocesan Council for Family Care		Adoption Worker	1906–54
Appleby, Dorothy, Miss	St Faith's, Maidstone and Tutor at Josephine Butler Memorial Home	Kent	Superintendent	
Applegate, B, Miss	Chester Diocesan Adoption Services			
Appleton, Miss	Hostel of the Good Shepherd, Colchester	Essex	Superintendent	April 1971–74
Archard, Peter, Mr	The Children's Society		Social Worker	1971–74
Armitage, Miss	Southwell Diocesan Council for Family Care		Social Worker	1950–53
Arscott, A M, Miss	Families for Children Adoption Agency		General Secretary	1970s

Name of Worker	Organisation or Home	Area	Role	Date
Ash, M, Miss	Avon & N. Wiltshire Swindon			1976
Ashby, Madge, Miss	St Albans Adoption Society	S. Bedfordshhire	Social Worker	1965–76
Ashby, P K D, Miss	St Albans Adoption Society	W. Herts	Social Worker	1957–60
Ashton, Alice, Ms	Oakhurst	Bexley		1956
Assumption, Sister	Sacred Heart Adoption Society	Westmeath (Eire)		
Athey, Sister	Red Gables	Haringey		1961
Atkins, M E, Ms	Church of England	Hackney	Welfare Worker	1976
Atkins, Mary, Miss	The Children's Society		Social Worker	1969–73
Atkins, Melanie, Ms	Adopt Anglia, project of Coram Family Adoption Society		Adoption Officer	From 1998
Atkins, Sylvia, Mrs	The Children's Society		Adoptions Social Worker	1962–70
Aung, Elizabeth, Miss	The Children's Society		Foster Care Social Worker	1973–74
Austin, Sister	Catholic Children's Rescue Society	Diocese of Salford	Moral Welfare Worker	
Ayton, G M	Chichester Diocesan Association for Family Social Work		Adoption Officer	
Bailey, M R, Mrs	Childlink			1971
Bailey, Mildred	Church of England, St Pancras Moral Welfare	Barnet and Storth Oaks	Warden, Guildford House	1955
Baker, J, Miss	Church of England	Willesden	Moral Welfare Worker	1972
Baker, J, Miss	National Adoption Society		Social Worker	1977
Balcomb, D	The Children's Society	N. Region	Social Worker	1979–81
Ball, Marlene	Chester Diocesan Adoption Services			
Ball, Patricia, Mrs	The Children's Society		Foster Care Social Worker	1971–72
Bann, Miss	Church of England	Lewisham & Lee	Welfare Worker	1963
Bannon, O M E, Mrs	The Church of Ireland Adoption Society		Organising Secretary & Social Worker	1981
Barham Smith, Mrs	Homeless Children's Aid & Adoption Society F B Meyer Children's Home Inc.		Welfare Worker	
Barham, W, Mrs	Family Care (Essex)	Redbridge		
Barker, E, Miss	Church of England	Stepney	Welfare Worker	1963

Name of Worker	Organisation or Home	Area	Role	Date
Barker, J, Miss	National Adoption Society		Social Worker	1977
Barlow, Dudley, Mr	National Adoption Society		Chief Registrar of Friendly Societies	
Barlow, Hilaro, Sir	National Adoption Society		Chairman	1921
Barnett, Rosemary, Miss	The Children's Society		Foster Care Social Worker	1972–73
Barritt, G, E, Rev	National Children's Home		Principal	1969 onwards
Barry, Jane, Miss	Church of Ireland Adoption Society	Northern Ireland		
Barry, M, Mrs	Dundee Association for Social Service		Senior Social Worker	1977
Bartlett, Karen, Ms	Catholic Children and Family Care, Wales	Cardiff	Social Worker	
Barton, Miss	Prospect House, Hoylake	Merseyside	Matron	
Barton, Sister	Bartletts, Chelmsford	Essex	Assistant Superintendent	
Bateman, Helen	The Children's Society		Social Worker	1976–77
Bayley, I, Miss	Family Care (Essex)	Havering		
Bayliff, Miss	Church of England	Finsbury and Holborn	Welfare Worker	1960
Bayliff, Miss	St Faith's	Camden		1960
Beard, Miss	Blackburn Diocesan Adoption Agency		Caseworker	Early 1960s
Beattie, Miss	St Nicholas M&B or Dunraven	Devon		
Beesley, E T, Mrs	F B Meyer Children's Home		Welfare Worker	
Beesley, Edward, T, Mr	Homeless Children's Aid & Adoption Society F B Meyer Children's Home Inc		General Secretary Welfare Worker	
Bell, Gwen, Sister	10 Rutford Road	Lambeth		
Bell, Michael, Rev	St Andrew's Children's Society Ltd, Edinburgh		Chairman	1977
Bellis, Mrs	Lancashire & Cheshire Child Adoption Council		Case Secretary	Nov 1962–77
Benbow, Maureen, Miss	The Grange M&B home, Blackburn	Burnley and Nelson area	Moral Welfare Worker	1960s
Benning, Sydney	The Children's Society	Southport	Social Worker	1979–81
Bergen, Miss	St Mary's	Wandsworth		
Bibby, P, Mrs	SSAFA – Forces Help		Deputy Director	1982
Biddle, Miss	Church of England	Hammersmith	Welfare Worker	

Name of Worker	Organisation or Home	Area	Role	Date
Biggs, Gladys, Mrs	The Children's Society		Welfare Officer	1948–69
Biggs, Mrs	Church of England	Gravesend	Moral Welfare Worker	
Bindloss, B, Miss	Families for Children Adoption Agency		Adoption Secretary	
Bird, Miss	Church of England	Haywards Heath MW	Moral Welfare Worker	
Birtles, Halcyon, Miss	The Children's Society	Bristol	Social Worker	1978
Biscardine, Mrs	St Olave's M&B Home	Devon		
Bishop, Miss	Cross Roads Club Berkhamsted	Herts	Superintendent	Early 1930s
Black, Miss	Church of England	Westminster, Finsbury and Holborn	Moral Welfare Worker	1963
Blackburn, Helen, M, Miss	National Adoption Society		General Secretary	1921–59
Blackburn, Miss	Catholic Children's Society	Arundel & Brighton, Portsmouth & Southwark		
Blackmore, Georgina, Mrs	The Children's Society		Social Worker	1973
Bloxham, Janet, Miss	The Children's Society	Leicester	Social Worker	1979–81
Blythe, J, Mrs	York Adoption Society			1978–83
Booth, Irene, Miss	The Children's Society	Staffordshire	Adoption Officer	1977–99
Booth, Pauline	Chester Diocesan Adoption Services			
Born, M, Miss	Church of England	Southwark, Newington	Moral Welfare Worker	1958
Boswell, E A, Mr	Manchester Adoption Society		Senior Adoption Worker	1977
Bourne, Miss	The Children's Society		Head of Boarding Out	Until 1962
Bowerbank, Mrs	Western National Adoption Society			
Bowes, B, Mrs	Avon & N. Wiltshire	Bath		1976
Bowker, N, Miss	Ely Diocesan Moral Welfare Association			1970s
Bowman-Stephenson, Thomas, Rev	National Children's Home		Principal	
Boyce, Miss	St Monica's, Westcliffe-on-sea	Essex		
Bradford, Mrs	Church of England	Hackney and Stoke Newington Harrow	Moral Welfare Worker	1959 1963
Bradley, Sister	Church of England	Harrow, Walton-on-Thames	Moral Welfare Worker	1963
Bradshaw, Pauline, Miss	The Children's Society		Foster Care Social Worker	1971

Name of Worker	Organisation or Home	Area	Role	Date
Breda, Sister	Catholic Children's Society	Arundel & Brighton, Portsmouth & Southwark		
Bremmer, Miss	Hostel of the Good Shepherd, Colchester	Essex	Assistant Superintendent	1967
Brenchley, Diana, Miss	Church of England	Kensington & Chelsea	Moral Welfare Worker	Left 1979
Brewster, M, Mrs	Durham Diocesan Family Welfare Council		Organising Secretary	1977
Bridge, Sue	Chester Diocesan Adoption Services			
Bridger, Brigadier	Adswood, Salford	Manchester	Matron	
Brightwell, Miss	Church of England	Amersham	Moral Welfare Worker	
Brister, M, Miss (deceased)	Oldham Adoption Society		Secretary and Case Worker	
Brocklesby, Edwina	St Francis Children's Society			
Bromhead, Ilka, Miss	The Children's Society		Boarding Out	1966
Bromhead, K, Miss	Church of England, Southwark WelCare	Southwark	Organising Secretary	1934–51
Broom, Major	Adswood, Salford	Manchester	Matron	
Broughton, Miss	Church of England	South Harrow	Moral Welfare Worker	1957
Browning, Roger	Church of Jesus Christ of Latter Day Saints		Adoption/Fostering Officer	1981
Bryant, Judith, Miss	National Children's Home		Social Worker	
Bullivant, Miss	Church of England	Middlesbrough	Moral Welfare Worker	
Bunting, Mary, Mrs	The Children's Society		Social Worker	1974–75
Burdett, M D, Mrs	National Adoption Society		Social Worker	1973
Burke, K, Miss	Catholic Children's Society	Arundel & Brighton, Portsmouth & Southwark		
Butler, Constance, Mrs	The Children's Society		Adoption Social Worker	1966–67
Butt, Miss	St Anne's St Joseph's	Lambeth Lambeth		From 1928 From 1939
Buttery, J, Mrs	Oldham Adoption Society		Case Worker	1969–71
Caley, Mrs	Church of England	Folkestone and Hythe (Canterbury)		1956
Callanan, Cathleen, Ms	Cork & Ross Family Centre, St Anne's Adoption Society	Eire	Social Worker	1996–
Cameron, Miss	London Diocesan Hostel, Guildford House	Barnet		From autumn 1951
Candy, Miss	Church of England	Barnet	WelCare	
Carcass, Nancy, Miss	Chester Diocesan Adoption Services	St Bridget's, Chester		

Name of Worker	Organisation or Home	Area	Role	Date
Carey, Mr John	Mission of Hope for Children's Aid and Adoption		Principal Adoption Worker	
Carey, Veronica, Ms	St Mary's Adoption Society	Kerry, Eire	Social Worker	
Carothers, Mrs	Church of England	Islington Chelsea	Moral Welfare Worker	1957 1963
Carpenter, Rosemary, Mrs	St. Albans Adoption Society	Mid Hertfordshire	Social Worker	1976–77
Carrington, Mrs	St Agnes, Withington	Manchester	Matron	
Carter & Bell 10a Idol Lane, Eastcheap, EC3	Homeless Children's Aid and Adoption Society, F B Meyer Children's Home Inc.		Hon Solicitors	
Carter, Canon	Plymouth Diocesan Catholic Children's Society		Administrator	1948–60
Cartwright, J, Miss	Family Care (Essex)	Redbridge		
Cartwright, J W, Miss	Free Church Maternity Home	Bournemouth	Social Worker	1953
Cartwright, J W, Miss	Church of England	Doncaster	Welfare Worker	1957
Cartwright, J W, Miss	Adopt Anglia, Project of Coram Family Adoption Society			From 1968
Catlow, Linda, Mrs	Manchester Adoption Society	Manchester	Secretary	
Cavanagh, Jackie, Mrs (née O'Regan)	St Anne's Adoption Society	Eire	Social Worker	1987–95
Challenger, F M, Miss	Church of England	St Pancras	Welfare Worker	1960
Champion, Margaret, Miss	Church of England		Welfare Worker	
Chaplin, Sister	Marie Vickers House	Brighton		1923
Chapman, Christine	Chester Diocesian Adoption Services, St Bridgets M&B Home	Chester		
Chapman, G W, Miss	St Mary's	Lambeth		1958
Chapman, M, Miss	Plymouth Diocesan Catholic Children's Society	Plymouth		
Chapman, M T, Miss	Cornwall Social and Moral Welfare Association		Social Worker	1963–66
Chapman, M T, Miss	Plymouth Diocesan Catholic Children's Society		Director	1977
Chesterton, Miss	Church of England	Wandsworth, Putney and Tooting		
Chesterton, Miss	Church of England	Wandsworth, Putney and Tooting		
Cheveley, Deaconess	3 Bampfylde Road 12 Bexley Terrace	Torquay	Matron	1906–

Name of Worker	Organisation or Home	Area	Role	Date
Clancy, Helen, Ms	St Catherine's Adoption Society	Clare, Eire	Social Worker	
Clapham, Janice, Mrs	The Children's Society		Social Worker	1973–74
Clare, Mary, Sister (Deceased)	Catholic Children & Family Care Society, Wales	Cardiff	Social Worker	
Clark, Diane, Miss	The Children's Society		Adoptions Social Worker	1965–66
Clark, Eileen, Mrs	The Children's Society		Adoptions Social Worker	1963–77
Clark, Mrs (née Gill)	Beacon Lodge	Haringey		
Clarke, Miss	Church of England	Kingston, Surbiton and Malden	Welfare Worker	1963
Clarke, Susan, Miss	The Children's Society		Trainee Social Worker	1974–75
Clatworthy, Brian	Manchester Adoption Society	Manchester	Director	From 2000
Clements, Miss	Church of England	Mitcham		1963
Cliff, M, Miss	Hutchinson House, Buswood House	Waltham Forest	Matron	
Clough, Mr	The Solicitor whose address was used by the Bristol Women's Aid Association whose records are untraced.			
Coakley, Norma, Ms	St Anne's Adoption Society	Eire	Social Worker	1982–98
Coakley, Una, Ms	Cork & Ross Family Centre, St Anne's Adoption Society	Eire	Social Worker	1989–
Cobb, Evelyn, Miss	St Albans Adoption Society	N. Bedfordshire	Social Worker	1958 (6 months) 1973–1977
Cohn, Gertrude, Ms	British Adoption Project		Social Worker	
Colbeck, Joy, Mrs	St Albans Adoption Society		Adoption Records Secretary	
Colgate, Hugh, Mr	The Children's Society		Boarding Out Worker	1966–70
Colson, Miss	National Children's Adoption Association		Social Worker	
Combe, Margaret G, Mrs	Church of Scotland Committee for Social Responsibility		Adoption Supervisor	1977
Comfrey, Mrs	Catholic Children's Society	Arundel & Brighton, Portsmouth & Southwark		
Connelly, Susan, Miss	The Children's Society		Social Work Division	1973–74
Connor, Terry, Mr	Catholic Children's Society	Arundel & Brighton, Portsmouth, Southwark		
Cook, Miss	Church of England	Colindale	Welfare Worker	1952
Cook, Mrs	Church of England	Colindale		1936
Cooke, Enid A, Miss	Church of England	NW6 Harlesden	Moral Welfare Worker	1952 1949

Name of Worker	Organisation or Home	Area	Role	Date
Cooney, George	Catholic Children & Family Care Society, Wales	Cardiff	Administrator	
Cooper, Miss	Council for Christian Care, and St Nicholas Mother and Baby Home, previously Dunraven	Exeter		
Corcoran, Nina	Chester Diocesan Adoption Services, St Bridgets Mother & Baby Home	Chester		
Cornish, F, Mrs	Melbourne House	Exeter	Secretary	
Cox, Brenda	Chester Diocesan Adoption Services, St Bridgets Mother and Baby Home	Chester		
Cox, Miss	Church of England	Harlesden, Stourbridge, Redditch & Droitwich	Welfare Worker	1949 pre 1956
Cox, Shirley, Mrs	Catholic Children & Family Care Society, Wales	Cardiff	Social Worker	
Coyne, Phillip, Canon, The Very Rev	Father Hudsons Society		Administrator	
Crabtree, J, Miss	Four Deaneries Family Welfare Association			1977
Cragg, G H, Mrs	Blackburn Diocesan Board for Social Responsibility	Blackburn	Adoption Co-ordinator	Pre 1977
Crimmins, R M, Mr	Plymouth Diocesan Catholic Children's Society		Chief Officer	
Cron, Miss	Church of England	Atherstone & Monks Kirby, (Coventry)	Welfare Worker	Pre 1956
Cronin, Eileen	Catholic Children & Family Care Society, Wales	Cardiff	Social Worker	
Croot, Geoff	Children's Society			
Cross, Ernest, Dr	Homeless Children's Aid and Adoption Society, F B Meyer Children's Home Inc		Medical Officer	
Crowe, Margaret	Chester Diocesan Adoption Services, St Bridgets Mother and Baby Home	Chester		
Crowe, Mrs	Catholic Women's Aid	Cork, Eire		
Crowley, Marian, Sister	St Anne's Adoption Society	Eire	Social Worker	Late 70s, early 80s
Crutcher, M E, Mrs	National Children's Home		Secretary	1918–55
Cuddihy, Brian E, Father	Catholic Children & Family Care Society, Wales	Cardiff	Director	

Name of Worker	Organisation or Home	Area	Role	Date
Cuddy, Miss	Catholic Children's Society	Westminster		
Cullen, A D	Parents and Children Together	Newbury		
Cullen, J	Catholic Caring Services for Children and Community (Diocese of Lancaster)	Lancaster	Social Worker	
Cullinan, D J, Mrs	Child Link		Secretary	1960s
Cummings, Miss	Plymouth Diocesan Catholic Children's Society	Plymouth		
Cunneen, Annie, Ms	Mid-Western Health Board	Limerick, Eire	Social Worker	
Curtis, George	Catholic Children's Society	Westminster	Principal Officer	
Curtis, Miss	Red Gables	Haringey		1955
D'Arcy, C, Mr	Catholic Children's Society	Arundel & Brighton, Portsmouth & Southwark		
Daly, John	Catholic Children's Society (Shrewsbury Diocese) Ltd		Director	
Daly, Kerry, Mrs	The Children's Society		Social Worker	1974–75
Daly, Miss	Catholic Children's Society	Arundel & Brighton, Portsmouth & Southwark		
Dando, Nora, Miss	National Children's Home		Adoptions Liaison Officer	1956–
Darmon, Robert	The Children's Society		Social Worker	1977–78
Davies, M, Miss	Avon & N.W. Wiltshire	Bristol		
Davies, Miss	Church of England	Willesden		1950s
Davies, Miss	St Faith's, Loughton	Essex	Superintendent	Between 1962 & 1970
Davies, Pamela, Mrs	The Children's Society		Social Worker	1974–75
Davis, A, Miss	Cardiff M&B Home	Cardiff		
Davis, Mrs	Church of England	Wimbledon and Merton		1963
Davis, N C, Miss	National Adoption Society		Social Worker	1962
Davis, Sister (CA)	Sutton House, Kingston-upon-Hull	East Riding, Yorks	Matron	Until approx 1958
Davison, D, Mrs	The Children's Society	N. Region	Social Worker	1979–81
Dawson, Leila, Miss	The Children's Society		Welfare Officer	1951–68

Name of Worker	Organisation or Home	Area	Role	Date
Day, M, Miss	Church of England	St Pancras		1960
De'Ath, Phyllis, Miss	Church of England	Kensington & Chelsea Welcare		1976
Deevy, Jacqui, Ms	Mid Western Health Board	Clare (Eire)	Social Worker	1997–98
Denney, D, Mrs	Family Care (Essex)	Grays area		
Dent, Mrs	Phyllis Holman Richards Adoption Society		Director and Social Worker	
Dewhurst, Miss	Church of England	Hornsey	Moral Welfare Worker	1963
Dickson, Miss	Church of England	Streatham, SW17	Moral Welfare Worker	1963
Digby-Baker, J, Miss	Catholic Children's Society	Arundel & Brighton, Portsmouth & Southwark		
Dight, Margaret, Ms	Catholic Children's Society RC Diocese of Nottingham)		Principal Social Worker	
Dinsdale, Norma, Miss	The Children's Society		Boarding Out Worker	1968
Dixon, Sister	Church of England	Islington		1963
Dobson, Miss	St Mary's	Lambeth		
Dodson, Miss	Bartlets, Chelmsford	Essex	Superintendent	May 1972– July 1972
Dodson, Miss	Ellen Carville	Waltham Forest		Early 1972– September 1972
Doncaster, M A, Sister	Church of England	Hampstead		1960
Donnelly, D K, Mr	Sheffield & District Child Adoption Association			
Dougherty, T, Rev	Catholic Child Welfare (Diocese of Middlesbrough)		Administrator	
Dovelan, P, Miss	Catholic Children's Society	Arundel & Brighton, Portsmouth & Southwark		
Dowling, Miss	Beacon Lodge	Harringey	Matron	1949
Drinkwater, Keith	The Children's Society	Handsworth	Social Worker	1978
Driver, D, Mrs	Family Care (Essex)	Brentwood		1976–77
Duffy, Susan, Mrs	The Children's Society		Case Worker	1973–74
Dugdall, Caroline, Miss	3 Bampfylde Road or 12 Bexley Terrace (M&B) and Torquay Church Refuge	Torquay	Matron	1923–51

Where to find adoption records

Name of Worker	Organisation or Home	Area	Role	Date
Dunbar, Miss	Independent Adoption Service		Administrative Secretary	
Dunne, Miss	Parkinson House	Preston	Then a Mother and Baby Home (now flatlets)	During 1940s and 1950s
Dye, Diane, Miss	National Adoption Society		Social Worker	1986
Eason, Sister	Church of England	Hammersmith		1963
East, Miss	Hostel of the Good Shepherd, Colchester	Essex	Superintendent	Sept 1974 +
Eaton, Miss	St Albans Adoption Society	Hertfordshire	Social Worker	1956
Edward, G E D	Catholic Children's Society (Shrewsbury Diocese) Inc		Director	
Edwards, D, Miss	Adopt Anglia Project of Coram		Adoption Officer	From 1961
Edwards, Vera, Mrs	Catholic Children & Family, Care (Wales)	Cardiff	Social Worker	
Eileen, Sister	Catholic Children's Society	Arundel & Brighton, Portsmouth & Southwark		
Elders, Ann, Miss	Church of England	Salisbury	Moral Welfare Worker	1957
Elliot, Leoni, Miss	Phyllis Holman Richards Adoption Society		Director and Social Worker	
Ellis, Miss	Ely Diocesan M W Association		Organising Secretary	
Emerson, S, Mrs	Chichester Diocesan Association for Family Social Work		Organising Secretary	1977
Emmanuel, Sister	Catholic Family Care Society	N. Ireland	Social Worker	1977
Eskrigg, Miss	Lancashire & Cheshire Child Adoption Council		Hon Secretary	
Evans, Madge	Chester Diocesan Adoption Services	Crewe		
Evans, Margaret	St Francis Children's Society			
Evans, Miss	Church of England	Westminster		1963
Evans, Mrs (née Sister Pannier)	St Hilda's, Crewe	Cheshire	First Adoption Society	
Evans, Sister	Bartletts	Chelmsford	Superintendent	1957–70
Evanson, Janet, Miss	Church of England	Southwark WelCare	Director	1976–83

Name of Worker	Organisation or Home	Area	Role	Date
Everiss, Mrs	Adopt Anglia Project of Coram		Adoption Officer	From 1947
Evison, E W I, Miss	Church of England	Kensington		1960
Fahy, Fionnerola, Ms	St Brigid's Adoption Society	Eire	Social Worker	
Fairclough, V, Miss	St Helena's	Barnet	Owner	1948
Falk, Ms	National Children Adoption Association		Visitor	
Farmer, Mrs	Church of England	Charing Cross Road		
Farrah, Miss	St Francis Children's Society			
Faull, Miss	Parkhurst	Islington		
Featherstone, Miss	Families for Children Adoption Agency			
Feehan, Mrs	The Children's Society		Adoptions Social Worker	1960–73
Felton, Valerie, Mrs	The Children's Society		Adoptions Social Worker	1966–73
Ferguson, Miss	Haig Ferguson Memorial House	Edinburgh	Matron	
Ferguson, Robert	The Children's Society		Foster Care Social Worker	1972
Ferron, Mrs	Ely Diocesan M W Association			
Fever, Norah, Mrs	The Children's Society		Foster Care Social Worker	1973–78
Field, Miss	Families for Children Adoption Agency			
Fildes, Mary	Catholic Children's Resource Society (Diocese of Salford) Inc		Social Worker	
Finch, J, Sister	Family Care (Essex)	Waltham Forest		
Findlow, Grace, Miss	Church of England	Ealing		1963
Findlow, S, Miss	Church of England	Greenwich, Orpington		1960s
Fines, Chris	Parents for Children	Director		1985–88
Finney, Mrs	Catholic Children's Society	Arundel & Brighton, Portsmouth & Southwark		
Fitzgerald, Maureen, Mrs	The Children's Society		Boarding Out Worker	1967–70
Flatt, G	The Children's Society	E. Region	Social Worker	1979–81
Fleming, D M, Mrs	Oldham Adoption Society		Caseworker	1977
Fletcher, Miss	Church of England	Leeds	Moral Welfare Worker	1972

Name of Worker	Organisation or Home	Area	Role	Date
Flood, Susan, Miss	The Children's Society		Adoptions Social Worker	1971
Floud, Cynthia, Ms	Parents for Children		Director	
Flynn, Audrey, Sister	(Church Army) St Albans Adoption Society	Boreham Wood	Social Worker	1954–59
Flynn, Audrey, Sister	Chester Diocesan Adoption Services			Died 1978
Flynn, Edith, Ms	Christian Outreach Adoption Society		Adoption Officer	
Foster, N, Mrs	The Children's Society	NW Region	Social Worker	1979–81
Francis, Barbara	Chester Diocesan Adoption Services			
Frank, Miss	Putnam House	Aylesbury		1947–49
Frank, Miss	Beacon Lodge	Harringey	Matron	1941–47 1949–68
Franklin, Beryl, Mrs	St Albans Adoption Society		Social Worker	1966–77
Fraser, Miss	Haygarth-Witts, Memorial House, St Agatha's	Merton Newham		1962–64/5
Fraser, Pat, Ms	N. Yorks National Children's Home			
Freeman, Marie, Mrs	The Children's Society		Boarding Out Worker	1955–60
Freeman, Susan, Miss	The Children's Society		Boarding Out Worker	1969–70
Gabriel, Sister	Catholic Children and Family Care Society (Wales)	Cardiff	Social Worker	
Gallagher, Gabriel (Sister)	St Brigid's Adoption Society	Eire		
Galloway, James	Church of England	Westminster Welcare		1976
Gambles, Una	Chester Diocesan Adoption Services			
Gardiner, Isabel, M	Church of England	NW4, Hendon		1930s
Garland, Miss	Catholic Children's Society Westminster			
Gates, E, Sister	Association for Moral Welfare Work (Retford, Bawtry, Tuxford)			1950–64
Gathercole, V, Mrs	Avon & N. Wiltshire	Weston-Super-Mare		
Gauterin, Nora	Chester Diocesan Adoption Services			

Name of Worker	Organisation or Home	Area	Role	Date
Gear, Enid, Mrs	St Albans Adoption Society Family Care (Essex)	North Herts	Social Worker Principal Social Worker	1969–71 1987
Gentry, D, Mrs	Family Care (Essex)	Waltham Forest Area		
George, Sister	Crathorne (M&B Home)	Barnet		1923
Gibbons, Mrs	Morwenna, Penzance	Cornwall	Matron	
Gibson, D, Mrs	Family Care (Essex)	Southend Area		
Gibson, Mary, Mrs	The Children's Society		Social Worker	1973–74
Gill, Gwendoline, Mrs	The Children's Society		Welfare Officer	1959–72
Gill, Margaret, Ms	St Catherine's Adoption Society	Clare (Eire)	Social Worker	
Gill, Miss (later Mrs Clark)	Beacon Lodge	Haringey		
Gillespie, Alan	Voluntary Service	Aberdeen		1981
Gillett, Mollie, Miss	St Albans Adoption Society		Adoption Officer	1960–69
Giltinan, Donal	Voluntary Service, Aberdeen		Principal Social Worker	1977
Given, Miss	Sunnedon House (M&B Home)	Brentwood	Superintendent	1962–70
Glover, Lady	National Adoption Society		Chairman	1921–
Gobby, Miss	Church of England	Holborn and Finsbury	Moral Welfare Worker	1960
Goddard, Miss	Church of England	Rochester	Moral Welfare Worker	
Golding, Miss	St Olave's M&B Home	Devon		
Good, Father	St Anne's Adoption Society	Eire	Social Worker	1955–67
Goodeve-Docker, Miss	Church of England	Bath, Bristol	Moral Welfare Worker	
Goodeve-Docker, Mrs	Bristol Diocesan M W Association	Bath		
Goodman, Joy, Mrs	The Children's Society		Social Worker	1971–75
Goodwin, Norman	Chester Diocesan Adoption Services		Social Worker, Team Leader	
Gordon, Elizabeth, Miss	The Children's Society		Boarding Out Worker	1953–66
Gould, R D, Rev	Church of England	Hackney Welcare		1976
Graham, Jean, Miss	The Children's Society		Boarding Out Worker	1966–67
Gray, T, Miss	Church of England	Paddington and St Marylebone		1960

Where to find adoption records

Name of Worker	Organisation or Home	Area	Role	Date
Green, J, Miss	Families for Children Adoption Agency		Adoption Secretary	
Greenfield, Joanna, Mrs	National Children Adoption Association			1970s
Gregory, Arthur E, Rev	National Children's Home		Principal	1900–12
Gretton, Miss	St Monica's, Westcliffe-on-Sea	Essex		
Griffiths, B M, Miss	Parents and Children Together			
Griffiths, P, Miss	Catholic Children's Society	Arundel & Brighton, Portsmouth & Southwark		
Grove, Gwendoline, Dr	Southwell Diocesan Council for Family Care		Adoption Worker	1953–66
Grundy, Miss	Blackburn Diocesan Board for Social Responsibility		Organising Secretary	Probably 1940s/50s
Guess, Sister	Bow Hostel	Tower Hamlets		
Guest, L M, Sister (Church Army)	St Albans Adoption Society	South Bedfordshire	Social Worker	1954–59
Guest, P, Mrs	Avon & N. Wiltshire	Swindon		1976
Guest, Sister	Church of England	Luton	Moral Welfare Worker	
Guy, Ann, Ms	Catholic Care (Diocese of Leeds)		Senior Social Worker	
Guy, Jane, Miss	The Children's Society		Trainee Social Worker	1974–75
Guyler, Miss	Church of England	Reading and Bradfield		1958
Haines, Anne, Miss	St Albans Adoption Society	E. & N.E. Hertfordshire	Social Worker	1971–76
Hale, Miss	Beacon Lodge	Haringey		1945–46 1949–68
Hall, Miss	Girls' Hostel, Queen Street	Lancaster		1948–70
Hall, Vera, Mrs	Southwell Diocesan Council for Family Care	Adoption Worker		1966
Hallas	St Nicholas or Dunraven	Devon		
Halpin, Hilary, Mrs (deceased)	National Children Adoption Association		Organising Secretary	1966–78
Hamick, Miss	Church of England	Kensington	Moral Welfare Worker	1942–65
Hancock, Frances, Miss	The Girl's Hostel Devizes	Wiltshire	Matron	
Hancock, M, Miss	The Children's Society		Head of Admissions	1967

Name of Worker	Organisation or Home	Area	Role	Date
Hand, Pamela, Mrs	The Children's Society		Social Worker	1975–77
Hanlon, Stuart	Catholic Care (Diocese of Leeds)		Director	
Hannigan, Fr (Deceased)	Catholic Children and Family Care (Wales)	Cardiff		
Hannigan, J	Menevia Family Social Service		Administrator	1977
Hardwilk, K, Miss	Adopt Anglia Project of Coram Family Adoption Service		Adoption Officer	From 1950
Hardy, R, Mrs	Family Care (Essex)	Harlow Area		
Hare, S M, Miss	Church of England	Willesden		1960
Harman, Irene, Miss	National Children's Home			1956
Harmer, Miss	St Nicholas or Dunraven	Devon		
Harris, A (or R) M, Miss	Beechwood, Westcliff-on-Sea	Essex	Superintendent	To 1966
Harris, A M, Miss	Church of England	Chelmsford and Beechwood	Moral Welfare Worker	
Harris, Jacqueline, Miss	The Children's Society		Case Worker	1973–74
Harrison, Miss	Church of England	Tottenham		1959, 1963
Harrison, Nora, Sister	Lorna Lodge	Manchester	Superintendent	
Harrison, Sister	Hostel of the Good Shepherd, Colchester	Essex	Superintendent	To 1967
Hart, Edith, Miss	Mission of Hope for Children's Aid and Adoption		Welfare Worker	
Hart, June, Miss	The Children's Society		Boarding Out Worker	1967
Hawes, Mrs	Church of England	Hackney and Stoke Newington		1963
Hawkes, Ann, Miss	Cardiff M&B Home	Cardiff		
Hawkesley, Miss	Clements Hall, Hockley	Essex	Private Owner	
Hawkins, Miss	London Diocesan Hostel, Guildford House	Barnet	Housekeeper	
Haworth, Julie, Ms	W. Midlands National Children's Home			
Hay, Eileen, Miss	Children's Aid Society			1958–9
Hay, Mrs	Lancashire & Cheshire Child Adoption Council		Assistant Secretary then Case Secretary	1958–62

Where to find adoption records

Name of Worker	Organisation or Home	Area	Role	Date
Heal, M, Miss	Beechwood	Wandsworth		1960s
Hearne, Miss	Church of England	Acton and Chiswick		1963
Heather, Jocelyn, Mrs	The Children's Society		Adoptions Social Worker	1969–72
Hedley-Bell, T, Mrs	Manchester & District Child Adoption Society		Secretary	
Heeran, Rita, Miss	Church of England	Hackney		
Hennessy, Deirdre, Ms	Mid Western Health Board	Clare (Eire)	Acting Senior Social Worker	1981–90
Herdsman, Miss	Church of England	Camberwell and Dulwich		1963
Herrington, J M, Mrs	Doncaster Adoption and Family Welfare Society Ltd		Head of Agency	1990–98
Hewett, K M Miss	Avon & N. Wiltshire	Bristol		1976
Hewson, Marjery, Mrs	The Children's Society		Social Worker	1961–73
Heynert, P, Mrs	Children's Aid Society		Secretary	1957
Higginson, Joy, Ms	Children North East		Director	
Hildegarde, Sister	Sean Ross Abbey	Tipperary (Eire)		
Hiley, Jacqueline, Miss	The Children's Society		Social Worker	1973–74
Hilleary, Miss	Church of England	Paddington Chelsea Battersea	Moral Welfare Worker	1963
Hillier, A, Miss	Children's Society			
Hills, V, Miss	Parents and Children Together	Oxford		
Hilton, J, Miss	The Children's Society		Boarding Out Worker	1962–66
Hitcham, Maureen, Miss	St Cuthberts Care			
Hitchcock, M, Miss	Llansbury	Wrexham		
Hitchin, Joyce	Chester Diocesan Adoption Services	Chester		
Hobart, Miss	Catholic Children's Society	Arundel & Brighton, Portsmouth & Southwark	Social Worker	
Hogg, Frances, Miss	Church of England	Southwark WelCare		
Hogg, Ross, Miss	Church of England	Welcare Muswell Hill (Haringey)		
Holliday, Mabel, Miss	The Children's Society		Boarding Out Worker	1966–76

Name of Worker	Organisation or Home	Area	Role	Date
Holman, C C, Ms	Parents and Children Together	Oxford		
Holman, Claire, Miss	St Faith's, Maidstone	Kent	Superintendent	1949–55
Holman, Miss	Church of England	Oxford Dorking Worcester City & County		1956 1942–44 1944–49
Honeyands, Yvonne, Mrs	The Children's Society		Child Care Social Worker	1966–72
Hook, P, Sister	Family Care (Essex)	Chelmsford area		
Hooker, J, Newman, Mr	British Adoption Project		Social Worker	1965–69
Hooper, N, Mrs	Church of England	Enfield		1963
Hope, Sister	Nutford Lodge	Westminster	Matron	1942
Hopgood, Miss	Parkinson House	Preston		1940s & 1950s
Horgan, Margaret, Ms	St Brigid's Adoption Society	Eire	Social Worker	
Horrocks, A, Mr	The Children's Society		Head of Boarding Out	1968–
Howard, Tamsin, Miss	The Children's Society		Foster Care Social Worker	1972
Howarth, Mrs	Heworth Moor House	York	Matron	
Howell, Huw	The Children's Society		Boarding Out Worker	1966–67
Howell, Olive, Ms	Church of England	Willesden	Moral Welfare Worker	1963
Hudson, Miss	Fylde House St Agnes House	Blackpool Manchester		1960s pre 1960
Hughes, B, Miss	Church of England	York		1956
Hughes, Beryl, O	Chester Diocesan Adoption Services	Chester	Principal Social Worker	
Hughes, Dr	Red Gables	Haringey	Medical Advisor	
Hughes, R, Miss	Lahai Roi Adoption Society		Senior Assistant (Adoption and Fostering)	1977
Hugh-Smith, Miss	St Francis Children's Society			
Hulme, T, Mrs	Family Care (Essex)	Chelmsford	Adoption Social Worker	
Humphrey, Mrs	Clark's House, Oxford	Oxford	Warden	
Hunt, Margaret, Miss	Free Church Maternity Home	Bournemouth	Matron	1956
Hurley, Mary, Ms	St Anne's Adoption Society	Eire	Social Worker	1984–96
Hyde, O M, Mrs	Oldham Adoption Society		Case Worker	1977

Name of Worker	Organisation or Home	Area	Role	Date
Ibbotson, C A, Mrs	Doncaster Adoption and Family Welfare Society Ltd		Head of Agency	1998–
Ingles, M, Miss	Cornwall Social and MW Association		Adoption Officer	1977
Innell, Mrs (née Sister Edith Welding)	10 Rutford Road	Lambeth and Hackney		
Inskip, Miss	Family Care (Essex)	Chelmsford area		
Irving, Karen, Mrs	Parents for Children		Director	
Jackman, R M, Sister	Church of England	Paddington		1960
Jackson, Joan, Mrs	The Children's Society		Adoptions Social Worker	1966–68
James, Mary, Miss	Independent Adoption Service		Director	
James, Mrs	St Faith's, Loughton	Essex	Superintendent	pre 1962–October 1970
James, W B, Mrs	Church of England	York		Pre 1956
Jefford, Kathleen, Sister	(Church Army) St Albans Adoption Society	South Bedfordshire	Social Worker	1960–65
Jerome, Sister	Catholic Children and Family Care (Wales)	Cardiff	Administrator	
Jeyes, Miss	National Adoption Society		Social Worker	1960
Johnson, Dorothy, Miss	The Children's Society		Adoptions Social Worker	1967–69
Johnson, R H, Rev	Mission of Hope for Children's Aid and Adoption		Secretary	
Jones, A M, Miss	Derby Diocesan Council for SW Adoption Committee		Advisor Adoption and Fostering	1977
Jones, Doris, Ereri	Chester Diocesan Adoption Services			Died 1998
Jones, Doris, Sister	(Church Army) Portsmouth Diocesan Council for Social Responsibility	Portsmouth	Moral Welfare Worker	1951–76
Jones, H M, Miss	Melbourne House, Exeter		Matron	1935
Jones, Mary, Mrs	St Albans Adoption Society		Adoption Officer Social Worker, Barnet & District Watford & District	1972–77 1969–71 1967–69
Josephine, Sister	Catholic Children's Rescue Society (Diocese of Salford) Inc		Moral Welfare	

Name of Worker	Organisation or Home	Area	Role	Date
Kaniuk, Jeanne, Ms	Thomas Coram Foundation for Children (now Coram Family)		Principal Social Worker	
Kanzell, B, Mrs	National Children Adoption Association		Social Worker	1974
Kathleen, Sister	Catholic Children's Society	Arundel & Brighton, Portsmouth & Southwark		
Kay, Shirley, Mrs	Parents and Children Together		Administrative Secretary	
Keating, Miss	Penshanger Maternity Home	Herts	Matron	1943
Keavney, Angela, Sister	St Anne's Adoption Society	Eire	Social Worker	Late 1970s
Kebel, Elaine R, Miss	National Adoption Society		Social Worker	1971
Kemp, C Ann, Dr	Adoption Anglia, Project of Coram Adoption Service		Hon. Medical Officer	1977
Kemp, Doreen, Miss	Church of England	Hampton Heston Isleworth and Staines Hackney		1963–72
Kemp, Miss	Church of England	Hounslow	Moral Welfare Worker	Pre 1972
Kenneally, Mairead, Ms (see O'Hare)				
Kennedy, Marie, Ms	Mid Western Health Board	Limerick (Eire)	Social Worker	
Kennor, Miss	St Olave's M&B Home	Devon		
Keogh, Nuala, Sister	Menevia Family Social Services		Social Worker	1981
Kernock, Miss	Church of England	Leicester	Moral Welfare Worker	
Kerton, Miss	Church of England	Nottingham	Moral Welfare Worker	
Killick, F, Miss	The Children's Society	SE Region	Social Worker	1979–81
Kilvington, Jane, Dr	St Albans Adoption Society		Medical Advisor	
Kinder, Eleanor, Miss	Mansfield and District Association for Moral Welfare			1946–77
King, Audrey, Mrs	St Albans Adoption Society	Welwyn Gdn City & Hatfield, East & North East Hertfordshire	Social Worker	1965–77
King, L M, Miss	Burnley & Nelson House of Help	Burnley	Moral Welfare Care Worker	1945–50s
King, Mary, Miss	British Adoption Project		Director	1965–66

Name of Worker	Organisation or Home	Area	Role	Date
Kingston, Mary, Sister	Catholic Caring Services to Children and Community (Diocese of Lancaster)		Social Worker	1977
Kirtley, Ethel, Miss	3 Bampfylde Road & 12 Bexley Terrace	Torquay	Matron	1914
Kirton, Miss	Southwell Diocesan Council for Family Care		Social Worker	1945–76
Kitchen, Miss	Church of England	Willesden	Moral Welfare Worker	
Kneller, Ms	British Adoption Project		Social Worker	
Knight, M C, Miss	Church of England	Romford, St Agatha's, Newham	Moral Welfare Worker	1966–68
Knight, Miss	St Agatha's	Newham		1966–68
Knowles, Mrs	Bartletts, Chelmsford	Essex	Superintendent	May 72–May 76
Kubler, Miss (later known as Miss Ridley)	Beacon Lodge	Haringey		1907–20
Lamb, Mrs	Church of England	Poplar		1963
Lane, Susan, Miss	The Children's Society		Boarding Out Worker	1968–69
Laughton, Nurse	(Guildford House) London Diocesan Hostel	Barnet	Matron	
Launchbury, Miss	Cornwall Social & MW Association & Morwenna		Matron	
Lawn, Ruth, Miss	National Children's Home		Social Worker	
Lawrence, Marjorie, Miss	St Albans Adoption Society	Barnet & District	Social Worker, Principal Social Worker	1963–69
Laws, Miss	Hostel of the Good Shepherd, Colchester	Essex	Superintendent	1968–71
Laws, Miss	Ellen Carville (Shelter)	Waltham Forest		
Lawson, Mrs	Catholic Care (Diocese of Leeds)			
Lawton, Wilma, Mrs	St Albans Adoption Society	S. Bedfordshire	Social Worker	1971–73
Layman, Mrs	St Nicholas M&B Home previously Dunraven	Devon		
Leadley-Brown, Miss	Lancashire and Cheshire Child Adoption Council		Barrister & Hon. Secretary	
Leapman, E, Mrs	Avon & N. Wiltshire	Chippenham & Swindon		1976
Lee, Jean, Mrs	The Children's Society		Boarding Out Worker	1970
Lee, Margaret, Ms	Mid Western Health Board	Co. Clare (Eire)	Social Worker	1998–

Name of Worker	Organisation or Home	Area	Role	Date
Lee, Martin	Christian Outreach		Director	
Lennox, Angela, Sister	St Catherine's Adoption Society	Co. Clare (Eire)	Social Worker	
Leslie, Miss	Families for Children Adoption Agency			
Lewis, Diane, Mrs	Manchester Adoption Society		Secretary	
Lewis, E M, Miss	Swansea & Brecon Diocesan Council for Social Work		Organising Secretary	1979
Lewis, Jenny	Catholic Children and Family Care Society (Wales)	Cardiff	Social Worker	
Lewis, Marjorie, Sister	10 Rutford Road	Lambeth		
Lewis-Clarke, G, Miss	Family Care (Essex)		Adoption Social Worker	
Liddell, J D, Mrs	Church of England	Hammersmith WelCare		1974
Lillis, Mary, Ms	St Catherine's Adoption Society	Co. Clare (Eire)	Social Worker	
Linney, Catherine	Chester Diocesan Adoption Services			
Litshi	The Children's Society		Boarding Out Worker	1963–66
Litten, John, Rev	National Children's Home		Principal	1933–50
Louise, Sister	Catholic Children's Rescue Society (Diocese of Salford) Inc		Moral Welfare Worker	
Lovell, D	The Children's Society	Ipswich E. Region	Social Worker	1978–81
Lucas, P, Miss	Church of England	Willesden		1960
Luertwood, Susan, Mrs	The Children's Society		Adoptions Social Worker	1967–69
Lusk, J T, Miss	Family Care, Edinburgh		Director	
Lynas, Mrs	Browning House Leeds & Heworth Moor House, York	N.Yorks York		From 1 January 1957
Lynch	The Children's Society		Boarding Out Worker	1957–66
Lyons, Cliona, Ms	St Anne's Adoption Society	Eire	Social Worker	1972–76
Lyons, Heather, Mrs	Portsmouth Diocesan Council for Social Responsibility			1976–
Lyons, M, Mr	Catholic Children's Society	Arundel & Brighton, Portsmouth & Southwark	Principal Social Worker	
MacDonald, Mrs	Southwell Diocesan Council for Family Care		Social Worker	1944–52

Name of Worker	Organisation or Home	Area	Role	Date
Macdonald-Brown, J, Mrs	Doncaster Adoption and Family Welfare Soc. Ltd.		Administrative Secretary	1977–88
Macklin, B, Sister	Church of England	Hampstead		1960
Mallabar, M, Miss	The Children's Society	N Region	Welfare Officer	1947–74
Mallaby, E V, Miss	Newark Moral Welfare Associaiton		Social Worker	1938–62
Mallard, M, Mrs	Avon & N. Wilts	Bristol		1976
Manley, Miss	Church of England	Islington	Moral Welfare Worker	
Mann, Ethel	Chester Diocesan Adoption Services	Mid Cheshire		
Mann, Miss	Prospect House, Hoylake	Merseyside	Matron	
Mann, V, Sister	Church of England	Paddington		1960
Manning, Liz, Ms	Mid-Western Health Board	Limerick (Eire)	Social Worker	
Manns, Sister	St Anne's	Wandsworth	Sister in Charge	1920
Mansell, Miss	M&B Hostel, Wadham Gdns	Camden	Matron	
Markby, Rev	Red Gables	Haringey		
Markham, FA, Miss	Mission of Hope for Children's Aid and Adoption		Welfare Worker	
Markham, G, Mrs	Church of England	Willesden	Moral Welfare Worker	1972
Marklew, Mrs	Catholic Children's Society	Arundel & Brighton, Portsmouth & Southwark		
Marsh, O, Miss (deceased)	Exmoor House, Dulveston	Somerset	Warden	
Marshallsay, Nicholas	Church of England		Social Worker	
Martin, Miss	Church of England	Islington		
Martin, S, Miss	Catholic Care (Diocese of Leeds)		Senior Social Worker	1977
Martin, Sheila, Mrs	St Albans Adoption Society	Barnet & District	Social Worker	1971–77
Mary Stella, Sister	Chester Diocesan Adoption Services, St Bridgets M&B Home			
Mascall, Miss	Catholic Children's Society	Arundel & Brighton, Portsmouth & Southwark		
Maskens, Amy, Miss	St Albans Adoption Society	Mid Hertfordshire	Social Worker	1967–75

Name of Worker	Organisation or Home	Area	Role	Date
Mason, Norma	Chester Diocesan Adoption Services, Pasture Road Centre	Moreton		
Mason, Sister	Church of England	Islington WelCare		
Masters, Colin, Mr	Thomas Coram Foundation for Children (now Coram Family)		Director and Secretary	
Masters, K, P, Miss	Church of England	Islington	Moral Welfare Worker	1957
Masters, Mrs	St Barnabas	Westminster		
Mathers, Jeannette, Miss	The Children's Society		Boarding Out Worker	1966
Maureen, Sister	St Anne's Adoption Society	Eire	Social Worker	1973–89
Maw, C, Miss	Catholic Children's Society	Arundel & Brighton, Portsmouth & Southwark		
Maxwell, Pat, Sister	Catholic Children and Family Care Society (Wales)	Cardiff	Social Worker	
Mayne, Miss	Catholic Children's Society	Arundel & Brighton, Portsmouth & Southwark		
McCall, Janet, Miss (see Mrs Ransome Wallis)				
McCulloch, Meg, Miss	St Albans Adoption Society	Mid Hertfordshire	Social Worker	1952–67
McDermid, Eunice, Miss	The Children's Society		Boarding Out Worker	1970–72
McDonagh, Mary, Sister	St Brigid's Adoption Society	Eire		
McFarlane, Miss	Family Care (Essex)	Chelmsford Area		
McFarlane, Miss	Beacon Lodge	Haringey		
McGarry, K, Mrs	St Margaret of Scotland Adoption Society		Principal Social Worker	1977
McGinchy, Brian, Mr	Catholic Children and Family Care (Wales)	Cardiff	Social Worker	
McGuire, S, Mrs	Scottish Adoption Association		Director of Adoption Services	
McHugh, M J, Mrs	Oldham Adoption Society		Case Worker	1977
McLaren, V, Mrs	Family Care (Essex)	Chelmsford Area	Organising Secretary	Until Feb 1970
McLaverty, John	Church of Jesus Christ of Latter Day Saints			
McMullen, Miss	Perth and Dundee Association of Social Service		Organising Secretary	

Name of Worker	Organisation or Home	Area	Role	Date
McNally, A	St Cuthberts Care		Adoption Officer	1981
Mellor, D, Miss	Church of England	Huddersfield MWW		1961
Midgeley, J E, Miss	Families for Children Adoption Agency		Adoption Officer	
Miles, U E, Miss	Parents and Children Together	Bucks – Amersham area		
Miller, Edith, Miss	The Children's Society		Foster Care Social Worker	1972–73
Miller, Miss	Church of England	Bethnal Green	Moral Welfare Worker	
Mills, Irene, Miss	The Children's Society		Boarding Out Worker	1965
Mirzanie, Barri, Mrs	Church of England	Willesden		
Mitchell, Mary, Dr	Adoption Anglia, Project of Coram Family Adoption Society		Hon Medical Officer	1977
Mitchell, Mrs	The Children's Society		Adoptions Social Worker	1962–66
Moakes, Doreen, Ms	Sunderland National Children's Home			
Moffatt, M, Mrs	Catholic Children's Society	Arundel & Brighton, Portsmouth & Southwark		
Moloney, E, Mrs	Family Care (Essex)	Waltham Forest		
Montague, Ms	National Children Adoption Association		Visitor	
Moody, Carole, Miss	The Children's Society		Boarding Out Worker	1961–74
Moore, Brian	The Children's Society	N. W. Region	Social Worker	1978–81
Moore, Connie, Mrs	St Albans Adoption Society	Barnet & District	Social Worker, Senior Social Worker	1963–73
Moore, D E, Sister	Church of England	St Pancras		1960
Moore, Miss	Southwell Diocesan Council for Family Care		Social Worker	1937–44
Morain, Miss	Catholic Children's Society (Westminster)			
Morgan, Miss	St Faith's, Loughton	Essex	Superintendent	October 1970 –July 1974
Morgan, N, Mr	Chichester Diocesan Association for Family Social Work		Director	1977
Moriarty, Catherine, Ms	St Mary's Adoption Society	Kerry (Eire)	Social Worker	

Name of Worker	Organisation or Home	Area	Role	Date
Morris, H M, Miss	Church of England	Southwark WelCare	Organising Secretary	1912–24
Morrison, Ms	Beacon Lodge	Haringey		
Mousley, Geoffrey	Catholic Children's Society (Shrewsbury Diocese) Inc		Principal Officer	
Mowbray, Mrs	Church of England	St Marylebone		1960
Mtshali, Patricia, Ms	Catholic Children and Family Care Society (Wales)	Cardiff	Social Worker	
Muir, D, Mrs	Family Care (Essex)	Brentwood		
Mulberry, Sister	St Anne's	Wandsworth	Sister in Charge	1923
Murcer, B, Mrs	The Children's Society	Midlands Region	Social Worker	1979–81
Murcer, W	The Children's Society	S. E. Region	Social Worker	1979–81
Murphy, Anne, Ms	Southern Health Board	Cork/Kerry (Eire)	Social Worker	
Murphy, Breda, Sister (previously called Sr Ancilla)	Catholic Children and Family Care Society (Wales)	Cardiff	Social Worker	
Murphy, Clare, Ms	St Catherine's Adoption Society	Clare (Eire)	Social Worker	
Murphy, John, Father	Catholic Care (Diocese of Leeds)			
Murray, Gus, Mr	St Anne's Adoption Society	Eire	Social Worker	1988–90
Murray, Miss	Catholic Children's Society	Arundel & Brighton, Portsmouth & Southwark		
Murray, Ruth, Ms	Cork & Ross Family Centre & St Anne's Adoption Society	Eire	Social Worker	1978–
Napier, Helen, Mrs	Adoption Anglia, Project of Coram Family Adoption Society		Team Leader	1986–98
Nash, Miss	The Children's Society	Paddington	Adoptions Social Worker	1964–66
Nash, Rosalind, Mrs	The Children's Society		Foster Care Social Worker	1972
Neville, Mrs	Catholic Women's Aid	Cork (Eire)		
Newall, Pauline, (later Booth)	Chester Diocesan Adoption Services			
Newbery, R, Miss	Adoption Anglia, Project of Coram Family Adoption Society		Assistant Officer	1959–72

Name of Worker	Organisation or Home	Area	Role	Date
Newby, R	The Children's Society	Midlands Region	Social Worker	1975–81
Newhouse, Miss	Church of England	Oxford		1956
Newth, M, Miss	Church of England	Bermondsey	Moral Welfare Worker	1958
Niblett, D M, Miss	Church of England	Finsbury and Holborn		1960
Nicholson, Miss	Main Memorial	Camden	Superintendent	
Nightingale, M	The Children's Society	E. Region	Social Worker	1979–81
Noble, John	The Children's Society	Darlington	Social Worker	1978
Noone, Alice	Catholic Children's Rescue Society (Diocese of Salford) Inc		Social Worker	
O'Brien, A O, Mrs	Family Care (Essex)	Colchester		
O'Brien, Ita, Ms	Mid Western Health Board	Limerick (Eire)	Social Worker	
O'Connell, I, Miss	Catholic Children's Society	Arundel & Brighton, Portsmouth & Southwark		
O'Connor, John C, Rev	Catholic Family Care Society	N. Ireland	Director	1977
O'Connor, Nan, Mrs	Mid Western Health Board	Limerick (Eire)	Social Worker	
O'Dea, Carmel, Ms	St Catherine's Adoption Society	Co Clare (Eire)	Social Worker	
O'Derchee, Maureen, Sister	Southern Health Board	Cork/Kerry (Eire)	Social Worker	
O'Donohue, Maureen, Ms	St Catherine's Adoption Society	Co Clare (Eire)	Social Worker	
O'Farrell, Kevin, Mr	Mid Western Health Board	Co Clare (Eire)	Social Worker	1990–95
O'Hara, B, Miss	Catholic Children's Society	Arundel & Brighton, Portsmouth & Southwark		
O'Hare, Mairead, Ms (née Kenneally)	St Anne's Adoption Society	Eire	Social Worker	1976–80
O'Keeffe, Joan, Ms	St Catherine's Adoption Society	Co Clare (Eire)	Social Worker	
O'Leary, Finbar, Father	Catholic Children and Family Care (Wales)	Cardiff	Director	
O'Mahony, John K, Father	St Anne's Adoption Society	Eire	Social Worker	1967–88
O'Malley, P, Mrs	St Cuthberts Care		Fostering and Adoption Officer	1991
O'Meara, J, Mrs	Avon & N. Wiltshire	Chippenham		1976

Name of Worker	Organisation or Home	Area	Role	Date
O'Regan, Jackie, Ms (see Cavanagh)				
O'Sullivan, N, Miss	Catholic Children's Society	Arundel & Brighton, Portsmouth & Southwark		
Oakley, J, Miss	Father Hudson's Society		Secretary	
Oguntosin, Bolajoko, Mrs	The Children's Society		Foster Care Social Worker	1973
Oloman, Mrs	York Adoption Society			
Orton, Ethel, Miss	St Albans Adoption Society	Barnet & District	Social Worker	1954–59
Orton, Miss	Church of England			
Osborne, Margaret	Chester Diocesan Adoption Services	Chester		
Owen, F, Miss	St Elizabeth's House	Exeter	Matron	1935
Owen, Jean	Chester Diocesan Adoption Services	Chester		
Painten, C, Miss	Church of England	N. Berkshire		
Painter, Miss	Parents and Children Together, Oxford			
Pannell, Robert, Mr	The Children's Society		Boarding Out Worker	1970
Pannier, Sister (later Mrs Evans)	St Hilda's, Crewe	Cheshire	First Adoption Secretary	
Parker, C, Miss	Church of England	Reading and Bradfield		
Parker, J C, Mrs	Childlink		Assistant Secretary	1971
Parker, Maureen, Mrs	The Children's Society		Adoptions Social Worker	1967
Parr, Agnes, Mrs	Fellowship of St Michael of All Angels	Lambeth and countrywide	Founder	1903
Parsons, Miss	Church of England	Reigate and Redhill		1963
Paterson, L M, Miss	Family Care, Edinburgh		Senior Social Worker	
Paton, Miss	St Faith's Coventry	Warwickshire	Matron	Early 1940s– late 1960s
Patrick, Lesley, Mrs	St Albans Adoption Society	N. Bedfordshire	Social Worker	1963–73
Patton, M, Mrs	St Faith's Adoption Society			
Paul, Sister (now Sister Maureen, retired from Southern Health Board)	St Anne's Adoption Society	Eire	Social Worker	1973–89

Name of Worker	Organisation or Home	Area	Role	Date
Pauline, Sister	Catholic Children and Family Care (Wales)	Llanelli	Social Worker	
Pazzi-Axworthy, Mr & Mrs	St Albans Adoption Society		Legal Advisors	
Pearse, Elizabeth, Dr	St Albans Adoption Society		Medical Advisor	
Perfect, E, Miss	Church of England	Hampstead		1960
Perry, C	The Children's Society	SE Region	Social Worker	1979–81
Perry, Ms	Church of England	Burnt Oak		
Pettitt, Elsie, Miss	Cambridge Shelter for Girls	Cambridgeshire	Superintendent	1920–21
Philips, E, B, Miss	Church of England	St Pancras		1960
Phillips, Leonard, Dr	Homeless Children's Aid & Adoption & F B Meyer Children's Home Inc		Hon. Consulting Physician	
Phillips, Nurse	London Diocesan Hostel, Guilford House	Barnet		1957
Philomena, Sister	Catholic Children's Rescue Society (Diocese of Salford) Inc		Team Manager – Family Placement Services	
Pickard, Miss	Church of England	Fulham		1963
Piefinch, M, Miss	Church of England	Leatherhead		
Piggott, Miss	The Children's Society		Boarding Out Worker	1964–67
Pinder, Miss	St Francis Children's Society			
Pitman, Audrey, Miss	St Albans Adoption Society East & North East Herts Association for Church Social Work		Social Worker Social Worker	
Pitman, Margaret, Mrs	The Children's Society		Boarding Out Worker	1965–67
Plamer, J, Mr	The Children's Society		Head of Boarding Out	1962–68
Plastorier, Le, Sister	London Diocesan Hostel, Guilford House	Barnet	Superintendent	
Plater, Miss	St Francis Children's Society			
Plummer, D C, Mrs	National Children Adoption Association		Social Worker	
Pollock, Catherine, Miss	St Albans Adoption Society		Adoption Officer	1969–72
Polman, Miss	Church of England	Uxbridge	Moral Welfare Worker	
Poplar, I L C, Miss	Family Care (Essex)		Director	From April 1971

Name of Worker	Organisation or Home	Area	Role	Date
Porter, Anna, Mrs	St Agnes House	Hounslow	Matron	
Postans, E, Deaconess	Church of England	Hampstead		1960
Potter, C, Miss	Bartlett's, Chelmsford	Essex	Assistant Superintendent	1972–76
Potter, Joy, Mrs	St Albans Adoption Society	N. Hertfordshire	Social Worker	1964–69
Powell, Miss	Hostel of the Good Shepherd, Colchester	Essex	Superintendent	1967
Poynier, Canon	Catholic Children and Family Care (Wales)	Wales	Director	
Pratt, Miss	Church of England	Tottenham		1959, 1963
Prescote, Mhari, Mrs	The Children's Society		Boarding Out Worker	1969–70
Presnail, Kathleen, Mrs	St Albans Adoption Society	Watford & District	Social Worker	1972–76
Pretty, Miss	St Agnes, Charlton-on-Medlock	Manchester	Matron	
Price, B F, Miss	Church of England	Weston-super-Mare Bath and Wells		1956
Prince, Miss	Church of England	Worthing	Moral Welfare Worker	1958
Prior, Alice, Miss	3 Bampfylde Rd & 12 Bexley Terrace	Torquay	Matron	1919
Proctor, Elizabeth	Catholic Children's Rescue Society (Diocese of Salford) Inc			
Proctor, S, Miss	Cornwall Social & MW Association		Organising Secretary	
Pulman, Miss	Church of England	Uxbridge		1963
Purney, S E, Miss	Church of England	Southwark WelCare	Organising Secretary	1925–28
Pyefinch, Miss	Church of England	Wallington and Carshalton		1963
Quine, Joyce, Mrs	Manx Churches Adoption and Welfare Society	Isle of Man	Principal Social Worker	
Radcliffe, Miss	Church of England	York		
Radford, Miss	Church of England	Lambeth		1963
Randall, Mary, Miss	The Children's Society	London	Social Worker	1978–81
Rathbone, W, Mrs	The Children's Society		Adoptions Social Worker	1960–66
Rawson, J L, Mrs	Bradford Diocesan MW Council		Senior Social Worker	1977
Rayner, Lois, Miss	British Adoption Project		Director	1966–69

Name of Worker	Organisation or Home	Area	Role	Date
Raynes, M A, Miss	Church of England	Southwark WelCare	Organising Secretary	1951–64
Raynham, Betty, Miss	Church of England	Barnet		1976
Reaney, Pat, Miss (deceased)	British Adoption Project		Social Worker	1965–67
Redgrave, Ken	Chester Diocesan Adoption Services			
Redmond, R	The Children's Society	NW Region	Social Worker	1979–81
Rees-Pryse, Daphne, Miss	St Albans Adoption Society	N. Hertfordshire	Social Worker	1962–63
Reeve, V, Mrs	Plymouth Diocesan Catholic Children's Society			
Reeves, Julie, Mrs	The Children's Society		Adoptions Social Worker	1971–72
Regan, D, Miss	St Francis Children's Society		Principal Adoption Officer	1977
Remedios, Margaret, Mrs	The Children's Society		Adoptions Social Worker	1965–68
Retallack, Lila, Miss	Church of England	Southwark WelCare	Organising Secretary	1929–34
Reynolds, Miss	Church of England	Islington WelCare		1976
Richards, Jim	Catholic Children's Society (Westminster)		Director	
Richards, K, Mrs	Families for Children Adoption Agency		Adoption Secretary	
Richardson, Miss	Church of England	Clapham and Brixton		1963
Richardson, Pearl, Miss	The Children's Society	Swindon	Social Worker	1978
Richardson, Pearl, Miss	The Children's Society	Swindon	Social Worker	1979–81
Ridley, Miss (previously Miss Kubler)	Beacon Lodge	Haringey		1907–20
Ridyard, M, Miss	Church of England	Finsbury and Holborn Central Chapter		1960
Rigby, F, The Rev	Ashton-under-Lyne Adoption Society			
Rigden, M, Miss	Family Care (Essex)	Grays area		
Rigden, Miss	Beechwood, Westcliffe-on-Sea	Essex	Superintendent	1969–73
Ritson-Smith, Ms	Parents & Children Together		Administrative Secretary	
Rivers, P A, Sister	Church of England	Salisbury	Moral Welfare Worker	
Robinson, E V, Miss	Church of England	Epsom and Leatherhead		

Name of Worker	Organisation or Home	Area	Role	Date
Robinson, J, Miss	The Children's Society		Head of Adoption	1946–67
Robinson, Joyce, Miss	The Children's Society		Adoptions Social Worker	1946–67
Robinson, Miss	The Children's Society		Head of Adoptions Dept.	1967
Rogers, Miss	Church of England	Canterbury		
Rogers, R, Miss	Adoption Anglia, Project of Coram Family Adoption Society			4 months only from 1967
Roisin, Sister	Catholic Children & Family Care Society (Wales)	Cardiff	Social Worker	
Rowe, Sylvia, Mrs	The Children's Society		Foster Care Social Worker	1972
Roxburgh, Mrs	Families for Children Adoption Agency			
Russell Wells, Hilda, Miss	St Albans Adoption Society		Adoption Officer	1954–59
Russell, P D, Miss	Leicester Diocesan Board for Social Responsibility		Organising Secretary	1977
Ryan, Jacinta, Ms	St Anne's Adoption Society	Eire	Social Worker	1990–99
Saddington, J, Mrs	National Children Adoption Association		Social Worker	1971
Sales, D S, Miss	Church of England	Bournemouth		
Salter, E, Miss	Avon & N. Wiltshire		Principal Social Worker	
Saltwell, Mrs	Crathorne	Barnet	Superintendent	
Sanders, Miss	Church of England	Westminster, St Marylebone		1963
Sawbridge, M P T, Miss	British Adoption Project, Parents for Children		Social Worker	1967–69
Sayers, Joseph	Worthing & District Council of Social Service		Secretary	
Scargill, Veronica, Mrs	St Albans Adoption Society	N. Hertfordshire	Social Worker	1971–72
Scoones, Miss	Church of England	Godstone and Caterham		1963
Scott, J E C, Miss	Gloucester Diocesan Council for SW		Administrative Social Worker	
Scott, Marian	Chester Diocesan Adoption Services	Cheshire		
Scott-Cowell, Mrs	M&B Hostel, Wadham Gardens	Camden	Superintendent	

Name of Worker	Organisation or Home	Area	Role	Date
Scurrah, Miss	Church of England	Hornsey		
Seaburne-May, Mrs	Parents & Children Together		Administrative Secretary	
Setterington, S, Miss	Gloucester Diocesan Council for SW			
Seymour, E J, Dr	Mission of Hope for Children's Aid and Adoption		Hon Medical Consultant	
Shaftoe, Hilary	Chester Diocesan Adoption Services	Cheshire		
Sharp, M S, Miss	Cambridge Shelter for Girls	Cambridgeshire	Superintendent	1922–23
Shaw, A, Miss	Newark Moral Welfare Association		Adoption Worker	1938–62
Shaw, Joyce M, Mrs	Manchester Adoption Society		Secretary / Administrator	1981
Shaw, Marjorie, Sister (Church Army)	St Albans Adoption Society	W. Hertfordshire	Social Worker	1960–77
Shaw, Miss	St Margaret's	Plymouth	Matron	1935
Sheilds, D K, Sister	Church of England	Holborn and Finsbury		1960
Short, J A, Mrs	Nugent Care Agency	Isle of Man	Adoption Worker	
Shortland, M, Miss	Plymouth Diocesan Catholic Children's Society			
Sievewright, Shelia, Ms	St Anne's Adoption Society	Eire	Social Worker	1979–90
Simons, Miss	Beechwood, Westcliff-on-Sea	Essex	Superintendent	April 1974–
Simpson, A, Miss	The Children's Society	N. Region	Social Worker	1979–81
Simpson, E, Mrs (deceased)	Oldham Adoption Society		Case Worker	1965–69
Simpson, June, Miss	Church of England	Southwark WelCare	Director	1983–91
Simpson, Lomax, Dr (Deceased)	Messengers House Trust	Merton and London	Director	
Sinker, Miss	Church of England	Atherstone and Monk's Kirby (Coventry)		1956
Skingle, June, Miss	The Children's Society		Adoptions Social Worker	1971–72
Skinner, John	The Children's Society	S. E. Region	Social Worker	1979–81
Skinner, Ruth, Miss	St Albans Adoption Society	N. Bedfordshire	Social Worker	1958–67
Slack, S, Miss	Family Care (Essex)	Havering area		
Sloman, Miss	Stretton House	Lewisham		1955

Name of Worker	Organisation or Home	Area	Role	Date
Smethurst, Joan, Mrs	Parents & Children Together		Administrative Secretary	
Smith, Barham, Mrs (see Barham Smith)				
Smith, Chris	St Francis Children's Society			
Smith, D E, Miss	Church of England	Brent WelCare		1974
Smith, D, Miss	Church of England	Hendon	Moral Welfare Worker	
Smith, Dorothy, Miss	Church of England	Hendon WelCare Ripon		To 1956
Smith, Dorothy, Mrs	St Albans Adoption Society	W. Herts	Social Worker	1968–77
Smith, Hodson, Rev	National Children's Home		Principal	1912–33
Smith, Iris, Miss	The Children's Society		Case Worker	1974
Smith, Marjorie, Mrs		Blackburn & Burnley areas	Director	1976
Smith, M L, Miss	Hope House, Great Grimsby	N. E. Linconshire	Social Worker	
Smith, R F, Mr	Mission of Hope for Children's Aid and Adoption		Secretary	
Smith, S, Miss	Catholic Children's Society	Arundel & Brighton, Portsmouth & Southwark		
Smith, W J, Mr	St Margaret of Scotland Adoption Society		Principal Social Worker	1980s
South, Miss	Church of England	Bermondsey & Rotherhithe Southwark & Newington		1963
Southall, Mrs	Children Society			
Southwark, Miss	Catholic Children's Society	Arundel & Brighton, Portsmouth & Southwark		
Southworth, Frances, Mrs	The Children's Society		Boarding Out Worker	1967–68
Speirs, Jennifer, Ms	Family Care (Edinburgh)		Director	
Spencer, S, Mrs	Family Care (Essex)		Adoption Social Worker	1969–74
Spooner, Miss	Families for Children Adoption Agency			
Stanaway, Elaine	Catholic Children's Rescue Society (Diocese of Salford) Inc		Social Worker	
Stapley, Nigel	The Children's Society		Boarding Out Worker	1968–69

Name of Worker	Organisation or Home	Area	Role	Date
Steel, E, Miss	Church of England Moral Welfare Council			
Steel, Miss	St Faith's Adoption Society		Diocesan Moral Welfare Officer	
Sterry, Stella, Ms	Adopt Anglia, Project of Coram Adoption Society		Senior Social Worker	1977–93
Stevenson, Pam, Miss	The Children's Society	Tunbridge Wells	Social Worker	1979–81
Steventon, O, Mrs	The Children's Society		Boarding Out Worker	1951–67
Stowe, Rachel, Miss	St Albans Adoption Society	N. Bedfordshire	Social Worker	1971–77
Stower, Eileen, Mrs	The Children's Society		Adoptions Social Worker	1966–67
Strange, G, Miss	Family Care (Essex)	Havering area		
Straw, Beryl, Sister (Church Army)	Chester Diocesan Adoption Services, Scottish Episcopal Church Adoption Society	Cheshire	Senior Social Worker	
Street, Miss	Church of England	Stourbridge, Droitwich and Redditch (Worcester)		1956
Stringer, Kate, Ms	Church of Jesus Christ of Latter Day Saints			
Strong, J, Miss	Church of England	Southwell		
Stubbs, M, Miss	Ely Diocesan Home	Cambridgeshire	Matron	
Sturt, Sister	St Anne's	Wandsworth	Sister in Charge	1920
Tatton, Assisi, Sister	St Brigid's Adoption Society	Eire	Social Worker	
Taylor, Gilbert T E	Homeless Children's Aid and Adoption & F B Meyer Children's Home Inc & 54 Frederick Street Edinburgh		Hon Solicitors	
Taylor, Lorna, Mrs	The Children's Society		Foster Care Social Worker	1972–75
Taylor, Miss	Church of England	Haringey		1971
Taylor, O, Sister	Church of England	Paddington		1960
Taylor, P, Mrs	Plymouth Diocesan Catholic Children's Society			
Teather, M, Miss	Church of England	E. Newcastle	Moral Welfare Worker	1957
Temple, Margaret, Miss	St Albans Adoption Society	East Hertfordshire	Social Worker	1953–66
Thomas, Frances, E, Mrs	Oxford Diocesan Council for Social work Inc.		Principal Social Worker	1977
Thomas, Luther I R, Rev Canon	Diocesan Council for Social Work	Swansea and Brecon		

Name of Worker	Organisation or Home	Area	Role	Date
Thomas, Morlais	The Children's Society	Wales and SW Region	Social Worker	1979–81
Thomas, Phillis, Miss	Church of England	Southwark WelCare	Organising Secretary	1964–71
Thompson, Mrs	St Nicholas or Dunraven M & B Home (Council for Christian Care)	Devon		Between 1935 & 1974
Thorne, M, Mrs	British Adoption Project		Social Worker	
Thornton, Geoffrey	St Albans Adoption Society	S. Bedfordshire	Social Worker	1974–77
Thornton, M, Miss	Scottish Adoption Association		Senior Social Worker	
Thornton, P J, Mr	Leicester Diocesan Board for Social Responsibility			
Threakall, Miss	St Agatha's	Newham		Pre 1962
Tierney, Jackie, Mrs	Manchester Adoption Society		Administrator	2000
Tillbrook, Mrs	Families for Children Adoption Agency			
Todd, Miss	Church of England	St Edmonsbury and Ipswich	Moral Welfare Worker	1961
Toes, E, Miss	Church of England	North and Central Cheshire		
Townsend, E, Miss	Church of England	Bethnal Green and Shoreditch	Moral Welfare Worker	1956 1963
Toy, Alaric, Mr	The Children's Society		Boarding Out Worker	1966–67
Tracey, Mareve, Ms	St Mary's Adoption Society	Kerry (Eire)		
Treacher, Miss	Church of England	Charing Cross Road	Moral Welfare Worker	
Tribe, Mrs	Lancashire & Cheshire Child Adoption Council		Case Secretary	1945–57
Truesdale, D	The Children's Society	Midlands Region	Social Worker	1979–81
Tucker, Elizabeth, Mrs	The Children's Society		Adoptions Social Worker	1966–67
Tucker, V, Mrs	Avon and N. Wiltshire	Bristol		1976
Tuckey, Ruth, Ms	Catholic Children's Society	Arundel & Brighton, Portsmouth & Southwark	Senior Social Worker	
Tunley, John	The Children's Society	Cardiff	Social Worker	1979–81
Turner, Helen, Miss	St Albans Adoption Society	Barnet, Watford & District	Social Worker	1959–65
Turner, J, Michael	Catholic Children's Rescue Society (Diocese of Salford) Inc		Director of Social Work	

Name of Worker	Organisation or Home	Area	Role	Date
Turner, J, Mrs	Church of England	Derby		
Turner, Miss	Catholic Children's Society (Westminster)			
Tyner, Miss	Beacon Lodge	Haringey		1920–40
Upstone, Pauline, Ms	Church of Jesus Christ of Latter Day Saints		Adoption/Fostering Officer	
Urch, Miss (deceased)	Began the first shelter for battered wives at Ladyholme.			
Uren, Winifred, Mrs	The Children's Society		Foster Care Social Worker	1971
Urquart, Anne, Miss	Blackburn Diocesan Adoption Agency	Chorley	Case Worker	Late 1960s
Usher, Priscilla, Miss	Church of Ireland Adoption Society	N. Ireland		
Vale, Alison	Chester Diocesan Adoption Services			
Van Horrik, Hendrik	The Children's Society		Foster Care Social Worker	1972
Varley, Barbara, Mrs	The Children's Society		Foster Care Social Worker	1972–73
Vaughan-Williams, V M, Miss	Parents & Children Together	Newbury		
Verdult, Miss	Catholic Children's Society Westminster			
Veronica, Sister	Catholic Children's Society	Arundel & Brighton, Portsmouth & Southwark		
Vieyera, Mrs	Church of England	Barnet		
Vincent, E M, Miss	Church of England	Guildford		
Vine, D	The Children's Society	Wales and S. W. Region	Social Worker	1979–81
Wagstaff, Joan, Deaconess	Chester Diocesan Adoption Services		Adoption Secretary	
Wainman, J, Miss	Blackburn Diocese Adoption Agency		Organising Secretary	Few years prior to 1971
Walker Jean, Mrs, née Shackle	The Children's Society		Foster Care Social Worker	1973–76
Walker, E M, Miss	Church of England	Islington	Moral Welfare Worker	1957
Walker, K, Ms	Parents for Children		Director	
Walker, M, Miss	Church of England	Oxford		1968
Walker, M, Mrs	Avon and N. Wiltshire	Weston-Super-Mare		

Name of Worker	Organisation or Home	Area	Role	Date
Walker, Miss	Church of England	Uxbridge	Moral Welfare Worker	
Waller, Priscilla, Miss	The Children's Society		Boarding Out Worker	1966–68
Wallis, Adeline, Miss	Mission of Hope for Children's Aid and Adoption		Welfare Worker	
Wallis, Janet, Mrs (nee McCall)	Mission of Hope for Children's Aid and Adoption		Founder & first Co-director	1858–28
Wallis, Ransome, Mr	Mission of Hope for Children's Aid and Adoption		First Co-director	
Walsh, Jenn, Ms	St Brigid's Adoption Society	Eire	Social Worker	
Walsh, May, Mrs	Blackburn Diocesan Adoption Agency		Senior Social Worker	1977–86
Walters, M, Mrs	Leicester Diocesan Board for Social Responsibility			
Wamphray, Miss	Haig Ferguson Memorial Home	Edinburgh	Matron	
Warburton, Richard	St Francis Children's Society			
Ward, B, Miss	Adopt Anglia, Project of Coram Adoption Society		Adoption Officer	From 1957
Ward, Miss	Ellen Carville	Waltham Forest		
Warne, G, Miss	Church of England	Rochester		1963
Warwick, Pat	Chester Diocesan Adoption Services			
Waterhouse, J W, Rev	National Children's Home		Principal	1950–69
Waterman, J, Miss	St Albans Adoption Society	W. Hertfordshire	Social Worker	1956–57
Watson, J M L, Miss	Church of England	Kensington Moral Welfare	Organising Secretary	1958
Watts, Margaret, Mrs	St Albans Adoption Society	N. Hertfordshire	Social Worker	1973–76
Watts, Miss	Church of England	Hampstead		1960
Waugh, Mrs	Avenel	Edinburgh	Matron	1978
Weaver, Miss	Beechwood, Westcliff-on-Sea	Essex	Assistant Superintendent	1969–73
Webb, Angela, Miss	The Children's Society		Boarding Out Worker	1966–69
Webb, Tony, Mr	The Children's Society		Foster Care Social Worker	1972–74
Welburn, Pat, Ms	Catholic Child Welfare Society (Diocese of Middlesbrough)		Principal Officer	

Where to find adoption records

Name of Worker	Organisation or Home	Area	Role	Date
Welfare, Patience	The Children's Society	Suffolk, Co Durham, Tyneside, Northumberland	Field Social Worker	1960s–70s
Wells, Elizabeth, Miss	The Children's Society		Adoptions Social Worker	1955–72
Westwood, Miss	Burnley & Nelson House of Help	Burnley	Moral Welfare Care Worker	1945–50s
Wheeler, S, Miss	Mansfield and District Association for Moral Welfare			1949–60
Whiffen, Miss	St Anne's Heywood	Manchester	Matron	1948–70
Whishaw, Constance, Mary	St Barnabas Home for Orphans, 19 Montpelier Crescent, New Brighton Sunny Bank Orphanage	Arnside, Cumbria	In Kelly's Director as 'Lady Superintendent' but appears to have owned both orphanages and is said to have arranged about 1000 adoptions pre-1926. Gave St Barnabas to the Children's Society probably about 1898. Not known what happened to Sunny Bank.	1906
White, Alison, Miss	The Children's Society		Case Worker	1974
White, Barbara, Mrs	The Children's Society	N. Region	Social Worker	1978–81
White, Dorothy, Mrs	Catholic Child Welfare (Diocese of Middlesbrough	Middlesbrough	Administrative Secretary	
White, Margaret, Mrs	St Albans Adoption Society	N. Bedfordshire	Social Worker	1974–77
White, Mrs	Baptist Union Adoption Society			
White, Mrs	Bartletts, Chelmsford	Essex	Superintendent	1970–71
White, Sheila, Mrs	Church of England	Harrow		1973–74
Whitear, Penelope, Miss	The Children's Society		Boarding Out Worker	1967–68
White-Franklin, Mrs	National Children Adoption Association		Social Worker	
Whitehead, Miss	Church of England	Islington		1963
Whitely, Joan, Mrs	St Albans Adoption Society	Watford & District	Social Worker	1976–77
Whitfield, Barbara, Miss	The Children's Society	Berkhamsted	Social Worker	1978–81
Whitworth, Susan, Miss	The Children's Society		Boarding Out Worker	1967–68
Whyte, Helen, Mrs	The Children's Society		Adoptions Social Worker	1966–71
Wickham, G, Mrs	The Children's Society		Boarding Out Worker	1947–67
Wiggin, P	The Children's Society	N. Region	Social Worker	1979–81

Name of Worker	Organisation or Home	Area	Role	Date
Wiggins, Susan, Mrs	The Children's Society		Boarding Out Worker	1970–71
Wilcox, Miss	The Girl's Hostel, Lancaster	Lancashire	Superintendent	1973–4
Wilding, Edith, Sister (later Mrs Innel)	10 Rutford Road and Hackney M&B Home	Lambeth		1974
Wileman, J, Miss	Church of England	Kensington		1960
Wilford, Miss	Church of England	Sutton	Superintendent Moral Welfare Worker	1961
Wilkens, Mrs	Lancashire & Cheshire Child Adoption Council		Case Secretary	1943–45
Wilkins, Jennifer, Mrs	The Children's Society		Adoptions Social Worker	1966–67
Wilkinson, D R, Mrs	Swansea & Brecon Diocesan Council for Social Work		Hon Secretary	1979
Willcox, Miss	Girl's Hostel, Queen Street, Lancaster			1948–70
Williams, Miss	Ellen Carville	Tower Hamlets		
Williams, V, Miss	Church of England	St Marylebone		1960
Williamson, Miss	Church of England	Battersea and NW6	Moral Welfare Worker	
Willis, Marion, Miss	The Children's Society		Adoptions Social Worker	1965–67
Willmott, P, Mrs	Family Care (Essex)	Redbridge Area		
Wilmot, Miss	Church of England	Redbridge		
Wilson, Bertha, Miss	St Albans Adoption Society	Watford & District	Social Worker	1939–63
Wilson, Ivy, Mrs	The Children's Society		Adoptions Social Worker	1952–77
Wilson, Miss	Carisbrooke (M&B Home)	Lambeth		1963
Wilson, Miss	Beechwood, Westcliff-on-Sea	Essex	Superintendent	1966–69
Wilson, Patricia, Miss	The Children's Society		Case Worker	1974
Wilson, Rodney, Mr	The Children's Society		Foster Care Social Worker	1972–73
Wilyna, Marie, Mrs	The Children's Society		Boarding Out Worker	1968–71
Windmuller, Ilse	Catholic Children's Rescue Society (Diocese of Salford) Inc		Social Worker	
Winfield, T, Mr	Catholic Children's Society	Arundel & Brighton, Portsmouth & Southwark		

Name of Worker	Organisation or Home	Area	Role	Date
Winston-Fox, Ruth, Mrs	Jewish Board of Guardians		May have arranged some private adoptions	
Wolton, James	The Children's Society		Boarding Out Worker	1967–69
Wood, B, Miss	Church of England	Westminster		1980s
Wood, N, Miss	Family Care (Essex)	Colchester area		
Woodruff, Anne, Ms	SSAFA – Forces Help		Director	
Woodruff, Mrs	Lancashire & Cheshire Child Adoption Council		Case Secretary	May 1975–October 1958
Woods, Bernard, Rev	Catholic Caring Services to Children & Community (Diocese of Lancaster)		Director	
Woods, Jennifer, Mrs	The Children's Society		Adoptions Social Worker	1966–72
Wooley, Kathryn, Miss	The Children's Society		Case Worker	1974
Woolvern, Janet, Mrs	The Children's Society		Adoptions Social Worker	1964–66
Worthington, Mr	Church of England	London W9		
Wrenn, Mrs	St Anne's Adoption Society	Eire	Social Worker	1955–late 1960s
Wright, Dr	9 Weymouth Street, London, W1		Known to be arranging private adoptions in 1969	
Wright, M, Miss	Church of England	St Marylebone		1960
Wright, Sister	St Agnes House	Hounslow	Matron	
Wyatt, Miss	Church of England	Hampstead and NW6	Moral Welfare Worker	
Yems, Elizabeth, Mrs	The Children's Society		Foster Care Social Worker	1972–74
Yes, J P, Mrs	Parents & Children Together		Administrative Secretary	
Young, K, Miss	St Faith's, Loughton	Essex	Assistant Superintendent	1975

6 • Social services/social work departments

Local Authority	Categories and Location	Availability	Notes	Enquiries to

ENGLAND

Categories of records:

(a) Guardian *ad litem* (G ad L) in England and Wales; curator *ad litem* (C ad L) in Scotland

(b) Adoption placements

(c) Children received from care

(d) Records received from other bodies

(e) Records passed to other local authorities

Local Authority	Categories and Location	Availability	Notes	Enquiries to
Barking & Dagenham LB Civic Centre Dagenham Essex RM10 7BN Fax: 020 8252 8606	(a) (b) (c) Central records	Some missing	Guardian *ad litem* records and adoption placement records moved to Essex (1948) and Barking Children's Department (1964)	Senior Manager
Barnet LB 1255 High Road London N20 9HZ Fax: 020 8359 4531	(a) (b) (c) (d) Central Office	Incomplete. Some destroyed by flood. Some records are microfilmed.	Some parts of Barnet / Southgate formerly in Hertfordshire, so worth trying Herts SSD. Middx. & LCC pre-1965 records held by London Metropolitan Archives d) Guildford House. London Diocesan Hostel.	Post Adoption Social Worker, Family Placements Team, 34 Woodhouse Road, London N12 9NG
Barnsley MBC Wellington House 36 Wellington Street Barnsley S70 1WA	(a) (b) (c), Central Office from 1972 to date. Pre-1972 records in departmental storage base.	Pre-1972 ex-West Riding CC, no records		The Director SSD
Bath & N.E. Somerset Housing and Social Services 7 North Parade Buildings Bath BA1 1NY Fax: 01225 477907	(a) held with Bristol SS Inspection Unit (b) (c) (d) (e) SSD Headquarters	Probably intact	Previously part of Avon. Became a Unitary Council 1 April 1996.	Team Manager, SSD Headquarters
Bedfordshire CC SSD County Hall Cauldwell Street Bedford MK42 9AP Fax: 01234 228128	(a) (b) (c) (d) Also hold step-parent adoption records SSD	(a) none pre-1948 (b) mainly post-1948 (c) post-1978 (d) all Luton records pre-1 April 1997. Accessed through Luton		The Team Leader, SSD, Adoption & Family Finding Team, Houghton Close, off Oliver Street, Ampthill MK45 2TG
Bexley LB Adoption and Fostering Team Bexley Council Howbury Centre Slade Green Road Erith Kent DA8 2HX Fax: 01322 351428	(a) (b) (c) Central Office	(a) and (b) Few destroyed by damp (c) intact		Team Leader, Adoption and Fostering Team

Local Authority	Categories and Location	Availability	Notes	Enquiries to
Birmingham MD SSD Louisa Ryland House 44 Newhall Street Birmingham B3 3PL	(a) (b) (c) (d) SSD	(a) (b) (c) Records held since 1950 only, some missing; (d) not known if any missing		Senior Social Worker (Central Resource Exchange)
Blackburn with Darwen BC SSD Jubilee House Jubilee Street Blackburn BB1 1ET	Pre-1 April 1998 records archived with Lancashire CC, Eastcliff offices, Preston. Post-1 April 1998 SSD (a) none held (b) (c) 1 April 1998 (d) none	All post-April 1998 intact. All records should be accessed through Adoption and Fostering Manager.	Previously part of Lancs. Became a Unitary Council 1 April 1998. Adoption registers held for wider Blackburn with Darwen region (some of Hyndburn) from 1989 – can assist in identifying location of records locally.	Adoption and Fostering Manager
Blackpool BC SSD Progress House Clifton Road Merton Blackpool FY4 4US Fax: 01253 477577	(a) none held (b) intact (c) intact	All pre-1 April 1999 records held by Lancs. CC. All post-1 April 1999 with Blackpool. All should be accessed through Blackpool.	Previously part of Lancs. Became a Unitary Council 1 April 1998.	Senior Practitioner Adoption Services
Bolton MB Le Mans Crescent Bolton BL1 1SA Fax: 01204 365 953	(a) (b) (c) Family Placement Unit, Woodlands, Manchester Road, Bolton BL3 2PQ	None lost or destroyed		Team Leader, Woodlands
Bournemouth BC 9 Madeira Road Lansdowne Bournemouth BH1 1QN Fax: 01202 535794	(a) (b) (c) Pre-1 April 1997 with Dorset CC Post-1 April 1997 SSD HQ	No records lost. Only records since April 1997 held.	Previously part of Dorset. Became a Unitary Council 1 April 1997	Team Manager, Family Placement Team, SSD HQ
Bracknell Forest BC Social Services and Housing Department Time Square Market Street Bracknell RG12 1JD	(a) (b) (c) (d) From 1 April 1992. Accessible through Family Placement Team, Time Square	(a) (b) (c) Berkshire Adoption and Advisory Service, York House, Sheet Street, Windsor, Berks. SL4 1DD Holds: (a) 1939–1968 (b) (c) pre-1992 Letters from birth relatives seeking contact. Access through Record Office, Time Square. Bracknell Court adoption records held by East Berkshire Magistrates' Court, The Law Courts, Chalvey Park, Slough, Berks, SL1 2HJ and some information might be available if main file lost. (Senior Legal Advisor)	Previously part of Berkshire. Became a Unitary Council 1 April 1998 but Berkshire Record Office and Berkshire Adoption Advisory Service continue to run on a county-wide basis. Record office, Reading Borough Council, Arts & Leisure Department, 9 Coley Avenue, Reading RG1 6AF. Has (1) Boarded out children 1941-48, (2) Children in cottage homes 1941–48.	Family Placement Team, Time Square

Local Authority	Categories and Location	Availability	Notes	Enquiries to
Bradford MDC Olicana House Chapel Street Bradford West Yorkshire BD1 5RE	(b) (c) (d) Adoption and Fostering Unit, Bradford SSD, Aire Building, 35 Saltaire Road, Shipley, West Yorkshire BD18 3HH	(b) (c) Many missing, especially from 1950s or earlier. Some still in area offices. Some not yet in alphabetical order. (d) Mostly on microfilm; only a few missing.	(d) Bradford Diocesan MW Council; SSD hold files for Queensbury area 1 April 1973–1 April 1975	Unit Manager (Adoption and Fostering) SSD HQ
Brent LB Triangle House 328–330 High Road Wembley Middlesex HA9 6AZ Fax: 020 8937 4520	(a) (b) (c) Family Placement Service HQ	(a) (b) (c) Not known if any lost or destroyed. From 1947 (some); from 1965 (all categories); (d) Card index for all legalised adoptions through National Adoption Society. Some early records of Western National Adoption Society destroyed in the Second World War.	Records held from 1947 appear to be adoption records of children in care. Other pre-1965 records held by the Archivist, London Metropolitan Archives (d) National Adoption Society and Western National Adoption Society.	Service Manager, Family Placement Service, SSD HQ
Brighton and Hove Council SSD Fostering and Adoption Team 253 Preston Road Brighton BN1 6SE Fax: 01273 295445	(a) (b) (c) (d) All records pre and post 1 April 1997 held at East Sussex Records Office	No accurate records before 1948; (d) Includes some information about children in some residential establishments	Previously part of East Sussex. Became a Unitary Council 1 April 1997. (d) Chichester Diocesan Association for Family Welfare Records at East Sussex County Record Office – access through East Sussex or Brighton and Hove.	Fostering and Adoption Team, 253 Preston Road, Brighton BN1 6SE
Bristol CC SSD PO Box 30 Amelia Court Pipe Lane Bristol BS99 7NB Fax: 0117 903 7841	(a) (b) (c) From 1948 in area offices	For adoption records, contact Adoption Records Clerk, Avondale Road, Redfield, Bristol. None lost or destroyed.	Previously part of Avon. Became a Unitary Council 1 April 1996. Some Avon records may now be in Bristol.	Other enquiries to: Planning and Development Manager (Adoption), PO Box 30, SSD HQ
Bromley LB Civic Centre Stockwell Close Bromley BR1 3UH Fax: 020 8464 3333	(a) (b) (c) (d) Department of SS and Housing, HQ	(a) From 1954; (b) From 1955 when agency set up – all records preserved; (c) Intact since 1948	(d) Kent CC gave Bromley records to the Borough in 1965 on reorganisation. Pre-1948 records had to be destroyed due to war damage.	Service Manager (Family Placements), Department of SS and Housing
Buckinghamshire CC County Hall Aylesbury Buckinghamshire HP20 1EZ	(a) (b) (c) SSD HQ	(a) Incomplete selection 1926–48. Complete from 1948; (b) Almost complete (c) Almost complete; some from pre-1948.	During a boundary reorganisation, part of Bucks became Berkshire but relevant files retained by Bucks. Milton Keynes became a Unitary Council 1 April 1997 but their records prior to that date remain with Bucks.	Adoption Adviser or Adoption Administrator
Bury MB SSD Castle Buildings Market Place Bury BL9 0LT Fax: 0161 253 5494	(a) (b) (c) 18/27 St Mary's Place	Some records lost/destroyed since 1926	Pre-1974, Bury was part of Lancashire but all records now with Bury.	Service Manager Family Placements, 18/20 St Mary's Place, Bury, Lancs. BL9 0DZ

Local Authority	Categories and Location	Availability	Notes	Enquiries to
Calderdale MB **Horsfall House** **Skircoat Moor Road,** **Halifax** **West Yorks HX3 0HJ**	(a) (c) (d) In local teams in Elland and Ovenden	Incomplete	Authority formed by linking old Borough of HaliFax: to outer area formerly administered by West Riding CC, including Brighouse, Elland, Shelf, Hebden Bridge, Sowerby Bridge, Ripponden, Todmorden. (d) Former West Riding records. West Riding records of adoptions for 1958–72 with Wakefield MD. Files for Queensbury area 1 April 1973–1 April 1955 with Bradford SSD.	Family Placement Team, Ovenden Hall, Ovenden Road, Ovenden, HaliFax: HX3 5QG Fax: 01422 323 287
Cambridgeshire CC **PO Box 9** **Shire Hall** **Castle Hill** **Cambridge CB3 0AP**	(a) (b) (c) (d) SSD and former County Offices	Incomplete Still holds Peterborough records which can be accessed through Peterborough or Cambridge	(b) Agency since 1967 (d) Ely Diocesan Moral Welfare Association Peterborough became a separate Unitary Authority 1 April 1998.	Homefinding, Buttsgrove Centre, 38 Buttsgrove Way, Huntingdon PE18 7LY and Homefinding, 18/20 Signet court, Swann's Road, Cambridge CB5 8LA
Camden LB **79 Camden Road** **London** **NW1 9ES** **Fax: 020 7413 6799**	(a) (b) (c) (d) 115 Wellesley Road, London NW5 4PA	Intact since beginning in 1965	(d) Spurgeon's Homes Adoption Society, Baptist Union Adoption Society. Records of Camden children adopted by foster parents previously in LCC (Div 2) care, 1960–64. Other records may be at London Metropolitan Archives.	Adoption Counsellor, Children and Families, 115 Wellesley Road
Cheshire CC **Room 353** **County Hall** **Chester** **CH1 1BW** **Fax: 01244 603815**	(a) (b) (c) (d) Some Northwich Guardians records from 1911 and some pre-1948 records with County Archivist 1950-70 SSD HQ 1970-onwards individual local offices	Records incomplete. Those of 1948/9 only in list form.	(d) Pre-1970 records for Warrington and Halton	The Administrator, SSD HQ
City of London **Milton Court** **Moor Lane** **London** **EC2Y 9BL** **Fax: 020 7588 9173**	(a) (c) SSD HQ	None lost or destroyed	Until April 1976, child care handled by Tower Hamlets (LCC area 5).	The Director, SSD
Cornwall CC **County Hall** **Station Road** **Truro** **TR1 3AU** **Fax: 01872 323817**	(a) (b) (c) (d) Adoption and Family Finding Unit, 13 Treyew Road, Truro TR1 2BY	(a) Patchy (b) Complete from 1948 (c) Patchy from 1948 (d) Patchy prior to 1950; fairly complete 1950–65	(d) Cornwall Social and Moral Welfare Association	Principal Officer, Adoption and Family Finding Unit

Local Authority	Categories and Location	Availability	Notes	Enquiries to
Coventry City Council SSD Civic Centre Coventry CV1 5RS Fax: 01203 833 501	(a) (b) SSD. (c) Recorded in Central Register (d) At St Faith's M&B Home, Warwick Road, Coventry. Access to records open to SS personnel.	(a) Available back to 1927 (b) Since 1971 (c) From 1948 at least	(d) St Faith's Adoption Society or St Faith's Shelter	Administrative Assistant (Family Placement Service), Stoke House, Lloyd Crescent, Wyken, Coventry CV1 5NY
Croydon LB SSD Taberner House Park Lane Croydon CR9 2BA	(a) (b) (c) SSD Adoption, Fostering and Leaving Care	Some gaps 1926-45. (d) Some brief information from 1927.	G ad l former Surrey area incorporated 1965. (d) Christian Family Concern.	Service Manager, Adoption, Fostering and Leaving Care, Council Offices, 130 Brighton Road, Purley, Surrey CR8 4HA Fax: 020 8645 9303
Cumbria CC 3 Victoria Place Carlisle Cumbria CA1 1EH Fax: 01228 607108	(a) (b) (c) (d) At appropriate district office (there are 6) or at HQ (mainly old Cumberland files)	Cumberland Registers from 1948, but some files missing. Pre-1948 records unlikely to be available, though mainly summarised before destruction. Some records of Cumberland Children's Department Adoption Agency.	(d) Carlisle Diocesan Family Welfare Association; records from Carlisle Diocesan Board for Social Responsibility	Principal Social Worker (Adoption)
Darlington BC Central House Gladstone Street Darlington DL3 6JX Fax: 01325 346 474	Some records from 1946. Currently being catalogued. All enquiries to Adoptions Officers.		Part of Durham until 1 April 1997	Adoptions Officers, Central House
Derby City Council SSD Middleton House 27 St Mary's Gate Derby DE1 3NV Fax: 01322 716922	(a) (b) (c) (d)	(a)(b) Derbyshire CC and Derby City 1926 or earlier – 1948 and 1974 – 1 April 1997 held by Derbyshire. 1950–74 and post-1 April 1997 held by Derby City	Became a Unitary Council 1 April 1997. (d) Derby Diocesan Council for SW Adoption Committee	Assistant Director, Children's Services
Derbyshire CC County Hall Matlock Derbyshire DE4 3AG Fax: 01629 772213	(a) (b) (c) (d) SSD HQ	(a) (b) Derbyshire CC from 1926 or earlier – present (b) Pre-1948 – Some Education Department records not transferred but information sometimes available	(d) Derby City records 1926 – 48 and 1974 – 1 April 1997	Adoption Manager, County Hall
Devon CC The Annexe County Hall Topsham Road Exeter EX2 4QR Fax: 01392 382363	(a) (b) (c) (d) SSD HQ	Intact but see notes	(a) Few records before 1948 (b) Records date from 1960 (d) Plymouth & District Association for Girl's Welfare	Adoption Services Manager, Adoption Unit, Foxhole, Dartington, Totnes TQ9 6EB

Local Authority	Categories and Location	Availability	Notes	Enquiries to
Doncaster MBC SSD PO Box 251 The Council House Doncaster S. Yorkshire DN1 3AG Fax: 01302 737857	(a) (b) (c) SSD HQ			Head of Services, Children & Families, SSD
Dorset CC SSD County Hall Colliton Park Dorchester DT1 1XJ Fax: 01305 224642	(a) (b) (c) (d) SSD HQ. All records microfilmed.	Some lost due to fire. Pre-1948 records (papers) from former Health Department held.	(d) St Gabriel's Adoption Society. Holds the pre-1 April 1997 records of Bournemouth and Poole. They were previously part of Dorset.	Adoption and Fostering Team, SSD, Acland Road, Dorchester, Dorset DT1 1SH
Dudley MB Ednam House 1 St James Road Dudley DY1 3JJ Fax: 01384 815865	(a) (b) (c) (d) (e) at Central Office Permanent Placement Team	(a) (b) (c) Incomplete before 1974 (e) Some records going back to 1926	(c) and (e) Some records / types (a) and (b) From and to Hereford, Worcs. and Staffs	Service Manager Permanent Placement Team
Durham CC County Hall Durham DH1 5UG Fax: 0191 383 3685	(a) At District Centres (b) At Adoption and Fostering Unit (c) At District Centres and Adoption and Fostering Unit (d) At Adoption and Fostering Unit.	Available from 1949 only	As result of boundary adjustments, relevant records passed to Gateshead, Sunderland, Tyneside and Cleveland SSDs and Darlington.	Operations Manager (Children Looked After), SSD County Hall
Ealing LB Acton Town Hall Winchester Street Acton London W3 6NE	(b) (c) Pre-1965 London Metropolitan Archives; post-1965 SSD	Not known if complete		Fostering and Adoption Service
East Riding of Yorkshire Council County Hall Beverley HU17 9BA Fax: 01482 883913	(a) (b) (c) (d) Family Placements Team, 31/31A Lairgate, Beverley HU17 8ET	(a) Not intact, pre 1949 records destroyed. (b) Only records from 1974 when Humberside began acting as agency. (c) Not intact – records kept since 1950. (d) Some records held for Hull area (1974–1996)	Previously part of Humberside. Became a Unitary Council 1 April 1996. As it was impossible to separate some records on the disaggregation of Humberside, Hull and East Riding, each have access to the ex-Humberside database of archive records and frequently consult re: location of files.	The Director of SS, Housing and Public Protection
East Sussex CC PO Box 5, County Hall, St Annes Crescent, Lewes, East Sussex BN7 1SW Fax: 01273 481261	(a) (b) (c) (d) SSD HQ	No accurate records before 1948. (d) Includes some information about children in some residential establishments.	(d) Chichester Diocesan Association for Family SW. Access through E. Sussex or Brighton & Hove.	Administration Assistant (Adoption)

Local Authority	Categories and Location	Availability	Notes	Enquiries to
Enfield LB Civic Centre Enfield EN1 3XL Fax: 020 8379 3928	(a) (b) (c) Southgate Town Hall		After reorganisation, relevant case files returned to Barnet, Haringey and Herts CC.	Assistant Director, Adoption & Fostering Team, Southgate Town Hall, Green Lanes, Palmers Green N13 4XD Fax: 020 8379 2882
Essex CC PO Box 297 County Hall Duke Street Chelmsford Essex CM1 1YS Fax: 01245 268 580	(a) (b) (c) (d) Essex Record Office, Wharf Road, Chelmsford CM2 6YT Accessed through Adoption Resource Centre	Intact from : (a) 1947 (b) 1960 (c) 1948 (d) Intact Microfilmed and on CD Rom	Relevant records passed to London Boroughs in 1965. Full lists kept. No information on pre-1948 records when adoption was dealt with by the Education Department, which has no records. (d) Family Care. Thurrock records pre-April 1998 and some Southend.	The Administrator, Adoption Resource Centre, SSD, Eckard House, Easton Road, Witham CM8 2DW For all records up to 1 April 1998
Gateshead MB Civic Centre Regent Street Gateshead NE8 1HH Fax: 0191 477 6544	(a) Prior to 1984 at SSD HQ. Post-1984 at Sunderland G ad L Unit, 3 The Esplanade, Sunderland (b) Family Placement Unit, Prince Consort Road (c)(d) SSD HQ	Records from August 1961 to present day.	(d) Relevant records of Durham CC areas.	Group Leader, Family Support Services, Council Offices, Prince Consort Road, Gateshead NE8 4HJ
Gloucestershire CC Bearland Wing Shire Hall Gloucester GL1 2TR Fax: 01452 425149	(a) (c) Shire Hall and Area Offices; (b) Gloucester Area Office; 3 Cocks Lane, Gloucester; (d)Shire Hall	All intact. No records pre-1947. Some information pre-1948 of children in care (old Public Assistance records).	As result of an earlier re-organisation relevant records passed to the then existing Avon. (d) Gloucester Diocesan Council for SW.	Adoption Panel Administrator, SSD Block 4, Shire Hall, Westgate St, Gloucester, GL1 2TR
Greenwich LB Nelson House 50 Wellington St London SE18 6PY Fax: 020 8921 3112	(a) (b) In adoption Section SSD. Old records in archives (c) In stores or archives (d)Maintained by information (e) Officer in Social Service's Social Work and Assessment division, Nelson House			Adoption Team, 147 Powis Street, Woolwich, SE18 6JL
Hackney LB 205 Morning Lane, London E9 6LG	(a) post-1965 Adoption & Fostering Unit (b) (c) 1948–65 London Metropolitan Archives	Prior to 1948 not known.		Principal Manager, Adoption & Fostering Unit
Halton BC Grosvenor House Halton Leas Runcorn WA7 1LE	(a) (b) (c) (d) SSD HQ	Complete as far as known.	Previously part of Cheshire. Became a Unitary Council 1 April 1998.	Operations Manager, Children's Resources, Grosvenor House
Hammersmith & Fulham LB 2nd Floor Barclay House Effie Road Fulham London SW6 1EN Fax: 020 8576 5078	(a) (b) (c)	Some lost since 1926.		Adoption Team SSD HQ

Local Authority	Categories and Location	Availability	Notes	Enquiries to
Hampshire CC Trafalgar House Winchester SO23 8UQ Fax: 01962 877 681 See also Southampton & Portsmouth	(a) (b) (c) (d) HQ	Not complete	1. Southampton & Portsmouth became Unitary Councils on 1 April 1997. Hants holds Southampton records pre-1 April 1997 & Portsmouth records pre-1 April 2000 but enquiries about these records should be made to the respective City Council. 2. As well as past Children's Department files & Hampshire files – the store includes: Portsmouth Diocesan Council for Social Responsibility; National Free Church Women's Council 1919-1937 (index cards); Winchester Diocesan Council for Social Responsibility; Some Southampton & Hampshire Education files (G ad L)	1. The relevant City Council 2. The Adoption Section SSD HQ
Haringey LB Housing & Social Services Grosvenor House 27 The Broadway Crouch End London N8 8DY Fax: 020 8862 1108	(a) (b) Family Placements Section SSD (c) Family Placements Section, Central Records Records 1 April 1964–31 March 1965 with Hounslow SSD	Some lost	Relevant area records of Middlesex Children's Department at London Metropolitan Archives	Team Leader, Permanency Team, Family Placement, 40 Cumberland Road, London N22 4SA
Harrow SSD Family Placement Unit 429–433 Pinner Road Harrow Middlesex HA1 4HN Fax: 020 8863 0236	(a) (b) (c) (d) Some in Civic Centre Archives	(b) Holds records from 1949. London Metropolitan Archives holds Middlesex CC records 1933–65 some of which may be adoption records.		Team Leader (Family Placement Unit) or London Metropolitan Archives
Hartlepool BC CRF Services 35 Avenue Road Hartlepool TS24 8HD Fax: 01429 523906	(a) (b) (c) (d) Located in secure conditions in a central facility in Hartlepool	(b) Since 1986 when the predecessor authority (Cleveland CC) became an adoption agency. A number of very slim files dating back to the 1960s exist for some parts of the Borough.	Prior to 1986, most adoptions arranged by Durham Diocesan Family Welfare Council which has extensive records.	Post Adoption Co-ordinator
Havering LB Midland House 109–113 Victoria Road Romford Essex RM1 2LX	(a) (b) (c) (d) SSD HQ	Incomplete	(d) Some former Essex CC	Team Leader, Resource & Placements Service, Midland House
Hereford Council c/o Children's Resource Team Moor House Widemarsh Common Hereford HR4 9NA	(a) (b) (e) (d) Pre 1 April 1998 microfiched records held in Worcester. Also some not microfiched. Post 1 April 1998 either in one of 3 area offices or in Hereford Record Office.	Some lost or destroyed	Previously part of Hereford & Worcester. Became a Unitary Council 1 April 1998. Where the C of E Dioceses of Hereford and Worcester were involved it would be worth contacting Hereford SSD as well as Worcester SSD.	Adoption Team Manager, Moor House

Local Authority	Categories and Location	Availability	Notes	Enquiries to
Hertfordshire CC County Hall Hertford SG13 8DP	(a) (b) (c) (d) Many records microfilmed		(d) The St Albans Council for SW acted as their agent from the mid-1950s. Herts CC now holds their records. 1954–57. Some individual case notes pre-1954 when adoptions referred to National Adoption Society, Baptist Union, or NCH.	Post Adoption Worker, Family Placement Team, 120 Victoria St, St Albans, AL1 3TG Fax: 01727 848993
Hillingdon LB Civic Centre High St Uxbridge UB8 1UW Fax: 01895 277456	(a) (b) (c) Permanency Team, Children's Resources, 855 Uxbridge Road, Hayes, Middx UB4 8HZ	Since 1976	Not an adoption agency before April 1976. Pre-1948 records at London Metropolitan Archives.	Team Manager, Permanency Team
Hounslow LB Civic Centre Lampton Road Hounslow Middx TW3 4DN	(a) (b) (c) SSD Family Placement Section, 26 Glenhurst Road, Brentford, Middx TW8 9BX Fax: 020 8862 6010	(a) None before 1948 (b) (c) Intact	Records of Middx agency placements 1962-65 at London Metropolitan Archives.	Principal Officer, Family Placement Section
Isle of Wight CC 17 Fairlee Road Newport Isle of Wight PO30 2EA Fax: 01983 524330	(a) (b) (c) (d) (e) Central Records SSD, held at Family Centre	(a) Some G ad L records (for other authorities) lost (b) Records 1950–1958 patchy (c) In some early cases where children were in care for some time before adoption, files have been lost (d) Welfare Supervision records from 1955 (e) Files (from other authorities) current in 1950s and 1960s have not always been returned.	Became a single Unitary Authority 1 April 1995.	Family Placement Team Manager, Sandown Neighbourhood Office, The Barrack Block, Broadway, Sandown, Isle of Wight PO36 9BS
Islington LB Family Placement Unit 29 Highbury New Park Islington N5 2EN Fax: 020 7704 8585	(a) At Highbury House, 5 Highbury Crescent, N5 1RW, Children & Families Administration Team (b) At Family Placement Unit (c) At Children & Families Team – dependent on address of client. Either N. Area, 102 Blackstock Road, N4 2BX or S. Area, 292 Essex Road, N1 3AZ. Central records accessed by one of above. (d) (e) either (a) (b) (c) depending on nature of record	Not known if complete		Permanent Family Placement Team Manager, Family Placement Services, 29 Highbury New Park, London N5 2EN
Kensington & Chelsea LB SSD Town Hall Hornton St W8 7NX	(a) (b) (c) Stored in the archives at Kensington Town Hall	Most records pre-1965 held by London Metropolitan Archives. Some scanty (a) & (b) in Kensington & Chelsea Archives 1950–1985.	Authority became an adoption agency in 1977.	Team Manager, Family Placement Unit, Westway Aid & Information Centre, 140 Ladbroke Grove, London W10 5ND Fax: 020 7598 4411

Local Authority	Categories and Location	Availability	Notes	Enquiries to
Kent CC Records Centre Door 34 Commercial Services Building Gibson Drive W. Malling Kent ME19 4QG	(a) (b) (c) (d) (e)	Some records lost since 1926. Full records 1950 onwards.	(d) Records of Canterbury and Rochester Board for Social Responsibility (e) London boroughs of Bexley and Bromley passed on after 1965.	NCH Post Adoption Service, 12 Romney Place, Maidstone, Kent, ME15 6LE
Kingston-upon-Hull CC Brunswick House Strand Close Beverley Road Hull HU2 9DB Fax: 01482 616111	(a) (b) (c) (d) SSD Brunswick House	From Hull Divisional Office intact From Beverley Divisional Office (a) Pre-1949 records destroyed; (b) Only acted as agency from 1974; (c) Not intact. Records kept from 1950. From Grimsby Division (a) (c) Records not intact; (b) Intact. From Scunthorpe division (a) (c) Records not intact; (b) Agency only since 1974.	Previously part of Humberside. Became a Unitary Council 1 April 1996. Records 1974–1996 (the Humberside years) can be traced via each new Unitary Authority. (d) Holds old records of neighbouring authority (e) Relevant records handed to Lincoln SSD (d) Holds some Lincoln Diocesan records 1971–74 (e) Scunthorpe's pre-1948 records of children in care are with Lincs SSD	The Director, SSD
Kingston-upon-Thames LB Guildhall I High Street Kingston-upon-Thames KT1 1EU Fax: 020 8547 6004	(a) (b) (c) (d) Adoption Archives Guildhall I	Some Surrey CC records from the 1950s & 1960s, but Surrey CC has retained most of their pre-1965 records		Team Manager, Family Placement Team
Kirklees MC 2 Oldgate Huddersfield W. Yorkshire HD1 6QF Fax: 01484 225360	(b) (c) (d) All accessed through Family Placement Unit	(e) Pre-1974 records of W. Riding CC passed to Wakefield MDC		The Unit Manager, Family Placement Unit
Knowsley MB Municipal Offices Archway Road Huyton, Liverpool L36 9UX Fax: 051 443 3670	(a) (b) (c) (d) Astley House, Astley Road, Huyton, Liverpool L36 8HY	Some lost	(d) Lancs CC passed on relevant records 1972	Team Manager, Adoption & Fostering Services
Lambeth LB Mary Seacole House 91 Clapham High Street London SW4 7TF Fax: 020 7926 4783	(a) BITS (Business Information Technology Services) (b) Permanency co-ordinator (c) Individual cases mainly in Head Offices. Earlier records not in area offices can be traced through BITS.	Pre-1948 records with London Metropolitan Archives. All subsequent records in Archives. Some lost since 1965.	Some pre-1965 records may have been passed to Lambeth (individual cases) in response to special requests. NB: G ad L records are usually condensed and may not contain all the desired details.	BITS (Business Information Technology Services) SSD HQ
Lancashire CC Social Services HQ PO Box 162 East Cliff County Offices Preston PR1 3EA	(a) From 1944 (b) From 1967 (c) (d) All held centrally (e) On reorganisation in 1974, some locally held records passed to new Local Authorities.	(a) Incomplete (b) Intact (c) Intact (e) Not known if complete	(d) Records of Preston CB & Burnley CB. Records of Blackpool CB & Blackburn CB up to 1 April 1998 (These should be accessed through the present authority) (a) (b) (c) Former Borough records held centrally.	The Adoption Services Manager, Social Services Directorate, SSD HQ Fax: 01772 264910

Local Authority	Categories and Location	Availability	Notes	Enquiries to
Leeds CC SSD Fostering & Adoption 3rd Floor West 110 Merrion House Merrion Centre Leeds LS2 8QB Fax: 0113 247 8874	(a) (b) (c) (d) SSD Adoption Office	(a) From 1963 (b) Register from 1943. Records from 1949. (c) Incomplete from 1940.	Private placements in Falloden Nursing Home	Team Leader, Fostering & Adoption, Merrion House
Leicester City SSD 1 Grey Friars Leicester LE1 5PH, Fax: 0116 2568243	Pre & post 1 April 1997 (a) 400 Thurston Road (b) Eagle House (c)	Incomplete	Leicester City & Rutland were part of Leicestershire until 1 April 1997 when they became Unitary Councils. Since then, one adoption team has covered all three services and all the records are kept at Eagle House.	(a) The Panel Administrator, 400 Thurcaston Road, Leicester LE4 2RD (b) Team Manager (Adoption), Eagle House, 11 Friar Lane, Leicester LE1 5RB
Leicestershire CC County Hall Glenfield Leicester LE3 8RA Fax: 0116 2657440	(a) (b) (c) (d) at Eagle House	Incomplete	(d) Leicester Diocesan Board for Social Responsibility. Since Leicester City & Rutland became Unitary Councils on 1 April 1997, one adoption team has covered three services and the records are kept at Eagle House.	Team Manager (Adoption), Eagle House, 11 Friar Lane, Leicester LE1 5RB
Lewisham LB Laurence House 1 Catford Road London SE6 4SW Fax: 020 8690 9924	(a) (b) (c) Fostering & Adoption Unit	(a) Records only since 1965. Earlier records London Metropolitan Archives (b) Since 1965 (c) All since 1965; pre-1965, either with Lewisham or LMA.		Service Unit Manager, Fostering & Adoption Unit, Hollydate, 43–45 Bromley Road, Catford, London SE6 2UA
Lincolnshire CC Wigford House Brayford Wharf East Lincoln LN5 7BH Fax: 01522 554 006	(a) (b) (c) (d) All records kept in Lincoln – some on electronic filing system.	Not known if complete – definitely gaps prior to 1950s	Before reorganisation in 1974, Lincs. was split into divisions called Lincoln, Kesteven, Holland & Lindsey. Parts of Lindsey became Humberside. This means that some North & N.E. Lincs. records prior to 1974 are held here. (d) Lincoln Diocesan Board for Social work or Moral Welfare.	Adoption Records Section, SSD
Liverpool City Council Social Services Directorate 26 Hatton Garden Liverpool L3 2AW	(a) (b) (c) (d) SSD HQ		(d) Lancashire & Cheshire Child Adoption Council from 1943 only. Some missing.	Team Manager Adoption
Luton BC SSD Unity House 111 Stuart Street Luton LU1 5NP Fax: 01582 547734	(a) (b) (c) from 1 April 1997 SSD HQ Pre-1 April 1997 Central Office Bedfordshire CC	(a) None pre-1948 (b) Mainly post-1948 (c) Post-1978	Previously part of Bedfordshire. Became a Unitary Council 1 April 1997.	Team Manager, Adoption & Permanent Family Placement Team

Local Authority	Categories and Location	Availability	Notes	Enquiries to
Manchester City of Town Hall PO Box 536 Manchester M60 2AF	(a) (b) (c) (d) SSD HQ		(d) Manchester & District Child Adoption Society & Manchester Diocesan Board for Social Responsibility	Senior Manager, Family Placement, SSD, 25 Rochdale Road, Manchester M9 1DD
Medway Council Compass Centre Pembroke Chatham Maritime Chatham ME4 4YH Fax: 01634 331200	(a) (b) (c) SSD HQ	Pre-1 April 1998 records held by Kent. Post 1 April 1998 records held by Medway. All normally accessed through Medway.	Previously part of Kent. On 1 April 1998, Rochester-upon-Medway & Gillingham combined to become one Unitary Council.	The Adoption Section, SSD HQ
Merton LB Civic Centre London Road Morden Surrey SM4 5DX	(a) (b) (c) (d) SSD HQ	Not known if any lost or destroyed, apart from some destroyed in fire in 1976. Some in-care records may be available.	(d) Some pre-1948 records received from Surrey: Haygarth Witts, M&B Home	Adoption & Fostering Officer, London Borough of Merton, Worsfold House, Church Road, Mitcham, Surrey CR4 3BE Fax: 020 8545 4203
Middlesbrough Council Sandringham House 170A Overdale Road Park End Middlesbrough TS3 7EA Fax: 01642 300 849	(a) (b) (c) (d)	(a) From 1950 (b) From 1986 (d) Adoption records of Stockton-on-Tees from 1986. These should be accessed through Middlesbrough.	Previously part of Cleveland. Became a Unitary Authority 1 April 1996.	Family Placement Team Manager, (Permanence) SSD HQ
Milton Keynes Council Neighbourhood Services The Conference Suite Cripps Lodge Resource Centre Broadlands Netherfield Milton Keynes MK6 4JJ Fax: 01908 254309	(a) (b)	(a) Bucks & Milton Keynes GALRO Service (b) Prior to 1 April 1997 in Bucks archives. Post-1 April 1997 in Milton Keynes.	Previously part of Bucks. Became a Unitary Council 1 April 1997	Team Manager Placements, Milton Keynes Council, Learning & Development Directorate, Saxon Court, Avebury Boulevard, Central Milton Keynes
Newcastle-upon-Tyne City of 3rd Floor Shieldfield Building 4-8 Clarence Walk Newcastle NE2 1AL	(a) (b) (c) SSD HQ		Some records from Tyneside MD, Northumberland County. (d) Northern Counties Adoption Society.	Administrative Officer (Adoption Unit), 1 St James Terrace, Newcastle-upon-Tyne NE1 4NE Fax: 0191 230 2823
Newham LB Broadway House 322 High Street Stratford London E15 1AJ	(a) (b) (c) SSD Family Placement Unit	No records pre-1945		Family Placement Unit (Adoption Team) & SSD HQ
Norfolk CC County Hall, Martineau Lane Norwich Norfolk NR1 2DH Fax: 01603 615557	(a) (b) (c) At Adoption & Family Finding Unit	Records incomplete pre-1948		Team Leader, Adoption & Family Finding Unit, 3 Unthank Road, Norwich NR2 2PA

Local Authority	Categories and Location	Availability	Notes	Enquiries to
Northamptonshire CC **John Dryden House** **The Lakes** **Northampton** **NN4 7DF** **Fax: 01604 237767**	(a) (b) (c) County, (a) (b) (c) Borough, SSD HQ	County: approximately 1963 onwards only. Borough: most intact from 1948 onwards. (a) Often possible to obtain a copy of report from County Court.		County Manager, Services to Children & Families
North East Lincolnshire **Council SSD** **Fryston House** **Grimsby** **DN20 9AN** **Fax: 01472 325470**	(a) (b) (c) (d) Held in Grimsby Archives. Access via N.E. Lincs. Fostering & Adoption Service, Carnforth Crescent, Grimsby DN34 5EF.	(a) (c) Records not intact. Some pre-1974 records with Lincolnshire.	Previously part of Humberside. Became a Unitary Council 1 April 1996. Holds some Lincolnshire CC records pre-1974 from Grimsby area. Also Grimsby area records from Humberside.	Principal Care Manager, Fostering & Adoption, Carnforth Crescent, Grimsby
North Lincolnshire **Council** **The Angel** **Market Place** **Brigg** **North Lincs** **DN20 8LD**	(a) (b) (c) (d) North Lincs Fostering & Adoption Team, The Grove, 38 West Street, Scawby, N. Lincs, DN20 9AN Fax: 01652 657 287 Records actually housed in N.E. Lincs archives, Grimsby but all access to N. Lincs records through N. Lincs.	From Scunthorpe Division (a) & (c). Records not intact. Some records from old Humberside Agency placements. N. Lincs Agency since 1996.	Previously part of Humberside. Became a Unitary Council 1 April 1996. (d) Holds some old records from neighbouring authority. (e) Relevant records handed to Lincoln SSD. (d) Holds some Lincoln Diocesan records from 1971–74. (e) Scunthorpe's pre 1948 records of children in care with Lincs SSD.	The Director, Social & Housing Services SSD H.Q.
North Somerset DC **Housing & Social** **Services Department** **PO Box 52** **Town Hall** **Weston-Super-Mare** **N. Somerset** **BS23 1ZY** **Fax: 01934 888 832**	(b) (c)	None lost or destroyed	Became a Unitary Council 1 April 1996 when Avon handed over all N. Somerset records.	Service Manager, Child Care Provider Services
North Tyneside Council **Children's Services** **Camden House** **Camden Street** **N. Shields** **Tyne & Wear** **NE30 1NW** **Fax: 0191 200 6089**	(a) (b) (c) County Archives (d)		(d) Records from Northumberland CC pre-1974 for Whitley Bay, N. Shields, Wallsend and Longbenton.	Team Manager, Family Placement Team
Northumberland CC **County Hall** **Morpeth** **Northumberland** **NE61 2EF**	(a) (b) (c) County Archives & Tweed House	Some pre-1948 may be lost.		Manager, Adoption & Fostering Team, Tweed House, Hepscott Park, Stannington, Morpeth, Northumberland NE61 6NF Fax: 01670 534 451

Local Authority	Categories and Location	Availability	Notes	Enquiries to
N. Yorkshire CC County Hall Northallerton N. Yorkshire DL7 8DD Fax: 01609 773 156	(b) (c) (d) SSD HQ including those of York, up to 1 April 1996	1984 onwards complete	(d) N. Riding 1926–48 (incomplete), 1948–74 (complete). York Adoption Soc, 1943–84 (complete). Four Deaneries Family Welfare Association (not itself on adoption agency). York records pre-1 April 1996	Adoption Section
Nottingham City Council 14 Handsgate Nottingham NG1 7BE	(a) (b) (c) The Lindens, 379 Woodbrough Road, Nottingham NG3 5GX Fax: 0115 977 2529	Pre-1 April 1998 records with Nottinghamshire CC and should be accessed through them. Post-1 April 1998 accessed through Nottingham City.	Previously part of Nottinghamshire. Became a Unitary Council 1 April 1998	Assistant Director, Children's Services, SSD HQ
Nottinghamshire CC County Hall West Bridgford Nottingham NG2 7QP	(a) (b) (c) SSD HQ including those of Nottingham City until 1 April 1998.	(a) (c) Incomplete (b)Intact Adoption section holds (b) of Nottingham City 1948 – 31 March 1998. Probably complete. Nottinghamshire CC records microfilmed but pre-1948 incomplete and poorly microfilmed. County records from 1943. City Juvenile Court records from 1948. County Juvenile Court records from 1975 owing to earlier fire.	Computer database covering all enquiries and searching for siblings/parents/children	Adoption Officer
Oldham MBC PO Box 22, Civic Centre, West Street, Oldham OL1 1UW	(a) (b) (c) (d) Central Records	(a) (c) Not known if complete (b) Intact	(d) Oldham Adoption Society	Family Placement Team, Children's Central Resources, Marian Walker House, Frederick St, Oldham OL8 1SW
Oxfordshire CC SSD County Hall New Road Oxford OX1 1ND	(a) (b) (c) (d) SSD HQ	Incomplete. Date from first adoption in 1931.	(d) Some early records from Oxford City & Berks.	Service Manager, Family Placement
Peterborough City Council Bayard Place Broadway Peterborough PE1 1FD	(a) (b) (c)	Pre-1 April 1998 records with Cambridgeshire CC. Access through Peterborough or Cambridgeshire Post-01/04/98 SSD HQ.	Previously part of Cambridgeshire. Became a Unitary Council 1 April 1998.	Service Manager, SSD HQ

Local Authority	Categories and Location	Availability	Notes	Enquiries to
Plymouth CC **Civic Centre** **Royal Parade** **Plymouth** **PL1 2AA**	(a) (b) (c) (d) Kept centrally	(a) None before 1948 (b) (c) Complete	Previously part of Devon. Became a Unitary Council 1 April 1998 (d) Plymouth & District Association for Girls' Welfare	Adoption Agency Manager, SSD HQ
Poole BC **Civic Centre** **Poole** **BH15 2RU**	(a) (b) (c) Pre-1 April 1997 records held by Dorset. Post-1 April 1997 records held by Poole		Previously part of Dorset. Became a Unitary Council 1 April 1997	For post 1 April 1997: Adoption & Fostering Team Manager, Children & Families, 14a Commercial Road, Poole BH14 0JW. For pre 1 April 1997: Adoption & Fostering Team, Dorset SSD, Acland Road, Dorchester, Dorset DT1 1SH
Portsmouth CC **Civic Offices** **Guildhall Square** **Portsmouth** **PO1 2EP** **Fax: 0239 284 1631**	(b) (c) (d) Pre-1 April 2000 records held by Hampshire Post-1 April 2000 records held by Portsmouth	All records, including Portsmouth Diocesan Council for Social Responsibility, accessed through Adoption Manager, Portsmouth	Previously part of Hampshire. Became a Unitary Council 1 April 1997. Became a separate adoption agency 1 April 2000.	Adoption Manager, Adoption Section
Reading BC SSD **Abbey Mill House** **Abbey Square** **Reading** **RG1 3BE**	(a) (b) (c) (d) From 1 April 1992 – accessible through Family Placement Team.	(a) (b) (c) Berkshire Adoption Advisory Service, York House, Sheet Street, Windsor, Berks. SL4 1DD, holds: (a) 1939–1968 (b) (c) pre-1992. Small number of papers (1927–41) of the pre 1974 Reading Borough which acted as an adoption agency until 1950. Letters from birth relatives seeking contact. Accessible through Record Officer, Abbey Mill House.	Previously part of Berkshire. Became a Unitary Council 1 April 1998 but Berkshire Record Office & Berkshire Adoption Advisory Service continue to run on a county-wide basis. Record Office, Reading Borough Council, Arts & Leisure Department, 9 Coley Avenue, Reading RG1 6AF. Has Public Assistance Registers of: 1) Boarded out children 1941–48 2) Children in Cottage Homes 1941–48	Family Placement Team, Abbey Mill House
Redbridge LB **Fostering & Adoption Service** **235 Grove Road** **Chadwell Heath** **Romford** **Essex** **RM6 4XD,** **Fax: 020 8503 8072**	(b) (c) Active cases with SW Service; Adolescent Service; or Children with Disability Service. Closed cases – Fostering & Adoption Service.	Not known if complete. Some pre-1948 records held, but some possibly destroyed.	At re-organisation in 1965, all relevant records passed on by Essex CC.	Head of Service, Children & Families

Local Authority	Categories and Location	Availability	Notes	Enquiries to
Redcar & Cleveland BC **Council Offices** **Kirkleatham Street** **Redcar** **Cleveland**	(a) From 1950 (b) From 1986 when Cleveland became adoption agency.		Previously part of Cleveland. Became a Unitary Council 1 April 1996.	Child Placement Team Manager, SSD, Grosmont Resource Centre, 20 Grosmont Close, Redcar TS10 4PJ Fax: 01642 491630
Richmond-upon-Thames **LB** **42 York Street** **Twickenham** **Middlesex** **TW1 3BW** **Fax: 020 8891 7719**	(a) (b) (c) Before April 1980 at SSD, Hounslow where Richmond had joint agency arrangements. Departmental Archives from April 1980.	Intact as far as Richmond records concerned.	Borough was formed from parts of old Surrey CC and Middlesex CC, pre-1965 Surrey records remain with Surrey SSD. Records for Middlesex CC kept in Richmond Archives. Pre-1948: the Borough holds a few records mainly of Middlesex adoptions.	Team Manager or Team Clerk, Adoption and Fostering Team
Rochdale MBC **PO Box 67** **Smith Street** **Rochdale** **Lancs** **OL16 1YQ**	(a) GALRO Panel – now CAFCASS (b) (c) Active cases with Area Teams closed with Family Placement Team	(a) (c) Prior to 1974 some lost or destroyed – see notes. After 1974 intact. (b) Intact	Department holds records of Lancs CC before reorganisation, of which some destroyed by flood	Family Placement Team Manager, Foxholes House, Foxholes Road, Rochdale, Lancs. OL12 0ED Fax: 01706 715033
Rotherham MB **Crinoline House** **Effingham Square** **Rotherham** **S65 1AW**	(a) Central Office from 1950 (b) Central Office from 1984 (c) Area & Central Offices	Incomplete	Area extended under reorganisation but records of old West Riding CC not available.	Family Care Unit, Brooklands, Doncaster Road, Rotherham S65 1NN Fax: 01709 828561
Rutland Council **SS & Housing** **Department** **Catmose** **Oakham** **LE15 6HP** **Fax: 01572 758398**	(a) 400 Thurston Road (b) Eagle House (c) SSD (d) Pre and post 1 April 1997	Incomplete	Previously part of Leicestershire – became a Unitary Council 1 April 1997. Since then, one adoption team has covered Leicestershire, Leicester City & Rutland and all adoption records are kept at Eagle House.	Team Manager (Adoption), Eagle House, 11 Friar Lane, LE1 5RB
St Helens MBC **SSD** **The Gamble Building** **Victoria Square** **St Helens** **WA10 1DY**	(a) (b) (c) (d)		(d) Some relevant records from Lancs. CC	Team Manager Adoption & Foster Care Service, 73–75 Corporation Street, St Helens WA10 1SX Fax: 01744 611 550
Salford MB **Crompton House** **100 Chorley Road** **Swinton** **Manchester** **M27 2BP** **Fax: 0161 790 4892**	(a) (c) SSD HQ (b) Family Placement Team	(a) (c) Some lost since 1926. (b) None prior to 1948.	(a) (c) Some records with Lancs. CC, covering Eccles, Worsley, Swinton, Irlam (b) Records patchy 1948–55	(a) (c) Assistant Director Children's Services Division (b) Family Placement from Salford Team, Avon House, Avon Close, Little Hulton, Salford M28 0LA

Local Authority	Categories and Location	Availability	Notes	Enquiries to
Sandwell MBC Department of Social Inclusion & Health First Floor Kingston House 438 High Street West Bromwich B70 9LD	(a) Pre-1948 Central Office (b) Homefinding Team (c) Hollies Family Centre, Coopers Lane, Smethwick, Warley, W. Midlands B67 7DW Fax: 0121 569 5588	Intact. Microfilmed.	Warley and West Bromwich merged to become Sandwell MB.	Team Manager (Homefinding), Hollies Family Centre
Sefton MB Merton House Stanley Road Bootle Merseyside L20 3UU	(a) Central Office, or Area Office at Bootle and Southport back to 1948 (b) Central Office and Master Register of Adoptions for Lancs Div 2 (c) Mainly area offices since 1980; some at Central Office	(a) No information about adoptions 1926–48/49 (b) Some files missing but may be with Lancs CC	Borough formed from Bootle CB, Lancs Div and Southport CB. Master Adoption Register identifies cases and destination of files passed on in 1971 (mostly to Skelmersdale Area Office of Lancs CC).	Team Manager, Adoption/Permanence, Connolly House, 47 Balliol Road, Bootle, Merseyside L20 9AA
Sheffield MBC Redvers House Union Street Sheffield S1 2JQ Fax: 0114 273 4981	(b) (c) (d) (e) (a) South Yorkshire GALRO Panel, 34 Godstone Road, Rotherham S60 2PU	Some lost	(d) Sheffield & District Child Adoption Association	Family Placement Service, Sheffield City Council, 2nd Floor Castle Market Buildings, Exchange St, Sheffield S1 2AH
Shropshire CC The Shirehall Abbey Foregate Shrewsbury SY2 6ND	(a) (b) Observer House (c) Director of Health & Social Care, Shropshire CC, The Shirehall	(a) (b) Accessed through Service Manager (c) Accessed through Director of Health & Social Care, The Shirehall	Joint Adoption Service with Telford & Wrekin which were part of Shropshire until 1 April 1998	Service Manager, Joint Adoption Service, Observer House, Holywell Street, Abbey Foregate, Shrewsbury SY2 6BL Fax: 01743 248 639
Slough BC Town Hall Bath Road Slough SL1 3UQ	(a) (b) (c) (d) From 1 April 1992, Accessible through Family Placement Team HQ	(a) (b) (c) Berkshire Adoption & Advisory Service, York House, Sheet Street, Windsor, Berks SL4 1DD Holds: (a) 1939–68 (b) (c) pre-1992 Letters from birth relatives seeking contact. Accessible through Record Officer, HQ. Court copies of Slough adoption files held by East Berkshire Magistrates' Court, The Law Courts, Chalvey Park, Slough, Berks, SL1 2HJ and some information might be available if main file lost (Senior Legal Advisor).	Became part of Berkshire 1 April 1974. Became a Unitary Council 1 April 1998 but Berkshire Record Office and Berkshire Adoption Advisory Service continue to run on a county-wide basis. Record Office, Reading Borough Council, Arts & Leisure Department, 9 Coley Avenue, Reading RG1 6AF. Has Public Assistance Registers of: 1) Boarded out children 1941–48 2) Children in Cottage Homes 1941–48	Family Placement Team, HQ

Local Authority	Categories and Location	Availability	Notes	Enquiries to
Solihull MBC PO Box 32 Council House Solihull West Midlands B91 3QY Fax: 0121 704 8238	(a) (b) (c) (d) SSD HQ		(d) Some records of Warwickshire CC	Information & Assistant Manager, Social Services
Somerset CC County Hall, Taunton, Somerset TA1 4DY	(a) (b) (c) SSD HQ		Some pre-1973 records may still be in Bristol	Adoptions Co-ordinator, County Hall Fax: 01823 355156
Southampton City Council Civic Centre Southampton SO14 7NB	(a) (b) (c) Stored locally	Pre-1 April 1997 records with Hampshire but accessed through Southampton. Post-1 April 1997 with Southampton	Previously part of Hampshire. Became a Unitary Council 1 April 1997.	Permanence Team, 399 Hinkter Road, Thornhill, Southampton S019 6DS Likely to move Present tel: 02380 446450 Fax: 02380 438535
Southend-on-Sea BC SSD PO Box 59 Queensway House Essex Street Southend-on-Sea SS2 5TB Fax: 01702 613509	(a) G ad L services provided by a consortium (Southend, Thurrock & Essex) at GALRO Panel, PO Box 3591, 66–8 Duke Street, Chelmsford EM1 6JT (b) (c) From 1 April 1998	Pre-1 April 1998 records held by Essex Post-1 April 1998 SSD HQ	Previously part of Essex. Became a Unitary Council 1 April 1998.	The Manager, Adoption & Fostering Team, 283 London Road, Westcliff SS0 7BX
Southwark LB Mabel Goldwin House 49 Grange Walk London SE1 3DY	(a) (b) (c) Adoption and Fostering Unit	Not known if complete	Some pre-1965 records at Southwark, some held by London Metropolitan Archives.	Business Resource Manager, Children's Direct Services, Adoption & Fostering Unit, 47B East Dulwich Road, London SE22 9BZ Fax: 020 7525 4484
South Tyneside MBC SSD South Tyneside House Westoe Road S. Shields Tyne & Wear NE33 3RL Fax: 0191 427 9704	(a) (b) (c) SSD HQ	Incomplete records from 1948	Some pre-1974 records for Jarrow, Hebburn & Boldon with Durham SSD. Minimum records with a Sunderland connection possibly held there.	The Director
Staffordshire CC St Chad's Place Stafford ST16 2LR Fax: 01785 277 004	(a) (b) (c) (d) SSD HQ Including records of Stoke-on-Trent up to 1 April 1997	Some lost or destroyed	Some movement of records on 1974 re-organisation including Stoke-on-Trent (d) Burton-upon-Trent Association for the Protection of Girls Lichfield Diocesan Association for Family Care	Principal Child Care Manager, Family Placement
Stockport MB SSD Ponsonby House Edward Street Stockport SK1 3UR Fax: 0161 474 7895	(a) (b) (c) SSD HQ	(a) Intact, but records only go back to 1950 (b) Some, back to 1955 (c) Incomplete		Principal Assistant Children's Services

Social services departments

Local Authority	Categories and Location	Availability	Notes	Enquiries to
Stockton-on-Tees BC SSD Billingham Council Offices Town Centre Billingham TS23 2LW Fax: 01642 397147	(a) (b) (c) (d) Pre-1 April 1996 Middlesborough SSD, Sandringham House, Overdale Road, Middlesborough Post-1 April 1996 Area Offices		Previously part of Cleveland. Became a Unitary Council 1 April 1996.	Child Placement Team
Stoke-on-Trent CC Civic Centre Glebe Street Stoke-on-Trent ST4 1RJ	(a) (b) (c) (a) Accessed through Stoke-on-Trent from 1 April 1997	(a) Up to 1 April 1997 (Incomplete) accessed through Staffordshire (b) (c) 1948–74 accessed through Stoke-on-Trent 1974–91 April 1997 accessed through Staffordshire	Previously part of Staffordshire. Became a Unitary Council 1 April 1997.	The Team Manager Family Placement Services, Grove Road, Fenton, Stoke-on-Trent ST4 3AY
Suffolk CC St Pauls House, County Hall, Ipswich IP4 1LH Fax: 01473 583402	(a) Divisional offices or County Archivist (b) (c) Before 1974 at Shire Hall, Bury St Edmunds, or County Hall, Ipswich	Probably not complete	The present County comprises former E. Suffolk and W. Suffolk, and Ipswich County Borough	County Adoption and Fostering Officer
Sunderland MD SSD HQ 50 Fawcett St Sunderland SR1 1RF, Fax: 0191 553 7254	(a) (b) Fostering and Adoption Unit, HQ (c) Fostering and Adoption Unit, HQ or Area offices	Some lost		Fostering & Adoption Team, Penshaw House, Station Road, Penshaw, Houghton Le Spring DH4 7LB
Surrey CC A.C. Court High Street Thames Ditton Surrey KT7 0QA Fax: 020 8541 9654	(a)(b) (c) Archives (e)	Some lost since 1926	(e) LBs of Croydon, Richmond, Merton, Kingston, Sutton and Wandsworth records passed on.	County Permanency Team, Belair House, Chertsey Boulevard, Hanworth Lane, Chertsey, Surrey KT16 9JX
Sutton LB The Lodge Holywood Walk Carshalton Surrey SM5 3PB	(a) (c) (d) SSD HQ	All records kept from 1 April 1965 (d) Some records from Surrey CC from 1948.		Adoption & Fostering Team HQ
Swindon BC Housing & SSD Civic Annexe Euclid Street Swindon SN1 2JH Fax: 01793 465866	(a) (b) (c) (a) Civic Offices (b) (c) Clarence House, Clarence St, Swindon SN1 2JH	(b) Pre-1 April 1997 files held by Wiltshire CC, County Hall, Trowbridge BA14 8LE. All access through Swindon.	Previously part of Wiltshire. Became a Unitary Council 1 April 1997.	Written application to: The Head of Children & Families Services, SSD HQ
Tameside MB Council Offices, Wellington Road, Ashton-under-Lyne, Lancs OL6 6DL Fax: 0161 342 3793	(a) (b) (c) (d) HQ, Dukinfield Town Hall and West End Office	Pre-1974 may be incomplete owing to reorganisation.	(d) Holds records of former Lancs CC areas of Audenshaw, Denton, Droylesden, Ashton-under-Lyne, Mossley; Ashton-under-Lyne Adoption Society.	Service Unit Manager

Local Authority	Categories and Location	Availability	Notes	Enquiries to
Thurrock Council SSD **PO Box 140** **Civic Offices** **New Road** **Grays** **Thurrock** **Essex** **RM17 6TJ**	(a) (b) (c) SSD HQ	Pre-1 April 1998 records held by Essex but accessed through Thurrock. Post-1 April 1998 held by Thurrock.	Previously part of Essex. Thurrock became a Unitary Council on 1 April 1998.	The Manager, Family Placement Team, SSD HQ
Torbay BC **Social Services** **Directorate** **Oldway Mansion** **Torquay Road** **Paignton** **Devon** **TQ3 2TS** **Fax: 01803 208 406**	(a) (b) (c) (d) (e) Pre-1 April 1998 Devon SSD HQ Post-1 April 1998 Torbay SSD HQ	Intact, but see notes	Previously part of Devonshire. Became a Unitary Council 1 April 1998. No records before 1998 held by Torbay.	Child Care Officer, SSD HQ
Tower Hamlets LB **62 Roman Road** **Bethnal Green** **London** **E2 0QJ** **Fax: 020 7364 2277 or 2265**	(a) (b) (c) (d) Pre-1965 London Metropolitan Archives. Post-1965 SSD HQ.	Some destroyed		Team Manager, Permanent Placements, SSD HQ
Trafford MBC **Town Hall** **Talbot Road** **Stretford** **Manchester** **M32 OTH** **Fax: 0161 912 5027**	(b) (c) Adoption & Permanency Team, Stretford Public Hall, Chester Road, Stretford, Manchester M32 0LG		Before 1974 Trafford did not exist and work was done by old Lancs. & Cheshire Counties	Team Manager, Adoption & Permanency Team
Wakefield MB **8 St John's North** **Wakefield** **WF1 3QA** **Fax: 01924 307792**	(a) Guardian *ad litem* Unit, Wakefield & Kirklees GALRO Panel, PO Box 456, Dewsbury WF12 8ZX (b) Family Placement Manager (c) (d) Central Office (e) Files from 1971–1974 passed to appropriate authorities	(a) Some destroyed since 1926 (b) Intact (c) (d) (e) Some destroyed	W. Riding adoption records 1958–1972 held by Wakefield MB. Records of former Wakefield City Authority. (d) The Haven for Moral Welfare.	The Adoption Officer Family Placement Team, Children's Centre, 6 Springfield Grange, Flanshaw, Wakefield WF2 9QT
Walsall MBC Civic **Centre Darwall Street** **Walsall** **WS1 1RG**	(a) (b) (c) Family Placement Services Willenhall	(a) (b) (c) From 1950	Staffs CC still holds records of that part of present Walsall area which belonged to Staffs until 1974.	Team Manager (Permanence), Family Placement Services, SSD, 106 Essington Road, New Invention, Willenhall WV12 5DT Fax: 01922 646350
Waltham Forest LB **SSD** **Municipal Offices** **High Road** **Leyton** **London** **E10 5QJ**	(a) (b) After 1984 only (c) (d) Children's Placement Unit	(a) Records 1935–1948 (b) (c) Probably not intact, possibly destroyed in a flood in late 1960s (d) Not known if any are missing	No information on what Waltham Forest should have. Some records accidentally destroyed under old Adoption Law of retention for 25 years only. Not an adoption agency until 1984, files intact since then.	Adoption Administrator, SSD, Children's Placement Unit, Graylaw House, 394 High Road, Leyton, London E10 6QE Fax: 020 8539 8776

Local Authority	Categories and Location	Availability	Notes	Enquiries to
Wandsworth LB **Welbeck House** **Wandsworth High Street** **London** **SW18 2PU** Fax: 020 8871 8550	(a) (c) Pre-1965 London Metropolitan Archives Post-1965 Adoption & Fostering Unit (b) Adoption & Fostering Unit (e)	Intact	(e) Some records dating between 1948–1965 to Lambeth as result of reorganisation. Pre-1948 records, probably with London Metropolitan Archives.	Unit Manager, Adoption & Fostering Unit, 4th Floor, Welbeck House
Warrington BC **SS** **Bewsey Old School** **Lockton Lane** **Warrington** **WA5 5BF**	(a) (b) SSD HQ (c) Might be with Warrington, Cheshire or Wirral. Access through Warrington.	Almost complete	Previously part of Cheshire. Became a Unitary Council 1 April 1998.	Team Manager, Family Placement Team, SSD HQ
Warwickshire CC **PO Box 48, Shire Hall,** **Warwick CV34 4RD** Fax: 01926 412799	(a) (b) (c) General Office SSD	No records prior to 1948. Intact from 1948.		Head of Children's Services
West Berkshire DC **SSD** **Pelican House** **9–15 West Street** **Newbury** **RG14 1PL**	(a) (b) (c) (d) From 1 April 1992 accessible through Family Placement Team	(a) (b) (c) Berkshire Adoption & Advisory Service, York House, Sheet Street, Windsor, Berks SL4 1DD holds: (a) 1939–1968 (b) (c) Pre 1992 Letters from birth relatives seeking contact. Accessible through Record Officer, Pelican House.	Previously part of Berkshire. Became a Unitary Council 1 April 1998 but Berkshire Record Office & Berkshire Adoption Advisory Service continue to run on a county-wide basis. Record Office, Reading Borough Council, Arts & Leisure Department, 9 Coley Avenue, Reading RG1 6AF has: 1) Boarded out children 1941–48 2) Children in Cottage Homes 1941–48	Family Placement Team, SSD, Pelican House
Westminster LB **City Hall,** **Victoria Street,** **London** **SW1E 6QP** Fax: 0207 641 2249	(a) (b) (c) (d) SSD HQ	(a) (b) (c) None destroyed since 1965 when Westminster CC established. (d) Many up to mid-1940s lost in Second World War.	(d) National Children Adoption Association	Family Placement Unit
W. Sussex CC **County Hall,** **Tower Street,** **Chichester** **PO19 1QT** Fax: 01243 777100	(a) (b) (c) (d) SSD HQ	(a) Resisters and documents from 1939 (b) Since 1985 (c) Records at least from 1948 (d) Worthing Borough Register of names 1927–48. No documents.		Service Manager, Family Placements, Bognor Regis Health Centre, West Street, Bognor Regis, W. Sussex PO21 1UT
Wigan MBC SSD **Civic Centre** **Millgate** **Wigan** **WN1 1AZ** Fax: 01942 404113	(a) (b) (c) Enquiries to Ribble Road	Nothing known of pre-1948 files	Wigan now includes many areas of old Lancs, files being split up about 1971–72.	Resource Manager Family Placement, SSD, 80 Ribble Road, Platt Bridge, Wigan WN2 5EW
Wiltshire CC **SSD County Hall** **Trowbridge** **BA14 8JQ**	(a) (b) (c) County Hall	Written requests please	Records include those of Swindon pre-11 April 1997. Accessed through Swindon.	Assistant Director, Children & Families

Local Authority	Categories and Location	Availability	Notes	Enquiries to
Windsor & Maidenhead (Royal Borough of) Maidenhead Town Hall St Ives Road Maidenhead SL6 1RF Fax: 01628 796672	(a) (b) (c) (d) From 1 April 1992. Accessible through Family Placement Team, 4 Marlow Road	(a) (b) (c) Berkshire Adoption & Advisory Service, York House, Sheet Street, Windsor, Berks. SL4 1DD holds : (a) 1939–1968 (b) (c) Pre-1992 Letters from birth relatives seeking contact.\n\nAccessible through Record Officer, 4 Marlow Road	Previously part of Berkshire. Became a Unitary Council 1 April 1998 but previously part of Berkshire. Became a Unitary Council 1 April 1998 but Berkshire Record Office & Berkshire Adoption Advisory Service continue to run on a county-wide basis. Record Office, Reading Borough Council, Arts & Leisure Department, 9 Coley Avenue, Reading RG1 6AF has: 1) Boarded out children 1941–48 2) Children in Cottage Homes 1941–48\n\nWindsor & Maidenhead Petty Sessional Divisions' adoption records are held by East Berkshire Magistrates' Court, The Law Courts, Chalvey Park, Slough, Berks, SL1 2HJ and some information might be available if main file lost (Senior Legal Advisor).	Family Placement Team, 4 Marlow Road, Maidenhead SL6 7YR
Wirral MB SSD 63 Hamilton Square Birkenhead Wirral CH41 5JF Fax: 0151 666 3603	(b) (c) (d) (e) Held centrally at Conway Building	Records from 1945. Sparse between 1945 and early 50s.	The present Authority is an amalgamation of former Wallasey & Birkenhead Borough Councils & part of Cheshire County Council (circa mid 70s). Some listings are held of records held by Cheshire County Council, Lancashire & Cheshire Child Adoption Council.	The Adoption Team Manager, Conway Building, Conway Street, Birkenhead, Wirral CH41 6LA
Wokingham DC Community Services Wellington House Wellington Road Wokingham RG40 2QB	(a) (b) (c) (d) From 1 April 1992. Accessible through Family Placement Team, Wellington House.	(a) (b) (c) Berkshire Adoption & Advisory Service, York House, Sheet Street, Windsor, Berks. SL4 1DD holds: (a) 1939–1968 (b) (c) Pre-1992 Letters from birth relatives seeking contact. Accessible through Record Officer, Community Service, Lytham Court, Lytham Road, Woodley RG5 3PQ.	Previously part of Berkshire. Became a Unitary Council 1 April 1998 but Berkshire Record Office & Berkshire Adoption Advisory Service continue to run on a county wide basis. Record Office, Reading Borough Council, Arts & Leisure Department, 9 Coley Avenue, Reading RG1 6AF has: 1) Boarded out children 1941–48 2) Children in Cottage Homes 1941–48	Family Placement Team, Wellington House
Wolverhampton MD Civic Centre St Peter's Square Wolverhampton WV1 1RT	(a) (b) (c) (d) Adoption Agency Children's Services	Some destroyed	(d) Five files only of Lichfield Diocesan Association; remainder with Staffordshire SSD.	Children's Services Manager, 66 Mount Pleasant, Wolverhampton WV14 7PR

Social services departments

Local Authority	Categories and Location	Availability	Notes	Enquiries to
Worcestershire CC County Hall Spetchley Road Worcester WR5 2NP Fax: 01905 766 982	(a) (b) (c) (d) SSD HQ	All enquiries for Hereford & Worcester 1 April 1974 – 31 March 1998 to Worcester in first instance. All Worcester enquiries pre-1974 & post-31 March 1998 to Worcester. Some older records lost or destroyed.	Previously part of Hereford & Worcester. Hereford became a Unitary Council 1 April 1998. (d) Worcester Diocesan Association for MW Work	Principal Officer (Adoption), The Pines, Bilford Road, Worcester WR3 8PU
Wrekin (The) Council SSD Darby House PO Box 214 Telford TF3 4LE Fax: 01952 200519	(a) (b) Observer House		Previously part of Shropshire. Became a Unitary Council 1 April 1998 but retained a joint adoption service with Shropshire.	Service Manager, Joint Adoption Service, Observer House, Holywell Street, Abbey Foregate, Shrewsbury SY2 6BL Fax: 01743 248 639
City of York Council Children's Services Hollycroft Wenlock Terrace Fulford Road York YO10 4DU Fax: 01904 555 305	(a) (b) (c) Pre-1 April 1996. Archived with N. Yorkshire CC. Post-1 April 1996 SSD.			Placement Services, Hollycroft

SCOTLAND

In Scotland Curator *ad Litem* (C ad L) reports are often kept with Court records.

Aberdeen City Council SWD, 4 Albyn Place Aberdeen AB10 1YH Fax: 01224 620580	(a) (b) (c) SWD		Previously part of Grampian region. Became a Unitary Council on 1 April 1996.	The Manager, Children's Services, SWD, St Nicholas House, Broad Street, Aberdeen AB10 1EZ
Aberdeenshire Council Aberdeenshire Social Work Woodhill House Westburn Road Aberdeen AB16 5GB Fax: 01224 664992	(a)(b) (c). Many pre-1975 records are held by Aberdeen City Council although accessed through Aberdeenshire Council. Post-1975 records held in North, Central and South Aberdeenshire.	(a) Reports for Stovehaven area (formerly Kincardineshire) & Curator reports done by Probation Service destroyed but certain records back to 1930 still available. (b) (c) Some destroyed but in some areas still available. Some areas have complete records going back to 1930. Most records available from 1958.	Aberdeenshire part of the former Grampian Regional Council with Aberdeen City & Moray Councils; became a Unitary Council on 1 April 1996. It includes Banff/Buchan; Formartine; Garioch; Kincardine and Mearns and Marr and comprises the Grampian. Regional Council (1975–96) divisions of Banff/Buchan, Gordon and Kincardine and Deeside. (d) Voluntary Service, Aberdeen.	(1) Senior Social Worker (Fostering & Adoption North), Seafield House, 37 Castle St, Banff AB45 1DQ (2) Senior Social Worker (Fostering & Adoption Central), The Day Care Centre, Port Road, Inverurie AB51 3SP (3) Senior Social Worker (F & A South), Carlton House, Arduthie Road, Stonehaven AB39 2DL. Principal Planning Officer (Children's Services) Woodhill House.

Local Authority	Categories and Location	Availability	Notes	Enquiries to
Angus Council County Buildings Forfar Angus Fax: 01241 473366	(a) (b) (c) (d) Post- 1 April 1996 records	Incomplete. Pre-1996 records held at Friarfield House, Barrack St, Dundee. Accessed through Angus.	Angus, previously part of Tayside. Became a Unitary Council on 1 April 1996.	Adoption & Fostering Co-ordinator, Bruce House, Arbroath, Angus DD11 3TS
Argyll & Bute Council SSD 29 Lomond Street Helensburgh G84 7PW Fax: 01436 658755	(a) (b) (c) Regional Archives, Mitchell Library, North Street, Glasgow. Accessed through Argyll & Bute	Records from 1948	Previously part of Strathclyde region. Became a Unitary Council 1 April 1996.	Service Officer (Looked after Children), SSD HQ
Clackmannanshire Council Lime Tree House Castle St Alloa FK10 1EX Fax: 01259 452522	(a) (c) Local offices (b) Pre-1 April 1996 Stirling Council Post-1 April 1996 SSD HQ, Clackmannanshire		Previously part of Central Regional Council. Became a Unitary Council 1 April 1996.	Head of Child Care & Criminal Justice Service, SSD HQ
Dumfries & Galloway Council SSD Grierson House The Crichton Dumfries DG1 4ZH Fax: 01387 260 924	(a) None Held by SWD, most curator work done by a solicitor (b) (c) SWD HQ (d); (e) Whereabouts noted SWD HQ	Most records available from 1958, plus some earlier records	(d) Council includes former Dumfries & Galloway Regional Council, Dumfries County, Dumfries Burgh, Kirkcudbrightshire & Wigtownshire	Children's Services Manager
Dundee City Council Tayside House 28 Crichton Street Dundee DD1 3RN	(a) Kept with court records (b) Pre- & Post-1 April 1996 at Fairfield House, Barrack St, Dundee (c) Kept separately (d) Fairfield House	Early records incomplete	Previously part of Tayside region. Became a Unitary Council 1 April 1996. (d) Dundee Association for Social Service	Senior Officer, Adoption & Fostering, Social Work Department, 6 Kirton Road, Dundee DD3 0BZ Fax: 01382 436022
East Ayrshire Council Department of Educational & Social Services Council Offices John Dickie Street Kilmarnock KA1 1BY Fax: 01563 576937	(a) (b) (c) (d) Pre-1 April 1996 – Mitchell Library, North Street, Glasgow G3 7DN. Post-1 April 1996 Ayrshire Archives Centre, Craigie Estate, Ayr KA8 0SS		Previously part of Strathclyde. Became a Unitary Council 1 April 1996. (d) At Ayrshire archives, Kilmarnock Borough records 1956–71. Ayr County records 1952 onwards	Service Officer, Permanency Planning HQ
East Dunbartonshire Council 2–4 West High Street Kirkintilloch Glasgow G66 1AD Fax: 0141 77 76 203	(a) (b) (c) (a) Part of Court papers. (b) (c) Pre-1 April 1996 in archives section, Mitchell Library, Charing Cross, Glasgow Post-1 April 1996 SSD HQ	(a) Sheriff Clerk, Glasgow Sheriff Court, 1 Carlton Place, Glasgow G5 9DA or Sheriff Clerk, Sheriff Court House, Dunbarton G82 1QR	Previously part of Strathclyde. Became a Unitary Council 1 April 1996. All records accessed through East Dunbartonshire.	Duty Officer, Children & Families Section, SSD HQ

Local Authority	Categories and Location	Availability	Notes	Enquiries to
East Lothian Council **9 –11 Lodge Street** **Haddington** **East Lothian** **EH41 3DX** **Fax: 01620 824295**	(a) (b) (c) Brief details on Council's computerised database. Full records in microfilm or microfiche form with Scottish Adoption Association.	Some older records may be lost	Previously part of Lothian Region. Became a Unitary Council 1 April 1996.	Scottish Adoption Association, 2 Commercial St, Leith, Edinburgh EH6 6JA or East Lothian Centres, Department of SW & Housing, Brunton Hall, Ladywell Way, Musselburgh, East Lothian EH21 6AF and Department of SW & Housing, 6/8 Lodge St, Haddington EH41 3DX
East Renfrewshire Council **Social Work Department** **Lygates Office** **224 Ayr Rd** **Newton Mearns** **East Renfrewshire** **G77 6DR** **Fax: 0141 577 3377**	(a) Part of court records (b) All are sent to Mitchell Library, Glasgow (c) Accessed through East Renfrewshire		Previously part of Strathclyde Region. Became a unitary Authority 1 April 1996.	Head of Service, SWD, Eastwood Park, Giffnoch G46 6UG or Manager, Substitute Care Team, Lygates Office
Edinburgh City Council **Shrubhill House** **7 Shrub Place** **Edinburgh** **EH7 4PD** **Fax: 0131 554 5775**	(a) (b) (c) (d) (a) Part of Court records. Some old welfare supervision records held by Scottish Adoption Association (b) At Scottish Adoption Association, old records on microfiche (c) Adoption records to Scottish Adoption Association Others social work HQ	(b) (c) None lost or destroyed	Previously part of Lothian region. Became a Unitary Council 1 April 1996. d) Some from St Andrews with Scottish Adoption Association which also holds the records of: Scottish Episcopal Church Adoption Society 1959–78 and Church of Scotland Committee on Social Responsibility.	Planning and Commissioning Manager, SWD or Scottish Adoption Association, 2 Commercial St, Leith, Edinburgh EH6 6JA Fax: 0131 553 6422
Falkirk Council **Brockville** **Hope Street** **Falkirk** **FK1 5RW** **Fax: 01324 506 401**	(a) (b) (c) Pre-1 April 1996 Stirling Post-1 April 1996 SWD 7HQ	(a) (b) Some lost (c) None lost or destroyed	Previously part of Central Region. Became a Unitary Council 1 April 1996.	The Team Manager, Children & Care Resourcing
Fife Council **Social Work Service** **Fife House** **North Street** **Glenrothes** **Fife** **KY7 5LT** **Fax: 01592 413320**	(a) (b) (c) Central Archive Unit, Block Q11, Flemington Road, Glenrothes KY7 5QW	(a) None lost or destroyed from 1969 (b) (c) Pre-1975 Kirkcaldy Burgh records destroyed	Council area includes Fifeshire, Dunfermline and Kirkcaldy	Social Work HQ
Glasgow City Council **Nye Bevan House** **India Street** **Glasgow** **G2 4PF**	(a) (b) (c) Held at the Mitchell Library, Glasgow but accessed through Families for Children	Adoption records available from 1930. No Port Glasgow records prior to 1968. (a) Records not comprehensive	Previously part of Strathclyde region. Became a Unitary Council 1 April 1996.	Families for Children, 115 Wellington Street, Glasgow G2 2XT Fax: 0141 287 6069

Local Authority	Categories and Location	Availability	Notes	Enquiries to
Highland Council Social Work Services Kinmylies Building Leachkin Road Inverness IV3 6NN Fax: 01463 713237	(a) (b) (c) Social Work HQ	No information about pre-1948 records	Council includes Sutherland, Caithness, Ross and Cromarty, Skye, Lochalsh, Inverness, Nairn and Badenoch and Stathspey. For Uist and Barra, formerly in Invernesshire area, records in Social Work HQ. C ad L records in Inverness Sheriff's Office.	Chair, Adoption Panel, Social Work Services, Kinmylies Building
Inverclyde Council SW Services 195 Dalrymple Street Greenock PA15 1LD Fax: 01475 714060	(a) (b) (c) Pre-31 December 1999 – Mitchell Library, Glasgow. Post-31 December 1999 – not yet decided. Enquiries to Head of Social Work Services.	Pre-1974 incomplete. Enquirers originating in Port Glasgow, Greenlock, Gourock, Inverkip, Kilmacolm, Wemyss Bay should contact Service Manager	Previously part of Strathclyde. Became a Unitary Council 1 April 1996.	Service Manager Children & Families Support Services

Midlothian Council

(b) (c) Records up to 1971 for the previous Edinburgh, East Lothian, Midlothian and West Lothian authorities have been microfilmed. From 1971 onwards records have been microfiched. Until 1975, records include adoption placements within the area for Peebles CC. Records (a) have not been protected. C ad L reports are available within the court papers under the Scottish procedure.

Local Authority	Categories and Location	Availability	Notes	Enquiries to
Midlothian Council Midlothian House Buccleuch Street Dalkeith Midlothian EH22 1DH	(b) (c) Pre-1 April 1996 Shrubhill House, Edinburgh EH7 4PD. Post-1 April 1996 Scottish Adoption Association. All records accessed through Support Services Manager, Midlothian.	(b) (c) Some lost	Previously part of Lothian. Became a Unitary Council 1 April 1996.	Support Services Manager, Midlothian Council, Loanhead SWD, 4 Clerk St, Loanhead EH20 9DR Fax: 0131 448 2151 Or Scottish Adoption Association, 2 Commercial St, Leith, Edinburgh EH6 6JA Fax: 0131 553 6422
Moray Council Community Services Department Edgar Road Elgin IV30 6FF Fax: 01343 546367	(a) (b) (c) (d) (e)	Pre-April 1996 records for Moray Division of Grampian. Post 1996 records for Moray Council.	Previously part of Grampian region. Became a Unitary Authority 1 April 1996.	Social Work Manager, Children & Families, SWD HQ
North Ayrshire Council Elliot House Redburn Industrial Estate Kilwinning Road Irvine KA12 8TB Fax: 01294 317 701	(a) (b) (c) Pre-1 April 1996 Mitchell Library Glasgow Post-1 April 1996 N. Ayrshire Archives, Perceton House, Irvine, KA11 2AL Accessed through N. Ayrshire	Some adoption records for N. Ayrshire since 1972; microfiche adoption register records from Ayr division from 1932–1987; copy of information on babies adopted from Ayrshire Central Hospital from 1959–1977. Child in Care (Looked after Children) received into care from 1998.	Previously part of Strathclyde region. Became a Unitary Council 1 April 1996.	Principal Officer, Specialist Services SWD HQ

SCOTLAND

Local Authority	Categories and Location	Availability	Notes	Enquiries to
North Lanarkshire Council DSW Scott House 73–77 Merry Street Motherwell, ML1 1JE Fax: 01698 332 095	(a) Relevant Sheriff Court for 20 years. Then Scottish Records Office, New Register House, Edinburgh. (b) Pre-1 January 2000 Mitchell Library, North Street, Glasgow, G3 7DN. Post-1 January 2000 to be notified. (c) Area Team for 5 years. Then archived.		Previously part of Strathclyde. Became a Unitary Council 1 April 1996.	Principal Officer – Child Care DSW HQ
Orkney Islands Council Community SSD Council Offices Kirkwall Orkney, KW15 1NY Fax: 01856 876 159	(a) (b) SWD HQ	Complete since 1969	Became an independent Unitary Council 1 April 1996	The Director of Social Work
Perth & Kinross Council HQ Pullar House Kinnoull Street Perth PH1 5GD	(a) (b) (c) (d) Pre-1 April 1996 Friarfield House, Barrack Street, Dundee. Post-1 April 1996 (a) Held by curator ad litems (not centrally) (b) At A K Bell Library Archive, York Place, Perth PH2 8EP (c) Accessed through Children's Service, Perth & Kinross Council, Corporate HQ, Kinnoull Street, Perth	Early records incomplete	Previously part of Tayside region. Became a Unitary Council 1 April 1996. (d) Perth & Dundee Association of Social Service; Melville House, Perth	Adoption Officer / Planning Officer, Looked After Children, Perth & Kinross Council HQ, Kinnoull Street, Perth
Renfrewshire Council 4th Floor North Building Cotton Street Paisley PA1 1TZ Fax: 0141 842 5144	(a) (b) (c) Pre-1 April 1996 records at Regional Archives, Mitchell Library, North Street, Glasgow. Post-1 April 1996 with Renfrewshire	All records should be accessed through Renfrewshire	Previously part of Strathclyde region. Became a Unitary Council 1 April 1996. Covers Paisley, Johnston and Renfrewshire areas.	Head of Operations, Social Work Department, HQ
Scottish Borders Council Social Work HQ Newtown St Boswells Melrose TD6 0SA Fax: 01835 823 366	(a) (b) (c) (d) SWD HQ (e)	None lost or destroyed	Previously part of Borders. Since 1 April 1996 a single Unitary Council which includes former shires of Peebles, Berwicks, Selkirk and Roxburgh.	Service Manager, Family Placement Team, 1 Chapel Street, Selkirk TD7 4LB
Shetland Islands Council SWD 93 St Olaf Street Lerwick Shetland Islands ZE1 0ES Fax: 01595 744 460	(a) Solicitors act as Curators ad Litem although social workers also undertake reports. (b) (c) (d) (e) SWD Shetland		Previously part of Islands Council. Became a Unitary Council 1 April 1996.	Principal Officer, Children's Resources.
South Ayrshire Council Community Services 12 Main Street Prestwick KA9 1NX	(a) Ayr Sheriff Court (b) (c) (d) (e) Archivist, Craigie, Ayr	From 1950 onwards, most records available	Previously part of Strathclyde. Became a Unitary Council 1 April 1996.	Team Leader, Fostering & Adoption, Community Services, 12 Main Street, Prestwick KA9 1NX

Local Authority	Categories and Location	Availability	Notes	Enquiries to
South Lanarkshire Council Council Offices Almada Street Hamilton ML3 0AA	(b) (c) (d) Pre-1 April 1996 records archived at Regional Archives, Mitchell Library, North Street, Glasgow. Post-1 April 1996 South Lanarkshire Record Section, 30 Hawbank Road, College Milton, East Kilbride, Archivist Mr Frank Rankin	(c) Records passed to other local authorities when adoption is outwith child's authority. When adoption granted child's file amalgamated with adopters' file. The receiving authority would archive the record.	Previously part of Strathclyde region. Became a Unitary Council 1 April 1996.	Social Work Resources, Floor 9, Council Offices
Stirling Council Children's Services – Social Work Drummond House Wellgreen Place Stirling FK8 2EG	(a) Area Offices (b) (c) Older records are in Burghmuir, Stirling. Later records in Drummond House	(a) (b) Some lost (c) None lost or destroyed.	Includes former Central Regional Council up to 1 April 1996. That included Falkirk & Clackmannan.	Team Manager, Community & Residential Resourcing, Child Care
West Dumbartonshire Council Department of Social Work & Housing Services Council Offices Garshake Road Dumbarton G82 3PU	(a) (b) (c) (d) (e) Pre-1 January 1999 Glasgow City Archivist Section, Mitchell Library, North Street, Glasgow, G3 7DN Post-1 January 1999 W. Dunbartonshire Council, HQ	Most records from 1968 are available. Some earlier records.	Previously part of Strathclyde. Became a Unitary Council 1 April 1996.

Counselling by specially trained workers and by Barnardo's Scottish Adoption Advice Service. | Section Head, Child Care |
| Western Isles Council Council Offices Sandwick Rd Stornoway Isles of Lewes HS1 2BW | (a) (b) (c) Barra SWD, Isle of Barra

(a) (b) (c) Benbecula SWD, Balivanich, Benbecula

(a) (b) (c) Harris SWD, Tarbert, Harris

(a) (b) (c) (post-reorganisation) Lewis SWD, Stornoway, Isle of Lewis | Probably intact

None lost or destroyed

None lost or destroyed

None lost or destroyed | Previously part of Islands Council. Became an independent Unitary Council 1 April 1996. | Social Worker Adoption |

West Lothian Council

(b) (c) Records up to 1971 for the previous Edinburgh, East Lothian, Midlothian and West Lothian authorities have been microfilmed. From 1971 onwards records have been microfiched. Until 1975, records include adoption placements within the area for Peebles CC. Records (a) have not been protected. C ad L reports are available within the court papers under the Scottish procedure.

Local Authority	Categories and Location	Availability	Notes	Enquiries to
West Lothian Council W. Lothian House Almondvale Boulevard Livingston W. Lothian EH54 6QG Fax: 01506 777 030	(b) (c) (d) Scottish Adoption Association 2 Commercial Street, Leith, Edinburgh, EH6 6JA Fax: 0131 553 6422	(b) (c) Some lost	Previously part of Lothian Region. Became a Unitary Council 1 April 1996.	Scottish Adoption Association

Local Authority	Categories and Location	Availability	Notes	Enquiries to

WALES

Local Authority	Categories and Location	Availability	Notes	Enquiries to
Anglesey CC Isle of **Shire Hall** Llangefni Glanhwfa Rd Isle of Anglesey LL77 7TS Fax: 01248 750107	(b) (c) (d) SSD HQ	All records, some possibly still in Gwynedd, accessed through Anglesey	Previously part of Gwynedd. Became a Unitary Council 1 April 1996 when many records returned from Gwynedd.	Adoptions Office at SSD HQ
Blaenau Gwent CBC SSD, Municipal Offices **Civic Centre** Ebbw Vale **NP3 6XB**	(a) (b) (c) (d) Gwent Records Office County Hall Crosyceiliog Cwmbran Torfaen NP44 3XH		Previously part of Gwent. Became a Unitary Council 1 April 1996.	Senior Assistant Director, Children and Families, SSD HQ Fax: 01495 355285
Bridgend CBC SSD **Sunnyside** Bridgend **CF31 1AR**	(a) (b) (c) (d) Pre-1975 Glamorgan Record Office Cathays Park Cardiff Post-1975 SSD. All accessed through Bridgend	Some (a) and (c) lost since 1926	Previously part of Mid Glamorgan. Became a Unitary Council 1 April 1996. Glamorgan County Archivist has some pre-1948 records.	Principal Assistant, Adoptions Fax: 01656 648689
Caerphilly CBC Social Services and **Housing** Hawtin Park **Gellihaf** Pontillanfraith **Blackwood** NP12 2PZ Fax: 01443 864523	(a) (b) Pre-1996 records from Gwent held in Monmouthshire County Hall, Cwmbran. Pre-1974 records from Mid Glamorgan held in Glamorgan Record Office. The Glamorgan Buildings, King Edward VIII Avenue, Cathays Park, Cardiff, CF10 3NE.	(a) (b) (b) 1974–1996 records from Mid Glamorgan and Caerphilly records post-1996. SSD HQ. (c) Records from Gwent. Pre-1996 Cwmbran. Post 1996 Area teams Caerphilly. Records from Mid Glamorgan pre and post 1996. Area teams Caerphilly.	Previously part of Gwent. Since 1 April 1996 Caerphilly has been a Unitary Council formed of the Rhymney Valley area of Mid Glamorgan and the Islwyn area of Gwent.	Fostering and Adoption Team, 6 Piccadilly Square, Caerphilly CF83 1PB
Cardiff CC County Hall **Atlantic Wharf** Cardiff **CF15 UW**	(a) Panel Manager Cardiff and the Vale panel of Independent G ad L and reporting officers (b) (c) Trowbridge Centre	(b) (c) Intact	Previously part of South Glamorgan. Became a Unitary Council 1 April 1996. (e) Some adoption records passed to Vale of Glamorgan.	Team Manager Adoption, Trowbridge Centre, Greenway Rd, Trowbridge, Cardiff CF38 QS
Carmarthenshire CC Social Care and **Housing Dept** 3 Spilman Street **Carmarthen** SA31 1LE Fax: 01267 228908	(a) (b) (c) (d) Pre- and Post-1 April 1996. Adoption Archive, SSD HQ.	Not known if complete (b) 1940–1974	Previously part of Dyfed. Became a Unitary Council 1 April 1996. d) 1) Dyfed CC adoption records. 1974–1996 2) St David's Diocesan Moral Welfare Committee records	Assistant Director for Children Services, Adoption Archive, Department of Social Care and Housing, 3–5 Spilman Street, Carmarthen SA31 1LE

Local Authority	Categories and Location	Availability	Notes	Enquiries to
Ceredigion CC **Min-Aeron** **Rhiw Goch** **Aberaeron** **SA46 0DY** Fax: 01545 572619	(a) (b) (c) (d) Pre-1 April 1996. Adoption Archive Dept of Social Care and Housing, 3–5 Spilman St, Carmarthen, SA31 1LE Post-1 April 1996 SSD Aberaeron	Not known if complete	Previously part of Dyfed. Became a Unitary Council 1 April 1996.	Assistant Director, SSD
Conway CBC **Children and Family** **Services** **Civic Offices Annex** **Abergele Rd** **Colwyn Bay** **LL29 8AR**	(b) Pre-1996 records kept by Clwyd and now held by Flintshire. Relevant Gwynedd records passed to Conwy. Post 1996 records with Conwy.		Previously part of Clwyd and also of Gwynedd (Aberconwy area). Became a Unitary Council 1 April 1996 when many records returned from Gwynedd.	The Adoption Administrator, Family Placement Team, Children and Family Services, SSD HQ
Denbighshire CC **Ty Nant** **Nant Hall Rd** **Prestatyn** **Denbighshire** **LL19 9LG** Fax: 01824 706646	(a) (b) (c) Pre-1 April 1996 records. The County Office, Wepre Drive, Connah's Quay, Deeside, CH5 4HB. Post-1 April 1996. Children's Resource Centre.		Previously part of Clwyd. Became a Unitary Council 1 April 1996.	The Manager, Family Placement Team, Children's Resource Centre, SSD, Cefndy Rd, Rhyl, Denbighshire, LL18 2HG
Flintshire CC **SSD** **County Offices** **Connah's Quay** **Deeside** **CH5 4HB** Fax: 01352 701005	(a) (b) (c) Some since 1948	(a) Incomplete; pre-1948 Flintshire G ad L files not traced, but pre-1948 Denbighshire G ad L files available at Shire Hall (b) Complete (c) Some pre-1948 taken over by the children's departments of Denbighshire and Flintshire available; some details available in County Records offices	Previously part of Clwyd. Became a Unitary Council 1 April 1996. Still holds pre-1 April 1996 records for Wrexham, Denbighshire and part of Clwyd.	Adoption Agency Administrator
Gwynedd Council **County Offices** **Caernarfon** **LL55 1SH**	(a) North Wales Panel of G ad L, Glyn Marl Rd, Llandudno Junction (b) In Arfon Offices (c) Area Offices (d) Arfon Offices		(d) Bangor Diocesan Adoption Society. Held in Arfon Offices, Penrallt, Caernarfon LL55 1BN. Many lost in a fire some years ago.	Adoption Officer, SSD, Gwynedd Council, Penrallt, Caernarfon, Gwynedd LL55 1BN
Merthyr Tydfil CBC **SSD** **Ty Keir Hardie** **Riverside Court** **Avenue de Clichy** **Merthyr Tydfil** **CF47 8XD** Fax: 01685 384868	(a) (b) (c) (d) (b) SSD HQ (c) Pre- and post-1 April 1996		Previously part of Mid Glamorgan. Became a Unitary Council 1 April 1996.	Looked after Children Team Manager
Monmouthshire CC **County Hall** **Cwmbran** **NP44 2XH** Fax: 01633 644577	(a) (b) (c) SSD, Gwent Records Office, County Hall	Pre- and Post-1 April 1996 held by Monmouth	Previously part of Gwent. Became a Unitary Council 1 April 1996. Relevant information passed over by Powys CC in 1974, remains with Monmouth	Managers of Operations, SSD HQ

Local Authority	Categories and Location	Availability	Notes	Enquiries to
Neath Port Talbot CBC **Civic Centre** **Port Talbot** **SA13 1PJ**	(a) (b) (c) Adoptions Section, The Laurels, 87 Lewis Rd, Neath, SA11 1DJ Fax: 01639 641094	(a) (b) (c) Since 1 April 1996 all available for area. March 1974 – March 1996 W. Glamorgan placements and families living in local authority care. d) Incomplete records for Glamorgan CC	Previously part of West Glamorgan. Became a Unitary Council 1 April 1996. d) Glamorgan CC 1948–1974, c/o Archives Department, City and County of Cardiff, Atlantic Wharf, Cardiff	Adoptions Manager, Accommodation Service, The Laurels
Newport CBC **Civic Centre** **Newport** **South Wales** **NP20 4UR** **Fax: 01633 233372**	(a) (b) (c) Pre- and Post-1996 records, County Hall, Cwmbran, NP44 2XH		Previously part of Gwent. Became a Unitary Council 1 April 1996.	Head of Operational Services, SSD HQ
Pembrokeshire CC **County Hall** **Haverfordwest** **Pembrokeshire** **SA61 1TP** **Fax: 01437 769971**	(a) (b) (c) (d) Pre-1972 and Post-1996 with Pembrokeshire. 1972–1996 with Carmarthenshire	Not known if complete. Carmarthenshire has a register. Access 1972–1996 records through Carmarthenshire or Pembrokeshire	Pembrokeshire, Carmarthenshire and Cardiganshire became Dyfed in 1972. On 1 April 1996 Pembrokeshire became a Unitary Council.	Family Placement Team, The Elms, Golden Hill, Pembroke SA71 4QB
Powys CC **SSD** **St John's Offices** **Foreways** **Llandrindod Wells** **Powys** **LD1 5ES** **Fax: 01597 827555**	(a) (b) (c) SSD HQ (e)		(d) Relevant records to Mid-Glamorgan and Gwent when areas taken over by them. Present area includes previous Brecknock, Montgomeryshire and Radnorshire from 1 April 1996	Director, SSD
Rhonda **Cynon Taff** **CBC** **Education and Children's Services** **Maesycoed** **Lanelay Terrace** **Maesycoed** **Pontypridd** **CF37 1JG** **Fax: 01443 424018**	(a) (b) (c) (d) Pre-1977 Glamorgan Record Office, The Glamorgan Building, King Edward VIII Avenue, Cathays Park, Cardiff, CF10 3NE Post-1997 SSD	(a) (c) Some lost since 1926	Previously part of Mid Glamorgan. Became a Unitary Council 1 April 1996. d) Relevant records from Powys	Adoption Officer
Swansea CC **SSD** **County Hall** **Swansea** **SA1 3SN**	(a) (b) (c) (d) Pre-1 April 1996 Holds records of Swansea and Neath Port, Talbot Post-1 April 1996 Swansea records only	Incomplete apart from West Glamorgan records from 1974	Previously part of W. Glamorgan. Became a Unitary Council 1 April 1996. d) Area records of former Glamorgan CC; G ad L records of former Swansea City; West Glamorgan agency and G ad L records; Swansea and Brecon Diocesan Council for Social Work	Senior Adoptions Officer, Cockett House, Cockett Rd, Cockett, Swansea, SA2 0FJ Fax: 01792 583791
Torfaen CBC **County Hall** **Cwmbran** **NP44 2WN** **Fax: 01633 648794**	(a) (b) (c) (d) (e) Pre- and Post-1 April 1996 records County Hall	Not known if complete	Until 1 April 1996 Torfaen CBC was Eastern Valley area within Gwent. Now a Unitary Council.	Team Manager, Adoption

Where to find adoption records

Local Authority	Categories and Location	Availability	Notes	Enquiries to
Vale of Glamorgan BC Civic Offices Holton Road Barry CF63 4RU	(a) (b) Pre- and Post-1 April 1996 Haydock House (c) Pre-1996 records in Cardiff CC. Post-1996 Haydock House	(a) (b) Some records go back to 1930s but incomplete before 1948	Until 1 April 1996 was part of South Glamorgan. Now a Unitary Council.	(a) and (b) Senior Officer Adoption, Children and Families, Haydock House, 1 Holton Rd, Barry, CF63 4HA Pre-1 April 1996 (c) Operational Manager, (Fieldwork, Children and Families), County Hall, Atlantic, Wharf, Cardiff, CF1 5UW
Wrexham CBC Director of Personal Services The Guildhall Wrexham LL11 1AY	(a) (b) (c) Post-1 April 1996 Adoptions Administrator	Pre-1 April 1996 records with Flintshire CC. Adoption Administrator, County Offices, Connah's Quay, Deeside, CH5 4 HB	Until 1 April 1996 was part of Clwyd. Now a Unitary Council.	Adoptions Administrator, 3–9 Grosvenor Rd, Wrexham LL11 1DB

N. IRELAND

Local Authority	Categories and Location	Availability	Notes	Enquiries to
Eastern Health & Social Services Board Champion House 12–22 Linenhall Street Belfast BT2 8BS				Adoption Services Manager, 33 Wellington Park, Belfast BT9 6Dl
Northern Health and Social Services Board County Hall 182 Galgorm Road Ballymena Co Antriun BT42 1QB	(d) (e)			The Director, Social Services
Southern Health and Social Services Board Tower Hill Armagh BT61 9DR	(b) (c) (d) (e)	Records date back to 1950 in some Trusts	The Board's area consists of 3 Trusts	Assist Director of Social Services
Western Health and Social Services Board 15 Gransha Park Clooney Rd Londonderry BT47 1TG Fax: 028 7186 0311	Foyle H and SS Trust covers Londonderry, Limavady and Strabane. Riverview House, Off Abercorn Rd, Londonderry, BT48 6SB. Sperrin Lakeland H and Social Care Trust covers Omagh and Fermanagh. Family and Child Care Programme. Community Services Dept, Tyrone and Permanagh Hospital, Omagh, Co Tyrone, BT79 0NS.		The Board's adoption records are held by 2 Health and Social Services Trusts, Foyle and Sperrin Lakeland	Programme Manager

Social services departments

Local Authority	Categories and Location	Availability	Notes	Enquiries to

ISLE OF MAN (For law in Isle of Man see entry Chapter 2)

Local Authority	Categories and Location	Availability	Notes	Enquiries to
Government Office Douglas				Not involved with adoption
The General Registry Finch Road Douglas	Records of all adoptions			The Service Manager, Children and Families, Social Services Division, Hillary House, Prospect Hill, Douglas, Isle of Man IM1 1EQ Fax: 01624 686198

GUERNSEY (For law in Guernsey see entry Chapter 2)

Local Authority	Categories and Location	Availability	Notes	Enquiries to
States of Guernsey Children Board Perruque House Rue De La Perruque Castel Guernsey Channel Islands			Children sometimes adopted on the mainland; records might be held by Hampshire	Adoption and Permanency Officer, Garden Hill, Resource Centre, The Rohais, St Peter Port, Guernsey GY1 1FB

JERSEY (For law in Jersey see entry Chapter 2)

Local Authority	Categories and Location	Availability	Notes	Enquiries to
Children's Service Social Services Maison Le Pape The Parade St Helier Jersey JE2 3PU	(a) (b) (c)	(a) 1947–59 (b) 1959 onwards	Many children born in Jersey were placed in Guernsey or Southern England. Some records may be held by Guernsey or Hampshire.	Adoption Consultant, Children's Service Tel: 01534 623500

EIRE

Local Authority	Categories and Location	Availability	Notes	Enquiries to
Adoption Board Shelbourne House Shelbourne Road Ballsbridge Dublin 4 Fax: 00 353 1 667 1438				Senior Social Worker Tel: 00 353 1 667 1392

7 • Facilities in other countries

There are four main sources of help in any search which involves other countries. These are International Social Service, Overseas Adoption Helpline, Child Migrants Trust and certain websites.

International Social Service (address in Chapter 9) has branches or correspondents in over 100 countries. They have considerable knowledge of, and experience in, the variable adoption laws and the facilities available for searching in other countries.

For anyone about to begin a search which involves another country, a telephone call to ISS may be an excellent starting point. In a number of countries their staff are designated Section 51 counsellors.

Oveseas Adoption Helpline (address in Chapter 9) has built up a very comprehensive knowledge of other countries, contacts there and how best to proceed.

The Child Migrants Trust (address in Chapter 9) During the 19th and 20th centuries, up to 1967, about 130,000 children were sent to Australia, Canada, New Zealand and Rhodesia (now Zimbabwe). Many were told that they were orphans when they were not. Many went without their parents' knowledge or consent, had their names changed, and/or had no written personal identification. The Trust exists to help these migrants and their families.

Currently the Government is, through International Social Service, funding an Information Index to help those child migrants who wish to find their families, and a Support Fund to help those without means who have found their family to travel to the UK for a first time reunion. Details can be found in the Department of Health leaflet, *Former British Child Migrants*, available from the National Council of Voluntary Child-Care Organisations (address in Chapter 9).

The Australian addresses are:

Child Migrants Trust Inc.
228 Canning Street
North Carlton
Melbourne
Victoria 3054
Tel: 00 61 3 9347 7403
Fax: 00 61 3 9347 1791

Child Migrants Trust Inc
5 Thomas Street
Nedlands
Perth
Western Australia 6009
Tel: 00 61 3 9347 7403

Postal Address:
P O Box 674
Nedlands
Perth
Western Australia 6009
Fax: 00 61 8 9386 3695
Tel: 00 61 8 9386 3605

Websites In the following pages which include the countries most often involved in searching, web sites are given where known. Not everyone has access to the Internet although libraries often have computers and are very helpful to the uninitiated. The main sources of information and support in each country are given as well as a generalised summary of the position there. People who prefer to write for information should state that they do not have access to the internet.

For some services, such as searching, fees are payable so the financial position needs to be clarified from the beginning.

Embassies in some countries can be helpful in pin-pointing sources of information.

The Office of National Statistics (ONS), Adoption Section, is constantly updating and increasing the list of agencies overseas which are approved for Section 51 counselling.

Anyone adopted in England but now living abroad and wishing to be counselled locally should get leaflets ACR114 and 101 from ONS (Adoption) in Southport (address in Chapter 9).

AUSTRALIA

Each of Australia's 8 states makes its own adoption laws. All states enable adopted people, aged 18, to get information about their origins. The amount of information and the conditions for obtaining it, mandatory counselling, the right to veto the passing on of information, and help with searching vary and are likely to remain fluid as laws change. The rights of birth parents and relatives also vary in a comparable way.

There is no single central source of information but PARC (Post Adoption Resource Centre), P O Box 239, Bondi, New South Wales, 2026 Tel: 0061 2 9365 3444 Fax: 00 61 2 9363 3666 publishes a comprehensive information booklet.

www.bensoc.asn.au/parc
email parc@bensoc.asn.au

Facilities in other countries

State	Social Welfare Departments	Register Offices	Support Groups
Australian Capital Territory	The Adoption Information Service Family Services P O Box 1584 Tuggeranong ACT 2901 Tel: 00 61 2 6207 10080	RGACT P O Box 788 Canberra ACT 2601	Adoption Triangle (ACT) 18 Letters St Evatt ACT 2617
New South Wales	Family Information Services Level 13 Ferguson Centre 100 George St Parramatta NSW 2150 Fax: 00 61 2 6893507	191 Thomas Street Haymarket NSW 2001 Family Information Services Tel: 00 61 2 2138688	Post Adoption Resource Centre P O Box 239 Bondi NSW 2026 Fax: 00 61 2 93653666 Tel: 00 61 2 93653444
Northern Territory	Substitute Care and Children's Services P O Box 40596 Casuarina NT 0811 Tel: 00 61 8 89227077	RGNT P O Box 3021 Darwin NT 5794	
Queensland	Adoption Services Branch Department of Families, Youth and Community Care G P O Box 806 Brisbane 4001 Fax: 00 61 7 32100350 Tel: 00 61 7 32242544		Association for Adoptees 18 Wain Avenue Woodbridge 4114 Tel: 00 61 7 38083126 Mon – Friday 9 – 4 Jigsaw P O Box 912 New Farm 4005 Tel: 00 61 7 33586666 Fax: 00 61 7 38751161
South Australia	Adoption and Family Information Service P O Box 39 Rundle Mall Adelaide SA 5000 Tel: 00 61 8 82266694 Fax: 00 61 8 82266974	RGSA (from 1842) Edmund Wright House 59 King William St Adelaide SA5000	Jigsaw SA Inc P O Box 567 Prospect East SA5082 Tel: 00 61 8 83447529 Adopted Persons Support Group 52 Fordingbridge Rd Davoren Park 5113 Tel: 00 61 8 82874590 Association of Relinquishing Mothers (ARMS) Torrens Building 220 Victoria Square Adelaide 5000 Tel: 00 61 8 82216944
Tasmania	Adoption Information Service Department of Community and Health Services GPO Box 538 Hobart 7001 Fax: 00 61 3 62231343	RGT. Law Department 81 Murray Street Hobart TA 7000	Jigsaw (Tasmania) GPO Box 989K Hobart TA 7001

State	Social Welfare Departments	Register Offices	Support Groups
Victoria	Department of Human Services Adoption Information Service, GPO Box 4057 Melbourne 3001 Fax: 00 61 3 96162833	Office of the Government Statist Department of Property and Services 295 Queen Street Melbourne VIC 3000	Victorian Adoption Network (VANISH), 199 Cardigan Street, Carlton South 3053 Fax: 00 61 3 93494853 Association of Relinquishing Mothers (ARMS) 20 Beauvorno Avenue Keysborough 3173 Tel: 00 61 3 9789 4166 (A specialist search agency)
Western Australia	Family and Children's Services Adoption Branch 189 Royal Street East Perth WA 6004	RGWA Oakleigh Building 22 St Georges Terrace Perth WA 6000	Adoption Jigsaw WA Inc. PO Box 252 Hilarys WA 6025

CANADA

Much of the following information came from CANADopt's web site, www.nebula.on.ca/canadopt/. CANADopt seeks to provide a central location from which people can gather information specific to Canada and conduct their searches within Canada.

Each of Canada's 12 provinces has its own adoption laws and facilities and all are subject to change.

The adoption agencies are usually limited to helping people whose adoptions took place in Canada.

All provinces have a post adoption registry which encompasses the passing of non identifying information, the use of a "passive register" (the equivalent of the British Contact Register) and an Active Search Facility. In some there is a right to identifying information, and in some there is a right to veto passing on of such information. Counselling may be available or mandatory. There are variable fees.

Province	Post-adoption Services	Register Offices
Alberta	The Alberta Provincial Government Post Adoption Registry 9th Floor South Tower Seventh Street Plaza 10030 – 107 Street Edmonton Alberta Canada T5J 3E4 Tel: 00 1 780 427 6387 www.gov.ab.ca/cs/cs/services/adoptions/par.htm	Alberta Registries Vital Statistics, 3rd floor Box 2023 Edmonton Alberta, T5J 4W7
British Columbia	Adoption Reunion Registry c/o Family Services of Greater Vancouver 202-1600 West 6th Avenue Vancouver BC Canada V6J 1R3 Tel: 00 1 604 736 7917 Fax: 00 1 604 736 7916 www.adoptionreunion.net	British Columbia Vital Statistics Agency, PO Box 9657 Stn Prov. Govt, Victoria, BC V8W 9PR

Province	Post-adoption Services	Register Offices
Manitoba	Post Adoption Registry Manitoba Family Services 2nd Floor 114 Garry St Winnipeg MB R3C 4V5 Tel: Winnipeg 00 1 204 945 6962 Fax: 00 1 204 948 2949 or 00 1 204 945 6717	Vital Statistics Consumer and Corporate Affairs 254 Portage Avenue Winnipeg Manitoba R3C OB6
New Brunswick	Post Adoption Services Health and Community Services P O Box 5100 Fredericton, NB E3B 5G8 Tel: 00 1 506 453 2949	Vital Statistics Office Health and Community Services P O Box 6000 Fredericton NBE3 B5H1
Newfoundland and Labrador	Post Adoption Registry Department of Social Services Box 8700 Confederate Building St. Johns Newfoundland A1B 4J6 Tel: 00 1 709 729 3506	Vital Statistics Government Service Centre Department of Government Services and Lands 5 Mews Place Box 8700 St John's Newfoundland A1B 4J6
NorthWest Territories	Family and Children's Services Department of Social Services P O Box 1320 Yellowknife NWT X1A 2L9	Registrar General of Vital Statistics Department of Health and Social Services Bag # 9 Inuvik NT X0E 0T0
Nova Scotia	Adoption Disclosure Service Program Department of Community Services P O Box 696 Halifax Nova Scotia B3J 2T7 Tel: 00 1 902 424 2755 Fax: 00 1 902 424 0708	Vital Statistics Department of Business and Consumer Services P O Box 157 Halifax NS B3J 2M9
Ontario	Adoption and Operational Services Ministry of Community and Social Services Adoption Information Unit 2 Bloor St. West 24th Floor Toronto Ontario M4W 3H8 Adoption Disclosure Register Clerk International Adoptions: Relative Adoptions: Private Adoptions:	Registrar General P O Box 4600 Thunderbay Ontario P7B 6L8 Tel: 00 1 416 327 4730 00 1 416 327 4739 00 1 416 327 4740 00 1 416 327 4741
Prince Edward Island	Health and Community Services Agency P O Box 2000 Charlottetown Prince Edward Island C1A 7N8 Tel: 00 1 902 368 6511 www.gov.pe.ca/infopei/index.php3	Vital Statistics Health and Community Services Agency P O Box 3000 Charlottetown PE C0A 1R0

Province	Post-adoption services	Register Offices
Quebec	This is the office for Greater Montreal Area. There are smaller, local offices around the province. This location will give information on where to contact if the adoption was completed outside Montreal	
	Centre de Protection de l'Enfance et de la Jeunesse Service de l'Adoption 1001 Boulevard Maisonneuve Est 6e étage Montreal PQ H2L 4R5 Tel: 00 1 514 896 3200 Fax: 00 1 514 896 3190	Ministère de la Justice Direction de l'état Civil Service à la Clientèle 205 Rue Montmagny Quebec G1N 4T2
Saskatchewan	Post Adoption Registry Saskatchewan Social Services 11th Floor 1920 Broad Street Regina, SK S4P 3V6 Tel: 00 1 306 787 3654 Fax: 00 1 306 787 0925 www.gov.sk.ca	Vital Statistics Unit, Department of Health, 1942 Hamilton St, Regina, Saskatchewan, S4P 3V7
Yukon Territory	Department of Health and Social Services Government of Yukon Family and Children's Services Box 2703 (H-10) Whitehorse, Yukon Territory Y1A 2C6 Tel: 00 1 867 667 3002	Vital statistics Government of the Yukon Territory P O Box 2703 Whitehorse Yukon Territory Y1A 2C6

NATIONAL RESOURCES

National Archives of Canada
395 Wellington Street
Ottawa
Ontario K1A ON3
www.archives.ca
E-mail: jlozier@archives.ca

The Adoption Council of Canada
Box 8442, Stn T
Ottawa
Ontario K1G 3H8
Tel: 00 1 613 235 1566
E-mail: igrove@adoption.ca
An umbrella organisation similar
to BAAF

Adoption Reunion Searchline
63 Holborn Avenue
Nepean
Ontario
K2C 3H1
Tel: 001 613 825 1640
Fax: 001 613 825 7479

National Library of Canada
395 Wellington St
Ottawa
Ontario K1A 0N4

Parent Finders of Canada
3998 Bayridge Avenue
West Vancouver
British Columbia V7V 3J5
Tel: 001 604 926 1096
Fax: 001 604 926 2037
Email: reunion@parentfinders.org

Search and Research
39 Hopewell Avenue
Ottowa
Ontario
K1S 2YT
Tel: 00 1 613 730 1039
Fax: 00 1 613 730 034

Project Roots
Lloyd and Olga Rains
Prof. Pelstraat 59
2035 CS
Haarlem
Holland
Fax: 00 31 0842 1104 79
E-mail: rains@worldonline/nl
www.project.roots.com

A Canadian World War II veteran and his Dutch war bride have helped over 2000 war time children to be re-united with their Canadian fathers. Project Roots is entirely personal and voluntary.

If a person is, or was, a member of the Canadian Armed Forces their service records will be held by:

The Personnel Records Unit
National Archives Canada
Tunney's Pasture
Ottawa
Ontario
K1A ON3
Tel: 00 1 613 954 4135
Fax: 00 1 613 954 4138

National Archives cannot release any information about an individual except on proof of the person's death but they will forward a letter if they have an address on file.
There may be a small registration fee.

For former members of the Canadian Armed Services one could also try:

The Canadian Legion Magazine
Legion (Lost Trails)
Can Vet Publications Ltd
Suite 504
359 Kent Street
Ottawa
Ontario SL6 7DX
K2P 0R7

War Graves Commission
66 Slater Road
Suite 1707
Ottowa, Ontario
Canada
K1A 0P4
(Has records of persons killed in action)

INDIA

It is <u>extremely</u> difficult to trace people and records in India. The main source of help is the Central Adoption Resource Agency (CARA) which is part of the Ministry of Social Justice and Empowerment.

West Block 8
Wing 2
RK Puram
New Delhi
India
Website: www.adoptionindia.nic.in/

The records of the East India Company and its successor bodies, The India Office and The Burma Office (1600–1948) have now been amalgamated with the British Museum Oriental Collection and have become the Oriental and Indian Collections at the British Library, Euston Road, London NW1. They include registers of baptisms, marriages and deaths of Christians living in those countries, and information on civilians employed by the Indian army and other forces. Some are very incomplete. Eventually they will all be computerised.

Hodson's Index at the National Army Museum Reading Room, Royal Hospital Road, Chelsea, London SW3 4HT

(020 7730 0717) is a card index of almost all officers who served in the armies of the East India Company and the Imperial Indian Army between 1760 and 1939. It includes all ranks of officers but not warrant officers or non-commissioned ranks. Some have very scanty information.

The Reading Room also has East India Company and Indian army lists from 1795 to 1946 and these provide some information on people especially before World War II.

The British Association for Cemeteries in South Asia, 76 Chartfield Avenue, Putney, London SW15 6HQ (020 8788 6953) was begun by Captain Theon Wilkinson in about 1976. Its purpose is to record the many hundreds of European cemeteries, isolated graves and monuments in South Asia before they all disappear. To this end they have contacted many churches of all denominations throughout India, Pakistan, Burma and further afield. From these contacts they have been able to trace the background of many people buried there or whose families have now settled in Britain. They are building up a Records Archive of their own in the Oriental and India Office Collections in the British Library.

NEW ZEALAND

Information about adoption can be found on www.bdmgovt.nz and also from:

Adoption Information and Services Unit
New Zealand Children & Young Persons Service
P O Box 6901
Te Aro
Wellington
New Zealand
Tel: 00 64 4 381 9100
Fax: 00 64 4 381 9101

Adult Information Officer
Registrar General's Office
Private Bag
Lower Hutt
New Zealand

People adopted in New Zealand can, if they wish, at the age of 20, and after seeing a counsellor, be given a copy of their original birth certificate.

Birth parents have the right to receive identifying information with the consent of the adopted person.

Once an adopted person becomes 19 they can veto the release of identifying information to birth relatives.

A birth parent of a child adopted before 1 March 1996 can veto the release of identifying information contained in the original birth certificate. The birth parent of a child adopted after 1 March 1996 cannot veto the release of that information.

A veto remains in force for 10 years, but can be removed or renewed for an addition 10 years at any time.

The role of the counsellor is to inform, support and facilitate, but not to search.

Unless a veto has been registered, the Department of Child, Youth & Family (Adoption Information & Services Unit), at the request of the birth parent or adult adopted person, has the task of locating the other party and ascertaining his/her wishes with regard to information/contact.

NATIONAL RESOURCES

Birth Certificate Applications
Central Registry
Births, Deaths and Marriages
P O Box 31
115 Lower Hutt
New Zealand
Tel: 00 64 4 366 5311
Fax: 00 64 4 566 5311

New Zealand Electoral Rolls
www.elections.org.nz

Adoption Resource Centre
P O Box 60-246
Auckland Central
New Zealand
Tel: 00 64 9 811 8046

Adoption Support Link
P.O. Box 4164
Auckland
New Zealand
Tel: 00 64 9 424 1035

Adoption Support Link
15 Waiatawa Rd
Whangarei
New Zealand
Tel: 00 64 9 437 0655

Capital Adoption Search and Support Link
PO Box 38-304
Petone
Lower Hutt
New Zealand

The Christchurch Adoption Triangle
100 Harris Crescent
Christchurch
New Zealand
Tel: 00 64 3 352 2060

Jigsaw Inc.
P O Box 28-037
Remurera
Auckland
New Zealand
Tel: 00 64 9 523 3460

SOUTH AFRICA

The Child Care Act 1983 made it possible for designated people to obtain information from the record of the adoption enquiry.

a) An adopted person at 21.

b) An adopted person at 18 with the consent of the adoptive parents.

c) A biological parent, once the adopted person has become 21, with the written consent of the adoptive parents.

Main source of information:-

Department of Social Development
Registrar of Adoptions
Private Bag X901
Pretoria 0001
Tel: 00 27 12 312 7592
Fax: 00 27 12 312 7837

ACCREDITED CHILD WELFARE SOCIETIES

Bloemfontein Society for Child and Family Care
P O Box 1011
Bloemfontein 9300
Orange Free State

Pretoria Child and Family Welfare Society
P O Box 503
Pretoria 0001
Transvaal

Durban Child and Family Welfare Society
P O Box 47569
Greyville 4023
Natal

Johannesburg Child and Welfare Society
P O Box 2539
Johannesburg 2000
Transvaal

East London Child and Family Welfare Society
P O Box 11030
Southernwood 5312
Cape Province

Port Elizabeth Child and Family Welfare Society
P O Box 12269
Centrahil 6006
Cape Province

Pietermaritzburg Child and Family Welfare Society
P.O. Box 748
Pietermaritzburg 3200
Natal

USA

By 1927 all the states in the USA had adoption laws. Each state has its own laws and the polices and practices of different states and adoption agencies vary widely. Nearly all states still, in 2001, have sealed records.

Until 2001 there were three different categories of organisations or individuals who might be involved in arranging adoptions. These were:

- Licensed adoption agencies. The criteria for licensing could vary considerably from state to state. Some of the agencies are public and some private.

- Adoption Facilitators. In some states they could operate without being licensed and sometimes undertake home studies as well as giving advice to prospective adopters and birth parents.

- Adoption attorneys who required no special licence other than being a member of the bar.

The New Act which means that only adoptions made via licensed agencies will be acceptable under the Hague Convention, was passed in October 2000. It is expected that it will be ratified in 2001.

The National Adoption Information Clearing House (NAIC) is at:

330 C Street SW
Washington DC 20447
Tel: 00 1 202 (703) 352 3488 or
00 1 202 (888) 251 0075
www.calib.com/naic

Fax: 00 1 202 (703) 385 3206
E-Mail: naic@calib.com
To them we are indebted for the information that the following can be accessed on line:

The publication *Searching for Birth Relatives*
www.calib.com/naic/pubs/f_search.htm

Access to birth records by States
www.calib.com/naic/pubs/l_acestb2.htm

American Bar Association on Children and the Law
www.abanet.org/child/

Search support groups state by state to search the National Adoption Directory
www.calib.com/naic/database/nadd/naddsearch.cfm

TRACE (Trans-Atlantic Children's Enterprise) specialises in helping the children of American GI fathers to trace their paternal families.

The founder, Mrs Pamela Winfield, herself a GI bride, has written two books on the subject.

Membership Secretary
Mrs N J Clark-McCloud
1 Herons Flight
Bycullah Road
Enfield EN2 8EE
(No telephone calls but SAE please)

Ms Rachel James
PO Box 694
Youngstown
Ohio 44501
USA
E-mail: msrachel12@Juno.com

is willing to help adopted people whose fathers were American GIs stationed in the UK during World War II, but only if they came from N. Carolina or Ohio.

RED CROSS

The national Red Cross or Red Crescent Society will normally search for relatives only when they have been separated as a result of armed conflict or natural disaster. It would be only in exceptional circumstances that they would search for relatives separated by adoption, and then they might not have the appropriate staff to deal with the complications possibly involved. However, in exceptional circumstances, and where there are no other resources available, it might be worth a counsellor discussing the situation with the International Welfare Department, British Red Cross, 9 Crosvenor Crescent, London SW1X 7EJ (020 7235 5454).

Overseas Contacts

Barbados
The Child Care Board
Modern Living Complex
Whitepark Road
St Michael
Barbados

Netherlands
Fiom
Hertogenbosch
Kruisstraat 1
5211 DTs Hertogenbosch
Netherlands

National Office of the Child Care & Protection Board (Raad Voor de Kinderbescherming)
PO Box 19202
3501 De Utrecht
Netherlands
Fax: 00 31 30 2391450
Tel: 00 31 30 2392400
(The only agency that is allowed to make home-studies for adoptions by people from abroad.)

BAAF has a list of Licensed Adoption Agencies in the Netherlands.

8 • Searching

This section is mainly based on a NORCAP publication, *Searching for Family Connections*, and BAAF is very grateful for permission to reproduce an adapted version. The importance of an intermediary, if a birth parent's address is found, has not been touched on because it is assumed that the counsellor will have dealt fully with that in the first and any subsequent interview.

If adopted people wish to obtain more up-to-date information than their birth certificate provides, or if they would like to correspond with or meet their birth parents or other members of the birth family, they will have to pick up a trail at least 18 years old and possibly 40 or 50 years old. This chapter is designed to assist counsellors to help those people to undertake that search. Although the parent referred to throughout is the mother the information applies equally to the father.

The first really important thing is to stress the need to keep careful records of both successful and unsuccessful lines of enquiry, to avoid future uncertainties and duplication.

A useful first step is to ask the adopted person to take a large sheet of paper and jot down everything he or she can recall having been told about their birth family. Much of this may be inaccurate, but it could well contain a valuable fragment of truth. He/she will probably have been given the name of the society that arranged the adoption. The place of birth and the name of the court where the order was made will be on their birth certificate. These places may be able to provide new information. If the adoption society no longer exists, Chapter 3 of this book may show where its records are now held. Since 1976 all adoption records have to be retained for 75 years in England and Wales. (See page 191 for information on Scotland and page 192 for information about N. Ireland and Eire.)

The second step is to check the places the birth relatives would have been advised to contact if they were anxious to hear from the adopted person.

- The Government Adoption Contact Register.
- The General Register Office, Southport.
- The adoption society which arranged the adoption (if not already contacted).
- The social services/social work department which prepared the report for the court which granted the adoption order.
- The NORCAP contact register.
- The address given on the birth certificate.

If none of these enquiries reveals that the mother has already taken the initiative, the adopted person should not feel discouraged, or assume that the mother will not want to hear from them. Many birth mothers feel that the undertaking they gave when placing their child for adoption must never be broken, and would consider the smallest enquiry to be a breach of that promise. Other relatives may not have sufficient information to undertake any enquiries.

Public records available

There are two main avenues to search – the Electoral Registers and the indexes of the registers at The Family Records Centre. If possible, each should be used in conjunction with the other, but if one source is much more accessible than the other, it is possible to proceed along just one avenue with some measure of success.

Every one should have access to an original birth certificate if they were born in Britain. Some people will have a more recent address to use as a starting point but this may not be as reliable as the birth certificate address. It is probably unwise to spend too long pursuing enquiries about any address which is not documented on any official papers. The following route can be used to check any address.

The Electoral Registers at the time of the birth are probably the best starting point as they can show at once if the address on the birth certificate was that of the family home. The Registrar would have asked the person registering the birth for the usual address of the parent/s and would not have accepted a temporary or accommodation address if it was recognised as such. Births may be registered by a parent, person present at the birth, or the "householder" of the property where the birth took place. A birth father will be named on the birth certificate only if any of the following circumstances apply:

a) He is the husband of the mother

b) He has a parental responsibility for the child

c) The mother holds an affiliation order against him, or

d) He registers the birth with the mother.

One needs to contact the Electoral Registration Officer for the district concerned and find out where the register of electors for the year of birth and subsequent years can be seen. They are most likely to be available at the local county record office. In towns, the archival set of registers is normally lodged in the Local History (or Local Studies) section of the local public library. A comprehensive collection is available at the British Museum (see Chapter 9). There is a very useful book,

Electoral Registers since 1832; and Burgess Rolls by Jeremy Gibson and Colin Rogers (1990 2nd edn, Genealogical Publishing Company). The British Library's holdings are given in *Parliamentary Constituencies and their Registers since 1832* by Richard HA Cheffins (1998). These old electoral rolls should not be confused with the current register.

Electoral Registers are compiled each autumn and are effective from the following February. It would be best to check the Register on each side of the adopted person's date of birth. Even if members of the family are listed, the parents' name may not appear. Before 1969 only those over the age of 20 are shown and from 1969 those over the age of 17.

If it is established that this was the family home, the adopted person should check forward year by year and note all the names listed. A parent may appear in a later year with a "Y" against his/her name. The date of this entry should be noted as the "Y" indicates that the voter was between 20 and 21 in that year (if before 1969). If the voter became 18 after 1 January 1970 the date of the 18th birthday will appear next to the name – that is, the date on which the person first qualified to vote – useful information if it is necessary to obtain a birth certificate later.

If the whole family disappears from the Register, it probably means they moved house. Individual members ceasing to be listed could suggest children growing up and leaving home.

It is worth remembering that the spelling of a name is not always recorded accurately so it may be wise to try alternative spelling.

It may be found that the birth mother married and lived with her husband in her parents' home for one or more years or the father lived in his family home with his wife. It can also be useful to make a note of the names of any long-term neighbours. It may well help to visit the road. If it is obviously council housing, or has been redeveloped, the district council may be able to help with information from their re-housing records.

If, having worked forward to the present day, it is found that there are still relatives of the mother living at the original address, or that some old neighbours are still in the area, it may be a good time to make some enquiries using a "story". This will provide an explanation for the enquiries that is as near to the truth as possible, but which will not arouse any suspicions among neighbours, friends or relatives of the mother. The same story should be used with each person asked, in case they talk about it among themselves.

If possible it is better to make these enquiries by telephone or letter, not in person. There is always a slight chance that a strong physical resemblance will give the secret away. An acceptable "story" could be:

'My mother (i.e. the adoptive mother) was good friends with (name of birth mother from birth certificate). This was back in the (from date of birth, do not be too precise, e.g. early 1950s) when (name of birth mother) was working as (information from birth certificate – again do not be too precise e.g. machinist). We were having a clearout recently and found some photographs we think she would like and we wonder if you could tell us what happened to her.'

One of the addresses on the birth certificate may be that of a mother and baby home listed in Chapter 4 of this book. Even skimpy registers of the home may contain vital information.

Using the indexes of births, marriages and deaths

If the relatives' whereabouts have not yet been found, it may be time to try the other main search avenue, the General Register Office birth, marriage, death and adoption indexes. These can be found at:

- The Family Records Centre, 1 Myddelton Street, London EC1R 1UW.

The adoption index is available only at the Family Records Centre but it is the other indexes which are primarily needed and they are now available at many main reference libraries around the country and also at the NORCAP search room in Oxfordshire. The records in the libraries are on microfiche and have to be viewed with a microfiche reader – rather than using a VDU screen. The Family Records Centre has a list of the locations.

If the parents were not married at the time of the birth, there will be a need to establish whether they have since married, either to each other, or to other people. It will be necessary therefore to look at the marriage entries. Marriages are indexed in alphabetical order. The search should start from the last date when the parent was known to be single. (This may be the date of birth, or it may be the last year that the relative's name appeared on the Electoral Register.) All marriages are recorded twice – once in the name of the woman, as follows:

SMITH, Mary   JONES   BIRMINGHAM   123/AB

And once in the name of the man she married, as follows:

JONES, John   SMITH   BIRMINGHAM   123/AB

The two end columns will be the same, i.e. registration district and reference number. To get the full name of both parties there is a need to look up both entries. It will then be necessary to buy a full copy of the marriage certificate in order to confirm that it relates to the correct person. It is important to get the full copy because if the marriage is for the wrong person, a great deal of time may be wasted in pursuing someone who has no connection with the adopted person at all.

The marriage certificate will give the full names of the bride and groom, their ages, occupations, and addresses at the time of the marriage. It will also give the name and occupation of each of their fathers, and will note if the father is deceased. This can be very useful confirmatory information. The addresses given may provide another address to check with the Electoral Register.

Once evidence of a marriage has been found, one can start looking for the births of children of that marriage. The search should begin in the same quarter as that in which the marriage was found. If no marriage is found, a search may still be made for further births in each of the parent's individual names. Birth entries are listed as follows:

JONES (first name given) SMITH BIRMINGHAM 345/CD

The second column gives the mother's maiden name – which is very useful when identifying children of the correct marriage. If the name in that column is the same as the child's surname, it probably indicates that the mother was unmarried.

It is not necessary to purchase the birth certificates for all the children born. One only really needs the most recent, although many people choose to buy all the relevant certificates to build up a more complete picture, of their "other" family.

The address on the birth certificate of the youngest child will give another more up-to-date address to check against the Electoral Register.

If any of the children are old enough to marry it may be helpful to check to see if they have done so. If the son or daughter were living at the family home when they got married, their marriage certificate will again give a more up-to-date address to check against the Electoral Register. It is also worth checking out old copies of local newspapers that may contain a photograph and report of the wedding.

If it is suspected that any of the relatives' marriages may have ended in divorce, one could contact:-

- Principal Registry of the Family Division, First Avenue House, 42–49 High Holborn, London WC1V 6NP (Tel: 020 7949 7017).

For a small fee they will do a 10-year search. If a divorce entry is found they will send a copy of the divorce record. This will give the names of the petitioner, respondent, and in some cases a co-respondent which may be a useful clue when looking for a subsequent re-

marriage. In the case of a re-marriage, the bride will be entered under her previous married name.

There can be two major difficulties. If the mother's date of birth is not known, it may be impossible to be sure that the right person has been located so it is vital that her age is established.

Many pregnant woman sought help and advice from moral welfare workers (later called Wel-care workers). These workers were usually employed by R C or C of E dioceses, by other denominations or by ad hoc local organisations. Often their records, which might include vital facts such as the mother's age, have disappeared or been destroyed. However, it is always worth approaching the Diocese, or the present holders of the Diocesan records (entered where known in Chapters 4 and 6). Particulars of current dioceses can be found in the directory of Catholic Diocesan Children's Societies, obtainable from the Catholic Child Welfare Council, or in the Church of England directory of the Board for Social Responsibility, obtainable from Church House.

In earlier years, pregnant women often went to Mother and Baby homes for some time before the birth and often for 6 weeks after it. These homes had registers which normally included ages, and the present whereabouts of their records, when known, is given in Chapter 4.

The second major difficulty is if the mother has changed her name by Deed Poll or is unmarried but living with someone in a steady relationship. If she is using her new or her partner's name, and registering any children in that name, she may be extremely difficult to trace. Even when a marriage entry has been found, there may be no trace of her present whereabouts and eventually, but only when all other avenues have been explored, it may be necessary to check the death entries at the Family Records Centre. These are listed as follows:

JONES Mary (date of birth or age at death) BIRMINGHAM
789/EF

If there is an entry there, the full death certificate will give an address at the time of death, the name and address of the informant, and his/her relationship to the deceased who is most likely to be her nearest relative, i.e. husband, son or daughter.

The mother's full birth certificate or her marriage certificate would give details of her parents. Another use of the death indexes would be to get their death certificates as these would give the name and address of the person who registered the death which could have been the birth mother or one of her siblings.

The grandparents might have made wills which again would give names and addresses of the legatee members of the family and the executors. Copies of

Wills can be obtained from The Principal Probate Register (details in Chapter 9).

If all the usual sources of information have failed, it may be possible to trace other members of the family such as aunts or uncles or cousins. This can endanger the well-being of the birth mother and her relatives and needs detailed discussion with a counsellor or experienced intermediary.

New technology to assist searchers

Modern information technology has now provided new tools and is continually refining and developing. A fairly recent innovation is the annual compilation of Registers of Electors and telephone directories (plus possibly some other sources) to provide the UK Infodisk. Limited free access is available on the internet at 192.com but detailed access is via a subscription service or through the purchase of a CD ROM to use on a computer. The most effective version of this software is the "professional" edition. It is expensive, but NORCAP, several regional post-adoption services, and some other agencies do invest in this resource each year. They then recover the cost by making a small charge to conduct a specific search.

The Infodisk is useful only if the current name of the person sought is known.

The Infodisk can provide a printout of individuals of a particular name, residents of a specific address, residents of a street or post code, and the search can be UK wide, in Eire, or defined by county, town or village.

A most useful feature is the possibility of conducting a "linked" search. This is when a search is made for those addresses at which two or more specifically named individuals are both listed. Mary Smith may be a common name, and John Smith an equally common one, but there will actually be comparatively few households where both John and Mary Smith are living together. The potential benefit of this resource is enormous, and many searches that in the past have needed to be abandoned as impossible may now be viable.

Because it takes about a year from when the electoral rolls are compiled (in late summer) to publication (spring of the following year) through the data entry process to release of the new disk (early autumn), the information gained from the disk is not necessarily up to date. A check should therefore be made with the very latest Electoral Roll (the draft becomes available from November in each year and the full register takes effect the following February) before any contact is made.

Special circumstances

If the birth mother, her husband or her parents were in a particular profession such as medicine, the law, the Church, or nursing, some information might be available through professional lists. Similarly if they were from a particular community or religious group it might be worth an approach to a community or religious leader. With any of these there would be a very particular need for discretion and respect to avoid distress or embarrassment for the person sought.

It may seem to be especially difficult to find the birth mother's birth certificate if she was born abroad. However, if she was born to British parents living abroad, the birth would almost certainly have been registered at the local Embassy or Consulate and there is a section at the Family Records Centre in which these births are recorded.

People born and/or adopted overseas, or brought to the UK for adoption, may find that, like foundlings, they have great difficulty in gaining any concrete information about their origins from which to begin a search. Future legislation concerning the gathering and retention of information about such adoptions may make a search easier. Meanwhile, most post-adoption centres, many agencies and social services, the Overseas Adoption Helpline and the International Social Services will do their best to facilitate this special searching. NORCAP has members whose personal experience may be useful to other members, and they also have a group of foundling members.

It is essential to have some understanding of the depth of feeling involved in this kind of search and reunion. That is why it is so important that the adopted person should be free of any pressures either to go on or to give up, free to make their own emotional journey in their own way and time. During the search there will be moments of elation when things go well, and times of despair when there seem to be nothing but false leads. Many people give up the search, either permanently, or for a time after which they return to it with new heart. Perhaps all of this is good preparation for the final objective which can result in bitter disappointment or great happiness. After a successful search there may be even greater value in the support of a counsellor than there is before and during a search.

In Scotland

The Scottish system is fairly straightforward. The major difference between New Register House in Edinburgh and The Family Records Centre is that the actual entries are available to the public. Therefore, full details from, for example, a marriage certificate, can be obtained at the time of a search. Because of this, it is easier to avoid following up the wrong person on the day of a search.

However, a fee has to be paid by anyone going to Register House, even simply to look at the Indexes. The fee in 2001 is £18.00 per full day or £9.00 per half day. Copies of extracts are £7.00, but if an applicant can supply full particulars, including the register entry number and date of registration, the fee is £4.00. These fees are, of course, always subject to change.

Family Care in Edinburgh, in addition to its general work with families, provides a cluster of services for adopted people and their birth and adoptive families. It is responsible for the Scottish Contact Register and the Adoption Registry. The latter is a computerised record of many (not all) adoptions which were arranged through an agency. If an adopted person has their birth name and date, the agency may be identified. Where the information is available, a link is automatically made when an adopted person registers on the Contact Register. Family Care also advises adopted people about searching, and has carefully selected volunteers who will undertake searches for adopted people who, for one reason or another, are unable to go to the General Register Office themselves. The fee for one search is £50.00 to cover the administrative and register costs.

By prior arrangement, and on production of proof of identity, it is possible for an adopted person to go to the court which made the adoption order and read the papers there.

In Northern Ireland

The Adoption (Northern Ireland) Order 1987 became law on 18 December 1987 and became operative on 1 October 1989. Prior to that, adoption agencies were required to keep records for at least 25 years and court records were kept indefinitely.

In order to search in the General Register in Belfast, an appointment is necessary as space is limited and there can be a waiting list. Sometimes a social worker can get information more quickly. From 1 November 1998, all certificates of birth, death or marriage cost £7.00. There is a search fee of £3.00 for each five-year period. A search of birth, death or marriage indexes for a period not exceeding 6 hours costs £6.00.

In 1997, court records of adoptions were transferred from the Public Record Office of Northern Ireland (PRONI), 66 Balmoral Ave, Belfast BT9 6NY, to the local court offices. Initial contact should be made to the appropriate court office (see table).

PRONI also holds old school records, hospital records, Boards of Guardian records, land registries, etc. These may be subject to restricted access, so it is wise to make an application in writing ahead of any visit. Designated social workers within adoption agencies or the Health & Social Services Boards may be granted access on the enquirer's behalf.

The Church of Latter Day Saints, Holywood Road, Belfast holds an enormous number of records but probably only up to about 1950. It has limited opening times and is always very busy.

COURT OFFICE CONTACTS FOR ACCESS TO ADOPTION RECORDS

Office of Care and Protection
Royal Courts of Justice
P O Box 410
Chichester Street
BELFAST
BT1 3JF
Tel: 028 90235111

Chief Clerk
Craigavon Court Office
The Courthouse
Central Way
CRAIGAVON
Co Armagh
BT64 1AP
Tel: 028 38341324

Chief Clerk
Armagh Court Office
The Courthouse
The Mall
ARMAGH
BT61 9DJ
Tel: 028 37522816

Chief Clerk
Londonderry Court Office
The Courthouse
Bishop Street
LONDONDERRY
BT48 6PQ
Tel:028 71363448

Chief Clerk
Ballymena Court Office
The Courthouse
9-13 Ballymoney Road
BALLYMENA
Co Antrim
BT43 5EH
Tel: 028 25649416

Chief Clerk
Newtownards Court Office
The Courthouse
Regent Street
NEWTOWNARDS
Co Down
BT23 4LP
Tel: 028 91814343

Chief Clerk
Belfast Crown Court Office
Royal Courts of Justice
Chichester Street
BELFAST
BT1 3JF
Tel: 028 90235111

Chief Clerk
Omagh Court Office
The Courthouse
High Street
OMAGH
Co Tyrone
BT78 1UD
Tel: 028 82242056

Eire

The Adoption Board has information about any child who was adopted in Ireland even if he or she was born in England. The Board will give information about the Agency to the adopted person or to a birth relative.

The Department of Foreign Affairs, Hainault House, 69/71 St Stephen's Green, Dublin 2 may have some information about people who were sent to the USA to be adopted between the late 1940s and early 1970s.

Irish born adopted people who have become citizens of the USA are entitled, under The Freedom of Information/Privacy Act 1998, USA, to access to their immigration file. They need form G – 639 from the Immigration and Naturalisation Service, 425 Eye Street, N W Washington DC 20526, USA.

In 1990, the Adult Adoptees Association (AAA) was formed as a self support group for adopted people. A sister organisation evolved into the Adopted People's Association which, pending expected legislation, set up an Irish Contact Register, a database of voluntarily offered information.

Details are:

The Adult Adoptees Association
c/o Wynn's Hotel
35 Lower Abbey Street
Dublin 1

The Adopted People's Association
27 Templeview Green
Chase Hall
Dublin 13

Please enclose an SAE. Telephone: 00 353 1 867 4033, Mondays and Thursdays 2–4 pm.

The National Library of Ireland
Kildare Street
Dublin 2
Tel: 00 353 1 676 6690

If searchers can find the name of the person for whom they are searching, then the organisation can often be helpful in an intermediary capacity.

The Genealogy section of the National Library of Ireland is at Kildare Street, Dublin 2
Fax: 00 353 1 676 6690.

The Natural Parents Network of Ireland
PO Box 6714
Dublin 4

The Association of Professional Genealogists of Ireland can provide the names of genealogists who would make a search for a fee.

c/o The Genealogy Office,
2 Kildare Street,
Dublin 2
Fax: 00 353 1 662 1062.

Barnardo's Advice Service (Chapter 2) cannot do searching but will be as helpful as possible to anyone who is searching. It has a telephone advice service.

GENERAL

On 15 May 2001, nine reputable organisations experienced in searching for missing or out of contact people, set up a tracing website:

www.look4them.org.uk

It gives details of the main tracing organisations, describes the kind of enquiries they undertake, and is helpful in advising on individual searches.

Planning the search

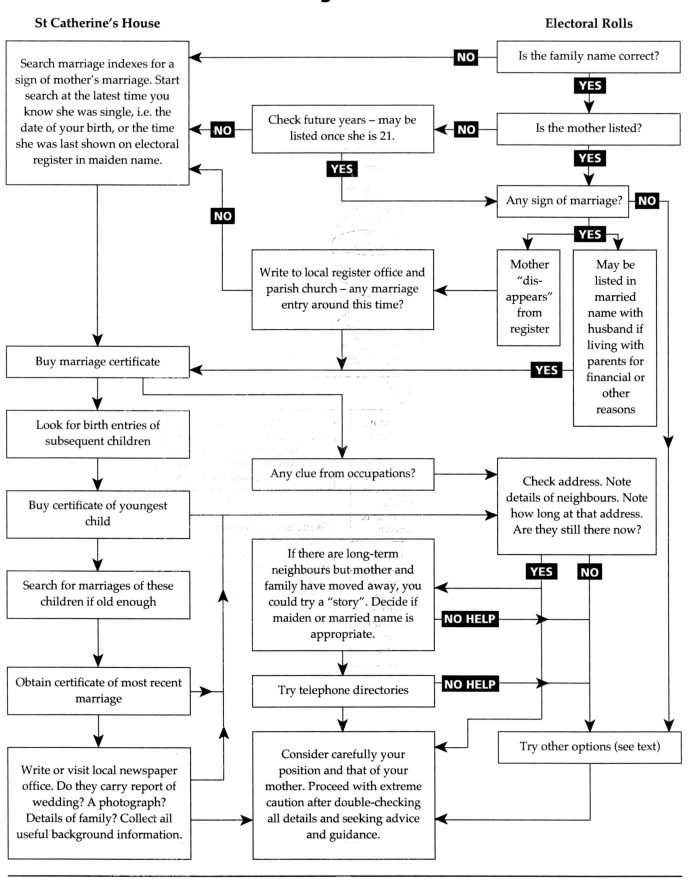

St Catherine's House

Search marriage indexes for a sign of mother's marriage. Start search at the latest time you know she was single, i.e. the date of your birth, or the time she was last shown on electoral register in maiden name.

Electoral Rolls

Is the family name correct? — **NO** →

YES

Is the mother listed? — **NO** → Check future years – may be listed once she is 21. — **NO** →

YES

YES → Any sign of marriage? — **NO**

YES

Mother "disappears" from register

May be listed in married name with husband if living with parents for financial or other reasons

Write to local register office and parish church – any marriage entry around this time?

NO

Buy marriage certificate ← **YES**

Look for birth entries of subsequent children

Any clue from occupations? → Check address. Note details of neighbours. Note how long at that address. Are they still there now?

Buy certificate of youngest child

Search for marriages of these children if old enough

If there are long-term neighbours but mother and family have moved away, you could try a "story". Decide if maiden or married name is appropriate. — **NO HELP** → **YES** **NO**

Obtain certificate of most recent marriage

Try telephone directories — **NO HELP** →

Write or visit local newspaper office. Do they carry report of wedding? A photograph? Details of family? Collect all useful background information.

Consider carefully your position and that of your mother. Proceed with extreme caution after double-checking all details and seeking advice and guidance.

Try other options (see text)

How adoptees can use their certificates
Original birth certificate

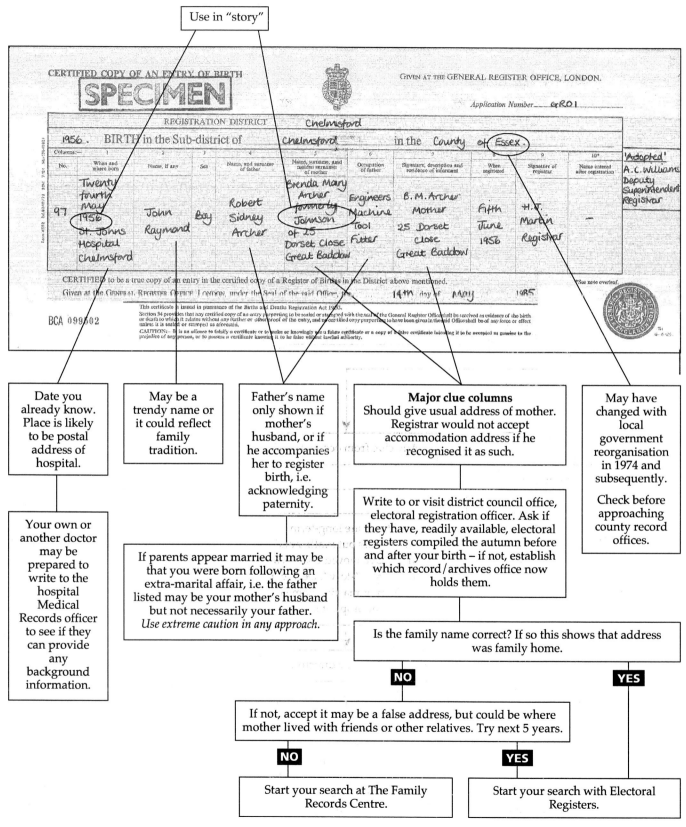

Use in "story"

CERTIFIED COPY OF AN ENTRY OF BIRTH

SPECIMEN

GIVEN AT THE GENERAL REGISTER OFFICE, LONDON.

Application Number...... GRO1

REGISTRATION DISTRICT — Chelmsford

1956. BIRTH in the Sub-district of — Chelmsford — in the County of Essex.

No.	When and where born	Name, if any	Sex	Name, and surname of father	Name, surname, and maiden surname of mother	Occupation of father	Signature, description and residence of informant	When registered	Signature of registrar	Name entered after registration
97	Twenty fourth May 1956 St. Johns Hospital Chelmsford	John Raymond	Boy	Robert Sidney Archer	Brenda Mary Archer formerly Johnson of 25 Dorset Close Great Baddow	Engineers Machine Tool Fitter	B.M. Archer Mother 25 Dorset Close Great Baddow	Fifth June 1956	H.T. Martin Registrar	—

'Adopted' A.C. Williams Deputy Superintendent Registrar

CERTIFIED to be a true copy of an entry in the certified copy of a Register of Births in the District above mentioned.

Given at the GENERAL REGISTER OFFICE, LONDON, under the Seal of the said Office, the 14th day of May 1985

BCA 099502

This certificate is issued in pursuance of the Births and Deaths Registration Act 1953.

Section 34 provides that any certified copy of an entry purporting to be sealed or stamped with the seal of the General Register Office shall be received as evidence of the birth or death to which it relates without any further or other proof of the entry, and no certified copy purporting to have been given in the said Office shall be of any force or effect unless it is sealed or stamped as aforesaid.

CAUTION:— It is an offence to falsify a certificate or to make or knowingly use a false certificate or a copy of a false certificate intending it to be accepted as genuine to the prejudice of any person, or to possess a certificate knowing it to be false without lawful authority.

Date you already know. Place is likely to be postal address of hospital.

Your own or another doctor may be prepared to write to the hospital Medical Records officer to see if they can provide any background information.

May be a trendy name or it could reflect family tradition.

Father's name only shown if mother's husband, or if he accompanies her to register birth, i.e. acknowledging paternity.

If parents appear married it may be that you were born following an extra-marital affair, i.e. the father listed may be your mother's husband but not necessarily your father. *Use extreme caution in any approach.*

Major clue columns
Should give usual address of mother. Registrar would not accept accommodation address if he recognised it as such.

Write to or visit district council office, electoral registration officer. Ask if they have, readily available, electoral registers compiled the autumn before and after your birth – if not, establish which record/archives office now holds them.

Is the family name correct? If so this shows that address was family home.

May have changed with local government reorganisation in 1974 and subsequently.

Check before approaching county record offices.

NO | YES

If not, accept it may be a false address, but could be where mother lived with friends or other relatives. Try next 5 years.

NO | YES

Start your search at The Family Records Centre. | Start your search with Electoral Registers.

The certificate shown above is © Crown Copyright; reproduced with the permission of the Controller of Her Majesty's Stationery Office.

Searching

How adoptees can use their certificates
Birth certificate after adoption

CERTIFIED COPY OF AN ENTRY IN THE RECORDS OF THE GENERAL REGISTER OFFICE

SPECIMEN

Given at the GENERAL REGISTER OFFICE

Application Number G 803

(1) No. of entry	(2) Date and country of birth of child (see footnotes)	(3) Name and surname of child	(4) Sex of child	(5) Name and surname, address and occupation of adopter or adopters	(6) Date of adoption order and description of court by which made	(7) Date of entry	(8) Signature of officer deputed by Registrar General to attest the entry
43744	Eighteenth May 1958 England	Barbara Catherine Jackson	Female	Dennis George Jackson 24 Birkenhead Drive Mansfield Notts Chemist and Muriel Barbara Jackson his wife of the same address	Thirty first January 1959 Mansfield County Court	Second March 1959	P Williams

CERTIFIED copy of an entry in the Adopted Children Register maintained at the General Register Office. Given at the General Register Office, under the Seal of the said Office, the *14th* day of *May* 19 85

GA 131682

This certificate is issued pursuant to the Adoption Act 1958 Section 20. By Section 20 of the Act, a certified copy of an entry in the Adopted Children Register, if purporting to be sealed or stamped with the seal of the General Register Office shall, without any further or other record of the entry or record be received as evidence of the adoption to which it relates and, where the entry contains a record of the date or country or district and sub-district of birth of the adopted person, this certified copy shall also be received as evidence of that date or country or district and sub-district respectively as if the copy were a certified copy of an entry in the Registers of Births.

CAUTION—It is an offence to falsify a certificate or to make or knowingly use a false certificate or a copy of a false certificate intending it to be accepted as genuine to the prejudice of any person, or to possess a certificate knowing it to be false without lawful authority.

Quote this number in any correspondence with Registrar General C.A. Section

Quote these details when writing to court office requesting sight of adoption order and guardian *ad litem* report (if available).

The certificate shown above is © Crown Copyright; reproduced with the permission of the Controller of Her Majesty's Stationery Office.

9 • Useful addresses and notes on records

General Register Offices

ENGLAND AND WALES

The Family Records Centre (replacing previous offices at Somerset House and St Catherine's House)

1 Myddelton Street
London EC1R 1UW
Tel: 020 8392 5300
Hours: 9am–5pm   Mondays, Wednesdays, Fridays
10am–7pm   Tuesdays
9am–7pm   Thursdays
9.30am–5pm   Saturdays

Among other records, the Centre holds:

- Indexes of births, marriages and deaths in England and Wales since 1837.

- Indexes of legal adoptions in England and Wales since 1927.

- Indexes of births, marriages and deaths of some British citizens abroad since the late 18th century, including deaths in the two World Wars.

- Microfilm copies of Census of Population Returns 1841–1891.

- Miscellaneous foreign returns of births, deaths and marriages from 1627–1960.

- On-line indexes to Scottish registration and census and divorce records via the Scottish link. When the required information has been identified through the index the application and payment for any certificate has to be made to the Scottish Registry.

The Centre no longer holds the current electoral rolls or telephone directories.

Postal requests for birth, marriage or death certificates should go to ONS (Office for National Statistics) at the General Register Office in Merseyside (see below).

Copies of the births, marriages and deaths records are now available on microfiche in various parts of the country and the centre has a list of these.

The General Register Office (Adoptions Section)
For all Section 51, Adoption Act 1976 enquiries, and arrangements for people adopted in England and now living abroad to be counselled there.
Tel: 0151 471 4313

The Adoption Contact Register
Smedley Hydro
Trafalgar Rd
Southport
Merseyside PR8 2HH

SCOTLAND*
(For further details see Chapter 8)

The General Register Office for Scotland
New Register House
Edinburgh EH13YT
Tel:0131 334 0380

NORTHERN IRELAND*
(For further details see Chapter 8)

Registrar General
Oxford House
49–55 Chichester St
Belfast BT14HL
Tel: 028 90 252000

EIRE *
(For further details see Chapter 8)

The General Register Office
8–11 Lombard Street East
Dublin 2
Tel: 00 353 1 671 1863

The Adoption Board
Shelbourne House
Shelbourne Rd
Ballsbridge
Dublin 4
Fax: 00 353 1 667 1438

ISLE OF MAN*
(For legal position see Chapter 2)

The Registrar
General Registry
Douglas
Isle of Man
Tel: 01624 675212

GUERNSEY*
(For legal position see Chapter 2)

The Registrar General
Griffe
Guernsey

JERSEY*
(For legal position see Chapter 2)

Superintendent Registrar
States Building
Royal Square
St Helier
Jersey

Marriage certificates in Jersey give the places of birth of bride and groom. Births of French Nationals are registered with the French Consulate. The Adoption Register began in 1948.

* The law in these countries is different from that in England and Wales.

Register of electors

Registers for individual constituencies for the current year can be consulted at the local public library or at the main post office for the area concerned. A set for the whole country (held for two years and then discarded) is available at the Office for National Statistics (ONS, Segensworth Road, Titchfield, Fareham, Hants PO15 5RR. Tel: 01392 813074 (direct line)). Public libraries may check the odd address but cannot do extended searches and ONS insist on a personal visit (a "how to find us" leaflet is available from them).

Non-current registers are best consulted at the British Library (96 Euston Road, London NW1 2DB) which has a complete set of registers for the whole country from 1947 and an extensive (ca 20,000) collection of earlier registers. It is advisable to telephone 020 7412 7536 in advance to discuss your requirements. Admission is by reader's pass and those without a pass will have first to obtain one. A free handout explaining the service, *United Kingdom Electoral Registers,* is available from the Library's Social Policy Information Service. Alternative sources locally are the county record offices or, in the larger towns, the local public library (usually the Local History Section). Holdings (other than the British Library's) are recorded in *Electoral Registers Since 1832...*by Jeremy Gibson and Colin Rogers (1990). The British Library's holding is given in *Parliamentary Constituencies and their Registers Since 1832...* by Richard H.A. Cheffins (1998).

Current (or near-current) registers are available electronically in the form of a CD-ROM called UK-InfoDisk (available from I-CD Publishing (UK) Ltd., 50 Sullivan Road, London SW6 3DX). The same data are available online at www.192.com. These offer the chance to search by name but interface in both cases is hard to use. The British Library offers a name search service through a different database (ring the above number and ask for the "CAMEO search service"). The cost of the search is approximately £12.50–£15.00.

The Guildhall Library, London has extensive electoral rolls but only for the City of London. Similarly it has City Parish Registers.

Jersey Library has microfiche records of the Jersey Evening Post, electoral registers for each parish, and ratepayers lists for each parish.

Telephone directories

Most main libraries have copies of directories for the whole country but they may not always be the latest edition.

BT Archives
3rd floor
Holborn Telephone Exchange
268–270 High Holborn
London WC1V 7EE
Tel: 020 7492 8792

BT Archives has all the earlier directories for England, Wales, Scotland and Northern Ireland. They like people to telephone beforehand, and are open Monday to Friday 10am–4pm.

The Guildhall Library, London has directories from 1880, virtually complete from 1957. It also has files of Directories from the 1950s for Eire, Guernsey and Jersey.

Current directories for some other countries can be seen at:
Westminster City Library
35 Martin St
London WC2
Tel: 020 7641 4636
Directories can also be accessed on www.teldir.com/eng.

Trades and professions

Many trades and professions keep lists of members. Librarians and archivists are helpful in locating them. The Guildhall Library, London, has a number of professional and trade directories for limited specific professions and trades.

Kelly's and other street directories

The largest collection of street directories is at:

The Guildhall Library (London)

Tel: 020 7606 3030
Monday – Saturday 9.30am – 5pm

Hospitals

Hospitals can be excellent sources of basic information. When they have closed, it has sometimes been difficult to discover where their records have gone. There is now a database called HOSPREC which collates information about the nature and whereabouts of records relating to hospitals throughout the country. There are copies in the public search rooms at the Public Record Office, and at the Wellcome Trust (see addresses). It can also be accessed on www.wellcome.ac.uk under Hospital database. These places do NOT hold the records of the individual hospitals, but they can often establish who does.

A number of major hospitals have an archival facility in which the records of closed hospitals in their area are available. e.g. Barts and the London NHS Trust hold the records of the Mother's Hospital, Hackney.

Local archivists often hold the records of closed hospitals in their area. e.g. The London Metropolitan Archives hold the records of the British Lying in Hospital for Women, Woolwich, and a number of others.

Archivists and local historians

In addition to the above, archivists and historians often hold records of old school admission registers, local children's homes and organisations, Poor Law records, and information about no longer existent buildings. They are usually interested and very helpful in quite a wide variety of ways.

Wills

The Principal Probate Registry
First Avenue House
42–49 High Holborn
London WC1V 6NP
Monday – Friday 9.30am – 4.30pm. It is advisable to arrive at least 1 hour before closing time.

Wills can be seen free and copies obtained for £5.00.

Records

PRESERVATION OF RECORDS

In **Scotland** records are retained permanently.

In **England and Wales**, since 1959, Adoption agencies have had the obligation to keep adoption records for at least 25 years, and for 75 years since the beginning of 1976. Courts have no similar statutory obligation, but do have an internal instruction from the Lord Chancellor's Department. The time for which records have been retained has varied greatly, but should be for 30 years up to November 1976 and for 75 years thereafter. Adoption records held by a court can usually be disclosed only "with the leave of the Court". Unfortunately there is no consistency in the approach of the Courts to applications for access to court records, although it is possible that this issue will be addressed in forthcoming reform of the law. A refusal by a Court

to consider on its merits an application for access might merit appeal to a higher court.

HIGH COURTS AND SOLICITORS

The Chief Master, Chancery Division, has records of adoptions that have been heard in the High Court up to 1971. Post 1971 they would be held by the Family Division of the Royal Courts of Justice. Among the information may be the name of the firm of solicitors which represented the adopters, and they may have more information. Much of this would be subject to client confidentiality, but there seems to be no reason why they should not divulge the name of any agency involved.

GUARDIAN AD LITEM REPORTS

Before Children's departments were formed in 1948, Guardian *ad litem* enquiries were usually made by Education Officers, Probation Officers or (occasionally) adoption agencies. In a few cases, records were not handed over to social services by education departments; probation records are destroyed after 10 years, and Guardian *ad litem* reports prepared by probation officers may be destroyed very soon after the court hearing.

LONDON BOROUGHS

In the Greater London area, the London boroughs became responsible for adoption work in 1965. Pre-1965 adoption records are usually held by London Metropolitan Archives.

(See preface to London – Chapter 4.)

LOCAL AUTHORITIES

During the 20th century, local authorities have at various times been absorbed, amalgamated and split up. Pre-1996 areas for agencies are given in Chapter 1. Subsequent changes have been noted in Chapter 6. While some records may have been lost during these changes some others, previously lost, have emerged. The multiplicity of changes does mean that it is sometimes necessary to try several areas for elusive files or information.

SPECIAL POST-ADOPTION FACILITIES

Although correct at the time of going to press, the days and times given for advice lines are, of course, subject to change.

ENGLAND

After Adoption Manchester
12–14 Chapel Street
Salford
Manchester M3 7NN

Advice Line: 0161 839 4930
Mon, Tues, Wed, Fri: 10am –
4.30pm
Thurs: 10am – 7.30pm

After Adoption Yorkshire
31 Moor Road
Headingley
Leeds LS6 4BG

Advice Line: 0113 230 2100
Mon, Tues, Thurs: 10am – 1pm
Wed: 4pm – 7pm

Durham Family Welfare
Agriculture House
Stonebridge
Durham DH1 3RY

Advice Line: 0191 386 3719

**East Anglia Diocesan
Children's Society**
c/o 4 Mason Road
Swanton Morley
Dereham
Norfolk NR20 4NN
Tel/Fax: 01362 638 229

Created July 1995. Sect 51
Counselling in place of St
Francis Children's Society or
other Catholic Agencies

The Families' House (formerly
St Faith's Trust)
125 Ber Street
Norwich NR1 3EY
Fax: 01603 614 049

Advice Line: 01603 621702
Tues: 10am – 1pm

Post Adoption Centre
5 Torriano Mews
Torriano Avenue
London NW5 2RZ

Advice Line: 0207 4852 931
Mon, Tues, Wed, Fri: 10am –
1pm
Thurs: 5.30pm – 7.30pm

Support After Adoption
14 Strelley Road
Nottingham NG8 3AP

Advice Line: 0115 915 0572
Mon: 9.30am – 1pm
Tues: 6pm – 9pm
Thurs: 1pm – 4pm

Able to help only people who
have a link (although this may
be tenuous) with Nottingham.

**SWAN (South West Adoption
Network)**
Leinster House
Leinster Avenue
Knowle
Bristol BS4 1NL

Advice Line: 0845 601 2459
Mon: 10am – 12pm; 1.30pm –
3.30pm; 6pm – 8pm
Tues, Wed: 10am – 12pm:
1.30pm – 3.30pm

**West Midlands Post Adoption
Service**
4th Floor
Smithfield House
Digbeth
Birmingham B5 6BS

Advice Line: 0121 666 6014
Mon, Tues, Wed: 10am–4pm
Mon: 6pm – 8pm

WALES

After Adoption in Wales
The Multicultural Centre
7 Neville St
Cardiff CF11 6LP

Advice Line: 029 20666597
Mon: 1.30pm – 3.30pm; 4.30pm –
6.30pm
Tues, Thurs: 1.30pm – 3.30pm
3rd Wed each month: 1.30pm –
4pm

SCOTLAND

**After Adoption Counselling
Centre**
Birth Link
Family Care
21 Castle Street
Edinburgh EH2 3DN

Advice Line: 0131 225 6441

Barnardo's
Scottish Adoption Advice
Service
16 Sandyford Place
Glasgow G2 2NB

Advice Line: 0141 339 0772
Mon, Tues, Thurs, Fri: 9.30am –
4.30pm
Wed: 9.30pm – 7pm

Scottish Adoption Association
2 Commercial Street
Leith
Edinburgh EH6 6JA

General and Advice Line: 0131
553 5060

ISLE OF MAN

**Manx Churches Adoption and
Welfare Society**
11 Circular Rd,
Douglas
Isle of Man IM1 1AF

Advice Line: 016224 625161
Tues, Wed: Thur: 10am – 3.30pm

NORTHERN
IRELAND

**South and East Belfast
Health and Social Services
Trust**
1 Wellington Park
Belfast BT9 6DT
Tel: 028 90 381 505

EIRE

**Barnardo's Adoption Advice
Service**
Christchurch Square
Dublin 8

Advice Line: 00 353 1 454 6388
Tues: 2pm – 5pm
Thurs: 10am – 2pm

Many closed and current
agencies in Eire offer post-
adoption counselling and help.

Voluntary self-
help groups &
organisations

ENGLAND

**NORCAP (National
Organisation for the
Counselling of Adoptees and
Parents)**
112 Church Road
Wheatley
Oxon OX33 1LU
Advice line: 01865 875 000
Fax: 01865 875686
Mon, Wed, Fri: 10am – 4pm

A self-help group for adult
adoptees, their birth and
adoptive families. It maintains a
long-standing Contact Register.

Talk Adoption
12 Chapel Street
Manchester M3 7NN
www.talkadoption.org.uk
E-mail:
HelpLine@talkadoption.org.uk
Advice line: 0808 808 1234

Tues – Fri: 3pm – 9pm
For people under 26 years who
have a link with adoption, both
before and after adoption,
whether as an adopted person, a
parent, a friend or a relative.

**NPN (Natural Parents'
Network)**
11 Green Lane
Garden Suburb
Oldham
Lancashire OL8 3AY
(S.A.E please)

Advice line: 01273 307597
Mon-Thurs: 9.30am – 12.30pm
Fri: 7pm – 9pm

Parentline Plus
520 Highgate Studios
53–79 Highgate Road
Kentish Town
London NW5 1TL

Advice line: 0808 800 2222
Incorporates Parent Line UK;
Parent Network and National
Stepfather Association.
Available for any parent.

Adoption UK (previously PPIAS)
Manor Farm
Appletree Road
Chipping Warden
Banbury
Oxfordshire OX17 1LH
Tel: 0870 7700 450
Fax: 01295 660123
E-mail:
admin@adoptionuk.org.uk

Supporting families before, during and after adoption.

Grandparents' Federation
Moot House
The Stow
Harlow
Essex CM20 3AG
Tel: 01279 444 964

ATRAP (Association for Transracially Adopted People)
c/o Post Adoption Centre
5 Torriano Mews
Torriano Avenue
London NW5 2RZ
Tel: 020 7284 0555

An independent support group for black adults of diverse ethnic heritage and nationalities who have been fostered or adopted into white families.

Intercountry adoptions

AFAA (The Association for Families who have Adopted from Abroad)
30 Bradgate
Cuffley
Herts EN64 RL

Advice Line: 01707 87 87 93
Pre-adoption helpline; Post-adoption support group

ARC (Adopted Romanian Children's Society)
Woodlands
14 Hanoverian Way
Whitleley
Sareham
Hampshire PO15 7JT
E-mail:
Woodlands4@supanet.com

BIR (Born in Romania)
31 Court Lane
Wolstanton
Newcastle
Staffordshire ST5 8DE
Tel: 01782 858915 9am – 10pm

Children Adopted from China
26 West Avenue
Exeter
Devon EX4 4SD
Tel: 01392 274433

Pre and post adoption support for families adopting from China.

Guatemala
P O Box 16911
London SE3 9WB
Tel/Fax: 020 8318 0836.
Morning hours.

A pre- and post-adoption support group for people adopting from Guatemala and particularly their children.

OASIS (Overseas Adoption Support and Information Services)
Dan Y Graig Cottage
Balaclava Road
Glais
Swansea SA7 9HJ
Tel: 01792 844329

A support group of inter country adopters.

Overseas Adoption Helpline
64–66 High Street
Barnet EN5 5SJ
Adive Line: 08705 168742
Fax: 020 8440 5675
E-mail: info@oah.org.uk

NORTHEN IRELAND

Adopt
Peskett Centre
2/2A Windsor Road
Belfast BT9 8FQ
Tel: 02890 382 353

A similar organisation to NORCAP. Members help with tracing.

EIRE

The Adult Adoptees' Association – See Chapter 8

The Natural Parents' Network of Ireland – See Chapter 8

USEFUL ADDRESSES

Adoption Board (Eire)
Senior Social Worker
9th Floor, Hawkin's House
Hawkin's Street
Dublin 2
Tel: 00 3 53 1671 5888

Adoptive Parent's Association
Albain
Piercetown
Dunboyne
Co Meath
Tel: 00 353 8252043
Sec: Tomriland
Annamoe
Bray
Co Wicklow
Tel: 00 353 0 4044 5183

Ariel Bruce
24 Stanley Street
Southsea
Hants PO5 2DS
Tel: 02392 614 075
www.arielbruce.com
E-mail: arielbruce@aol.com
Qualified social worker very experienced in tracing internationally.

The Association of Professional Genealogists of Ireland
c/o Genealogy Office
2 Kildare Street
Dublin 2
Fax: 00 353 1 662 1062

The British Library
96 Euston Rd
London NW1 2DB
Tel: 020 7412 7536

British Red Cross
International Welfare Department
9 Grosvenor Crescent
London SW1 7EJ
Tel: 020 7235 5454

Catholic Child Welfare Council
St Joseph's
Watford Way
Hendon
London NW4 4TY

Publishes the Directory of Catholic Diocesan Children's Societies and other Caring Services in England and Wales.

Central WelCare Office
(Southwark Diocese)
Trinity House
4 Chapel Court
Borough High Street
London SE1 1HW
Tel: 020 7939 9422

Child Migrants Trust
28A Musters Road
West Bridgeford
Nottingham NG2 7PL
Tel: 0115 982 2811
Fax: 0115 981 7168
www.nottscc.gov.uk/child-migrants

Church Army
Winchester House
Independent Rd
Blackheath
London SE3 5LF

Always acted on behalf of other organisations and has no records.

Church of England Board for Social Responsibility
Church House
Great Smith Street
London SW1P 3NZ

Deed Poll Enrolment
Central Office of the Supreme Court
Royal Courts of Justice
Strand
London WC2A 2LL

For 4 years, after that stored at the Public Record Office, Kew.

Department of Health
Adoption and Permanency Section
Wellington House
133–135 Waterloo Rd
London SE1 8UG
Tel: 020 7972 4545

Where to find adoption records

Department of Health Publications
PO Box 777
London SE1 6XH
Ref 220905KCHI for document called *Intermediary's Service for Birth Relatives*

Federation of Family History Societies
PO Box 2425
Coventry CV5 61X
(No telephone)

Guildhall Library
Aldermanbury
London EC2P 2EJ
Telephone 020 7332 1868/1870

Home Office Immigration and Nationality Directorate
Block C, Whitgift Centre
Croydon
Surrey CR9 1AT
Tel: 0870 6067766
Immigration Rules and Procedures
Tel: 0870 6081592 enquiries and individual cases

Hyde Park Family History Centre
64 – 68 Exhibition Road
London SW7 2PA

Sponsored by the Church of Jesus Christ of Latter Day Saints. Has extensive birth, marriage and death records, mainly on microfilm up to 1980.

Immigration and Nationality Department
Nationality Division
India Building
3rd Floor
2 Water Street
Liverpool L2 0QN

Can assist on matters concerned with nationality and citizenship.

Intercountry Adoption Lawyers Association
The Old Magistrates Court
71 North Street
Guildford GU1 4BJ
Tel: 01483 252525

International Social Services Adoption
3rd Floor, Cranmer House
39 Brixton Road
London SW9 6DD
Advice Line: 020 7735 8941
Weekdays: 10.00am – 1.00pm

International Social Service Resource Centre
Quai du Seujet 32
1201 Geneva
Switzerland
Tel: 00 41 22 9067700
Fax: 00 41 22 9067701
www.childhub.ch/iss

Endeavours to put together the available information concerning the protection of children in adoption world-wide.

Jewish Care
221 Golders Green Road
London NW11 9DQ
Advice Line: 0208 922 2222
Weekdays: 10am – 1.00pm

London Metrapolitan Archives
40 Northampton Road
London EC1 OHB
Tel: 020 7332 3820
Fax: 020 7833 9136

Lord Chancellor's Department
HQ 54 Victoria Street
London SW1
Tel: 020 7210 8500

Methodist Press and Information Service
Methodist Church
Administrative HQ
Methodist Church House
25 Marylebone Road
London NW1
Tel: 020 7486 5502

Methodist Press and Information Service
Methodist Archives and Research Centre
John Rylands University Library of Manchester
Deansgate
Manchester M3 3EH

National Council of Voluntary Child Care Organisations
Unit 4, Pride Court
80–82 White Lion Street
London N1 9PF
Tel/Fax: 020 7713 5937
www.ncvcco.org
E-mail:
migrant@voluntarychild.org

Nazareth House Archives
Nazareth House
Hammersmith Road
London W6 8DB

Newspaper Library
Colindale Avenue
London NW9
Tel: 020 7412 7353
Reader Information Line: 020 7412 7676

Office of National Statistics (ONS) – Adoption Section
General Register Office
Smedley Hydro
Trafalgar Road
Southport PR8 2HH
Tel: 01704 569824

Overseas Adoption Helpline
64/66 High Street
Barnet EN5 5SJ
Advice Line: 0870 5168742
Monday – Friday 9.00am – 1.00pm and 2.00pm – 5.00pm)

Public Records Office
Ruskin Avenue
Kew
Surrey TW9 4DU
Tel: 020 8876 3444 ext. 2350

Has a Hospital Records database which can be accessed on www.pro.gov.uk

Public Records Office (Northern Ireland)
66 Balmoral Avenue
Belfast BT 6AN

Rainer Foundation
The Galleries of Justice
Shire Hall
High Pavement
Lace Market
Nottingham NG1 1HN
Tel: 0115 952 0555
Fax: 0115 993 9828

Red Cross (see British Red Cross)

Royal Courts of Justice
Strand
London WC2A 2LL

Salvation Army
Social Historian
International Heritage Centre
101 Queen Victoria Street
London EC4P 4EP

Good records. Their search for relatives service is not available to adopted people or birth relatives.

Sisters of St Vincent de Paul
Provincial House
The Ridgeway
London NW7

Society of Archivists
40 Northampton Rd
London EC1R OHB
Tel: 020 7278 8630

Society of Genealogists
14 Charterhouse Buildings
Goswell Road
London EC1M 7BA
Tel: 020 7251 8799

The Wellcome Trust
183 Euston Rd
London NW1 2BE
Tel: 020 7611 8888